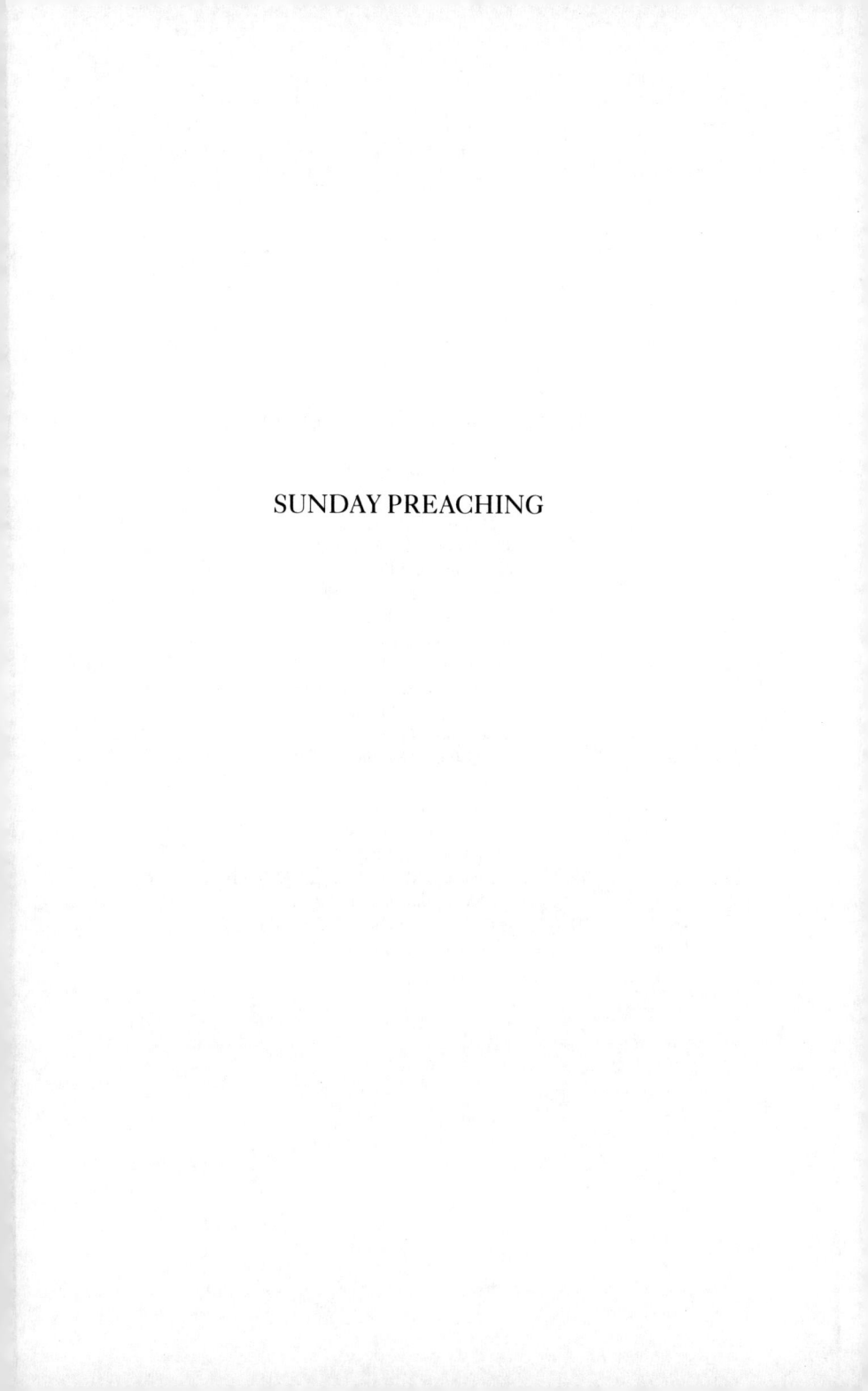

SUNDAY PREACHING

OTHER BOOKS BY CHARLES E. MILLER, C.M.

To Sow the Seed*
A Sense of Celebration
Making Holy the Day
Communicating Christ**
Repentance and Renewal***
Announcing the Good News**
Breaking the Bread**
Until He Comes***
Living in Christ
Love in the Language of Penance
Opening the Treasures
The Word Made Flesh**
As Rain That Falls
Mother and Disciple
Ordained to Preach
Together in Prayer
*with Oscar J. Miller, C.M.
**with Oscar J. Miller, C.M. and Michael M. Roebert
*** with John A. Grindel
All titles, with the exception of the first three,
have been published by Alba House.

SUNDAY PREACHING
*Brief Homilies for the Sundays
of the Three Cycles*

Charles E. Miller, C.M.

"Since brevity is the soul of wit,
And tediousness the limbs and outward flourishes,
I will be brief."
(*Hamlet* Act II, Scene II)

"By your gift I will utter your praise in the vast assembly."
(Ps 22:26)

ST PAULS

Alba House

Library of Congress Cataloging-in-Publication Data

Miller, Charles Edward, 1929-.
  Sunday preaching: brief homilies for the Sundays of the three
cycles / Charles E. Miller.
    p. cm.
  ISBN: 0-8189-0782-7
  1. Church year sermons. 2 Catholic Church — Sermons. 3. Sermons,
American I. Title.
  BX1756.M554S86 1997
  252'.6—dc21   97-7378
                                                              CIP

Nihil Obstat:
Reverend Monsignor David A. Sork
Censor Deputatus

Imprimatur:
✠ Roger Cardinal Mahony
Archbishop of Los Angeles
October 4, 1996

The Nihil Obstat and Imprimatur are official declarations that a book or pamphlet is free of doctrinal or moral error. No implication is contained therein that those who have granted the Nihil Obstat and Imprimatur agree with the contents, opinions or statements expressed.

Produced and designed in the United States of America by the
Fathers and Brothers of the Society of St. Paul,
2187 Victory Boulevard, Staten Island, New York 10314-6603,
as part of their communications apostolate.

ISBN: 0-8189-0782-7

© Copyright 1997 by the Society of St. Paul

Printing Information:

Current Printing - first digit   2   3   4   5   6   7   8   9   10

Year of Current Printing - first year shown
                        2002 2003 2004 2005 2006 2007 2008 2009 2010

Dedicated to my brother,
FATHER OSCAR MILLER, C.M.,
ordained Trinity Sunday, June 4, 1939,
who at the time of this writing
has served as an active, zealous priest
for over fifty-seven years,
and from whom I first learned
what it means to be a preacher.

Contents

Introduction ix
The Sunday Homily According to Church Documents xi

The A Cycle of Readings

The Season of Advent and Christmas 1
The Season of Lent and Easter 23
The Season of the Year 69

The B Cycle of Readings

The Season of Advent and Christmas 137
The Season of Lent and Easter 159
The Season of the Year 195

The C Cycle of Readings

The Season of Advent and Christmas 263
The Season of Lent and Easter 287
The Season of the Year 327

Solemnities, Feasts and Special Observances

Presentation of the Lord 396
Holy Thursday 398
Good Friday 402

Mother's Day 406
Solemnity of the Sacred Heart 408
The Birth of John the Baptist 410
Solemnity of St. Peter and St. Paul 412
Independence Day 414
Feast of the Transfiguration 416
Solemnity of the Assumption 418
Labor Day 422
Solemnity of All Saints 424
All Souls Day 428
Thanksgiving Day 430
Solemnity of the Immaculate Conception 432

[Note: the homilies for the Solemnities of the Trinity and the Body and Blood of the Lord (Corpus Christi) can be found following the homilies for the Solemnity of Pentecost in each of the three cycles.]

Introduction

An apology is in order. My sub-title, "Brief Homilies for the Sundays of the Three Cycles," is not accurate. This book actually contains what may be called "Homiletic Reflections on the Sunday Liturgies." I resorted to the sub-title only for the sake of succinctness. A homily is not what is on the printed page. A homily is "an integral part of a liturgical celebration." "It is a proclamation of God's wonderful works in the history of salvation, the mystery of Christ, which is ever made present and active within us, especially in the celebration of the liturgy" (*Constitution on the Liturgy*, 35, 52).

I offer this book of brief reflections as a help to priests in preparing their own homilies. These reflections are not meant to be preached, much less read aloud, as they stand. They are intended to serve only as a spark to ignite the fire of the Spirit who will guide the prayerful and studious priest in the development of his own homily. Each of these reflections is so brief that it could be preached as it stands in about three and a half to four minutes. An effective homily on Sunday should be between seven and ten minutes.

I make no apology for a repetition throughout of basic themes: the Incarnation, the priesthood of Christ in himself and in his people, the Paschal Mystery and the Eucharist as its sacrament, the importance of baptism, the Church as the universal family of God the Father in the Son and through the Holy Spirit, the Liturgy of the Word and the Eucharist as a single act of worship, the centrality of Sunday Eucharist, the vocation of Catholics to overcome the individualism and narcissism of our age by living the life of Christ as members of his body, the Church, and throughout the teaching and inspiration of the Second Vatican Council.

This book may also serve as a source of reflection for anyone who wishes to make the Sunday Scriptures a source of meditation, but throughout I have primarily had in mind my fellow priests to whom has been entrusted the proclamation of God's Word. The office of preaching is "a gift from God by which we are to utter his praises in the vast assembly" (Ps 22:26). May this simple book by God's grace be a help toward fulfilling the purpose of that gift.

Charles E. Miller, C.M.
St. John's Seminary
Camarillo, CA 93012
Trinity Sunday, June 2, 1996

> "I add my prayers to the warnings given you about going on too long in your sermons. We see from experience that such wordiness hinders their good effect and serves only to try the patience of the listeners, whereas a short, moving talk is often followed by good results."
> (St. Vincent de Paul, *Letter 2363*)

The Sunday Homily
According to Church Documents

"The homily should draw its content mainly from scriptural and liturgical sources. Its character should be that of a proclamation of God's wonderful works in the history of salvation, that is, the mystery of Christ, which is ever made present and active within us, especially in the celebration of the sacred liturgy" (*Constitution on the Liturgy*, 35).

"By means of the homily the mysteries of faith and the guiding principles of the Christian life are expounded from the sacred text during the course of the liturgical year. The homily, therefore, is to be highly esteemed as part of the liturgy itself; in fact, at those Masses which are celebrated with the assistance of the people on Sundays and feasts of obligation, it should not be omitted except for serious reason" (*Ibid.*, 52).

"The homily is an integral part of the liturgy and is strongly recommended; it is necessary for the nurturing of the Christian life. It should develop some point of the readings or of another text from the Ordinary or from the Proper of the Mass of the day, and take into account the mystery which is being celebrated and the needs proper to the listeners. There must be a homily on Sundays and holy days of obligation at all Masses that are celebrated with a congregation; it may not be omitted without a serious reason. — The homily should ordinarily be given by the priest celebrant" (*General Instruction of the Roman Missal*, 41-42).

"Among the forms of preaching the homily is preeminent; it is part of the liturgy itself…" (*Code of Canon Law*, Canon 767).

The A Cycle of Readings

*"You are the Christ,
the Son of the Living God."*
(Mt 15:16)

The Season of Advent and Christmas
Cycle A

"By his Incarnation and birth the Son of God
has united himself in a special way
with every human person. He worked with human
hands, he thought with a human mind,
he acted by human choice, and he loved with a
human heart. Born of the Virgin Mary he has become
one of us, like us in all things but sin.
He has shown us the way and if we follow it, life and
death are made holy and take on a new meaning."
(*Gaudium et Spes*, 22)

First Sunday of Advent, A

Hope, the Infant Virtue

Is 2:1-5; Rm 13:11-14; Mt 24:37-44

The virtue of Advent is hope. Charles Peguy, a poet who died in the First World War, wrote that faith is strong and powerful, and has motivated people to suffer and to die rather than abandon God and his Church. He wrote that charity is beautiful and warm, and has moved people to do heroic things out of love for God and his people. But hope in most of us, he felt, is but an infant. Advent is the season for the growth of hope.

St. Paul tells us that "hope is not hope when its object is seen. We hope for what we do not see" (Romans 8:24). And yet this virtue is not blind. It is not without foundation. Charles Dickens in his novel, *David Copperfield*, presented many luminous characters, one of which was a man by name of Wilkins Micawber. Whenever anyone asked him how he was, he had the same reply, "I am looking for something to turn up." He meant that he was waiting for some "position" to become available to him. His hope, however, was groundless since he had never in his life held a job, let alone a "position." Our hope is not like that.

Hope looks to the future but always with an eye on the past. Our hope for what God will do for us is based on what God has done for us. The biblical message is: what God has done is what God will do. We can trust God. He is consistent. The only surprise will be, not that God has abandoned his loving way of dealing with his people, but that he will surpass in the future all that he has done in the past.

The First Sunday of Advent calls us to look forward to the second coming of Christ, to wait in joyful hope for the coming of our Savior on that great day when he will right all wrongs, and when he will establish everywhere and for all time his kingdom of justice, love, and peace. "According to God's promise we await new heavens and a new earth in which righteousness dwells" (2 Peter 3:13).

As we look forward to the second coming of the Lord in glory, we look back to his first coming among us in his birth at Bethlehem. We acknowledge that "in times past God spoke in partial and various ways to our ancestors through the prophets; in these last days, he spoke to us through his Son" (Hebrews 1:1).

In the Fourth Eucharistic Prayer we acknowledge that "again and again God offered a covenant to his people and through the prophets taught them to hope for salvation." The hope proclaimed by the prophets of the Old Testament was based on God's actions by which he had freed the Israelites from slavery in Egypt and made them his people. This hope was fulfilled when God sent his only Son to free us from the slavery of sin and to establish with us the new and everlasting covenant. God had done not only what had been hoped for, but even more.

In Advent, through prayerful contemplation of all that God has done in the past, we receive the grace to nourish our hope, and to make it grow into a mighty and beautiful force in our life which may stand shoulder to shoulder with the great virtues of faith and love.

Second Sunday of Advent, A

Our God Has Been Made Visible
Is 11:1-10; Rm 15:4-9; Mt 3:1-12

The great Advent figure, John the Baptist, made an eccentric and spectacular appearance as a preacher in the desert of Judea. Although he attracted large crowds, he did not take advantage of his popularity, nor did he mislead the people. He was an honest man. He made it clear that someone greater was yet to come.

By the grace of God we know who that someone is. The Incarnation and birth of the Son of God has an effect on every aspect of our lives. His coming into our world was so significant that with his birth time stopped, so to speak, and we began counting time all over again. Advent is the season to meditate upon the meaning of the Incarnation, to follow the example of Mary who "treasured all these things and reflected on them in her heart" (Luke 2:19). The three Prefaces of the liturgy of Christmas offer us a simple, yet profound theology of the Incarnation. Reflecting on them will prepare us to celebrate Christmas.

The first Preface proclaims that in Jesus we see our God made visible. He is the image of the invisible God. As Jesus reminded Philip, "The one who sees me, sees the Father." If we want to know what God is like, we need only listen to the voice of Jesus and observe his actions in the Gospel. We do not have to invent a God according to our own liking or follow a God fashioned by someone else. Every Gospel we hear during the Mass throughout the year offers an insight into the true God. In human form Jesus is the truth of the Father.

The second Preface emphasizes the saving work which Jesus accomplished: "He has come to lift up all things to himself, to restore unity to creation, and to lead us from exile into the heavenly kingdom." Because of sin we were separated from God, but Jesus is the mediator who spans the gap forged by sin between God and his people. Even creation was "out of joint." In this world we were like exiles, far from our promised land, stumbling in the dark with no sure means to find our way. In human form Jesus is the Way to the Father and to our heavenly home.

The third Preface praises the Father: "Today in Christ a new light has dawned upon the world. Your eternal Word has taken upon himself our human weakness, giving our mortal nature immortal value." Pope St. Leo the Great in his Christmas homily sometime in the middle of the fifth century (he died in the year 460) reflected on the truth proclaimed in this Preface. He said, "Christian, acknowledge your dignity, and now that you share in God's own nature, do not return by sin to your former base condition. Do not forget that you have been rescued from the power of darkness and brought into the light of God's kingdom."

In his love Christ wishes to fill us with joy as we prepare to celebrate his birth. Through prayerful reflection on the meaning of his Incarnation we will be ready for a spiritually fruitful celebration of Christmas, so that when Christ comes "he will find us watching in prayer, our hearts filled with wonder and praise."

Third Sunday of Advent, A

Time, Christmas, and Liturgy
Is 35:1-6, 10; Jm 5:7-10; Mt 11:2-11

Time is a fascinating reality which we experience but which we do not comprehend. Many people enjoy movies which "play" with time, such as the "Back to the Future" series, and yet in our more sober moments we recognize that time once past cannot be recaptured. Or can it?

The Church, following its biblical foundations, teaches an extraordinary doctrine about time and the liturgy. The *Constitution on the Liturgy*, in commenting on the liturgical year during which we recall the events of the life of Christ, declares that these events "are in some way made present at all times and the faithful are enabled to lay hold of them and become filled with saving grace" (102). By God's almighty power which he exercises in the liturgy, the past is not buried for us.

A few years ago Pope John Paul II celebrated midnight Mass with fifteen thousand people in St. Peter's Basilica. In his homily he posed a challenging question, "Are we gathered here, as in every part of the world, on this December night merely to recall an event which has passed into history, just as every human birth passes into history and gradually becomes but a memory?"

Then the Pope answered his own question: "To us a Son is given. This is an event which is almost two thousand years old, and yet it cannot be considered an event of the past. This birth belongs to us today, tomorrow, and for all time. Let us once more receive this gift." Pope John Paul II was but echoing the homily of his predecessor, Pope St. Leo the Great, who at his Christmas Mass over fifteen and a half centuries earlier declared: "Although the state of infancy which the majesty of the Son of God did not disdain to assume, developed with the passage of time into the maturity of manhood, and although all his human acts undertaken on our behalf belong to the past, nevertheless today's feast of Christmas renews for us the sacred beginning of Jesus' life and his birth from the Virgin Mary."

Another Pope, Pius XII, gave this explanation in his encyclical, *Mediator Dei* in 1947: "The liturgical year devotedly fostered and accompanied by the Church, is not a cold and lifeless representation of the events of the past, or a simple and bare record of a former age. Rather it is Christ himself who is ever living and active in his Church. Here he continues that journey of immense mercy which he lovingly began in his mortal life, going about doing good with the design of bringing people to know his mysteries and in a way live by them. These mysteries are ever present and active (in the liturgy)" (165).

All of time for God is caught up in one moment of eternity: with God there is no past, present, or future. We can say that in a special way God holds in memory the events of the life, death, and resurrection of his Son. When we remember these events in the liturgy, we enter into the memory, the eternity of God.

St. Luke in his Gospel after telling us the story of the birth and childhood of Jesus wrote: "His mother kept all these things in memory" (2:51). When we follow her example, the birth of Jesus is a reality for us in the sacred liturgy.

Fourth Sunday of Advent, A

Christmas Makes the Difference
Is 7:10-14; Rm 1:1-7; Mt 1:18-24

The crib is up in the church. All the figures are there except one: quite appropriately the Christ Child is not yet in the manger. Noting the absence of the infant should get us thinking about life without Christ. We may well wonder how life would be affected if God had not sent his Son into the world as our savior. Someone said that without Christ life would be like living at Los Angeles International Airport. There amid all the confusion and rushing about, everything is a number. You are on flight 227 which is leaving from terminal 6 at 1:15, due to arrive at 8:32, and you are seated in row 33. The airplane you will fly is called a 747. Having accepted the impersonal approach implied in all those numbers, you entrust your life, with a considerable amount of faith, to the worthiness of the air craft, the careful maintenance of the ground crew, and the expertise of the pilots. You watch the attendants as they explain the safety procedures and you find it not a little alarming that there is a danger which makes such an explanation necessary. Once you are in the air and you have calmed your nerves, you nibble away at a bag of peanuts and sip from a plastic container of Coke (usually more ice than beverage). As you try to get comfortable, cramped as you are in the middle of a three-seat section, you think, "There has to be a better way."

Thank God there is a better way, not for air travel, but for life itself. Christmas makes the difference. The Second Vatican Council proclaims the significance of the coming of Christ: "By his Incarnation and birth the Son of God has united himself in some fashion with every human person. He worked with human hands, he thought with a human mind, he acted by human choice, and he loved with a human heart. Born of the Virgin

Mary, he has become one of us, like us in all things but sin. He has shown us the way and if we follow it, life and death are made holy and take on a new meaning" (*Constitution on the Church in the Modern World*, 22). In the third Preface for Christmas we acknowledge that "by taking upon himself our human weakness, he has given our mortal nature immortal value."

We are not a mere number with God. Because of Jesus we have been given a name, and that name is "Christian." To be a Christian means to be like Christ, a child of God the Father. Heaven is our home and we are on a journey there through this life. The means for this journey is not a 747, nor even a space ship. It is a person, Christ himself. "He has come to lift up all things to himself... and to lead us from exile into his Father's kingdom" (Second Preface of Christmas). We find him, not in the vast temple of impersonal numbers which we call an airport, but in the saving atmosphere of our parish church, especially during the celebration of the Holy Eucharist.

During the Mass we hear a calming message, not an alarming one, even though it contains a challenge for Christian living. Above all we are nourished for our journey with the sumptuous banquet of the body and the blood of the Lord. Life is different because of Christ. Christmas should fill our hearts with joy as we recognize in Christ the revelation of God's love for us.

Solemnity of Christmas, A

The Birth of Christ Our Priest
Is 62:11-12; Tt 3:4-7; Lk 2:15-20

For people of faith Christmas is the celebration of the birth of Jesus Christ, the Son of God, our Lord and Messiah, the Savior of the World. There are so many wonderful and touching aspects to this solemnity, it is no surprise that something can be missed. Christmas is also the birthday of Christ the Priest. Yes, Christ the Priest. A beautiful theology of the Church sees the womb of Mary as the splendid cathedral in which the Holy Spirit anointed Jesus as the Great High Priest.

Jesus as Priest is our mediator. Through his divinity to which he is begotten by God in eternity, he is in contact with his Father. Through the humanity which he took to himself in the womb of Mary, he is in contact with us. Divinity unites Christ with the Father; humanity unites him with us. Like a bridge, he spans the gap which separates the divine from the human.

God's grace flows from the Father through Christ to us. Our prayers rise from us through Christ to the Father. That is what it means to say that Christ is our Priest. Even though we may rarely think of Christ precisely as our Priest, the celebration of the Eucharist, which is the heartbeat of the Catholic Church, constantly reflects this truth. The eminence of all liturgy consists in the truth that it is the worship offered by Christ the Priest to the Father in union with his priestly people.

Our liturgical prayers of petition conclude by telling the Father that we are asking his help through our Lord Jesus Christ, his Son. We summarize the great eucharistic prayer by reminding the Father that all glory and honor are his through, with, and in Christ his Son. This expression of the role of Jesus as our Mediator reflects the doctrine that Jesus is our Priest.

We give the title "priest" to those who have been ordained to the episcopacy and the presbyterate, not because they have an independent existence in their ministry or even because the priesthood of Christ is multiplied in them, but because the mystery of the Incarnation continues through ordination. Jesus is in fact the only Priest of our religion.

An ordained priest never speaks in his own name or acts in his own person. In the sacrament of penance, he declares "I absolve you from your sins," but that first person singular is the person of Jesus Christ. The priest says over the bread and wine, "This is my body… this is my blood," but every Catholic recognizes that the Eucharist is not the body and blood of the priest but the body of Christ given up for us and his blood poured out for us.

Christ the Priest looks in two directions. First he looks toward his Father to whom his entire being is directed from the timelessness of eternity and with whom he is united in his divinity. Then he looks toward us with whom he has become united in his humanity from the moment of his Incarnation, and he urges us to follow him, the way to the Father, so that we may know the truth of the Father and live by the Father's life.

It is very touching to contemplate the infant who was born at Bethlehem. In fact, Bethlehem represents one of the most beautiful aspects of our faith. But we will miss much of the meaning of Christmas unless we see it as the birthday of Christ the Priest.

Solemnity of Christmas, A (alternate)

A Christmas Lullaby
Is 52:7-10; Heb 1:1-6; Jn 1:1-18

Each year on December 25th we join with people of faith around the world to celebrate Christmas. Together we focus on an infant, born in a little town in Judea which was nothing more than a insignificant outpost of the mighty Roman Empire. And yet we recognize that this birth changed all of human history and gave a new meaning and purpose to our lives. Despite the humble appearances, we believe that in Bethlehem the Eternal Son of God was born of the Virgin Mary.

The appeal of Christmas is not so much the truth that God entered our world and that divinity took on humanity, but the manner in which this was done. God could have become human as a full grown adult with a great display of power and majesty. Instead he chose to come amid the most humble of circumstances, born of a simple girl of Nazareth whose spouse could not even find a place for them to stay in their ancestral city.

We know the story well. For most of us it has been part of our Christmas celebration from the time we could kneel as a child before the crib of an infant. Is there anything more God could have done to invite us to embrace him in love than to come to us as Jesus did at Bethlehem?

The meaning of Christmas is so simply profound that our recognition of it overflows from human thought and seeps into our deepest emotions. The significance of Christmas is more felt than understood.

In the early nineteenth century an event occurred in the village of Oberndorf in Austria which led to an expression of the meaning of Christmas which people will probably cherish as long as this world endures.

A few days before Christmas in 1818 the organ in the church of St. Nicola broke down. It became clear that it was impossible to make repairs in time for the midnight Mass. The organist asked the parish priest, Father Josef Mohr, for permission to use a guitar at the Mass. He explained that they would keep the music simple but they did need some form of accompaniment.

Father Mohr agreed and mentioned that he had been working on a Christmas poem, one which his people could understand, for they were without much education as were the shepherds who were invited to the crib in Bethlehem. The priest handed him a piece of paper on which he had written a text which came to only twenty-six words in German. There was no title to the brief poem.

The organist went to work. Shortly before Christmas Franz Gruber had completed his melody. At midnight Mass in the church of St. Nicola in an Austrian village in the year 1818 people for the first time sang "Silent Night."

The carol needed no title. It had captured the spirit — the feeling — of Christmas. It was simple, humble, actually a lullaby to the Son of God. From Oberndorf, Austria it spread throughout the world and this Christmas will be sung in almost every language of the world by people of the Christian faith.

A German carol became universal because a Jewish baby, the eternal Son of God, was born in Bethlehem as our Savior.

Feast of the Holy Family, A

Don't Forget St. Joseph

Si 3:2-6, 12-14; Col 3:12-21; Mt 2:13-15, 19-23

On the Sunday after Christmas we celebrate the Feast of the Holy Family. A family is made up of at least three persons: father, mother, and child. Or is it? These days we speak of "one parent families," and that one parent in most cases is a mother. Where is the father? Even in some "two parent" families, the kids at times must ask, "Where is dad?"

Recognizing that generalizations admit of admirable exceptions, many people feel that we have lost something in our society regarding the beneficial effects of a loving and devoted father within a family. A loving, masculine influence tends to be lacking. A role model for boys is found outside the family, often in objectionable ways. No matter how dedicated a woman is, she should never be expected to be both mother and father to her children.

From the Gospel story of the conception, birth, and childhood of Jesus there emerges a quiet, modest figure who is the perfect model for fathers today. This Sunday's celebration of the Holy Family will do well not to forget St. Joseph.

The Preface for feast days of St. Joseph puts God's plan for this humble man into perspective. The priest prays to God the Father by saying: "Joseph is that just man, that wise and loyal servant, whom you placed at the head of your family. With a husband's love he cherished Mary, the virgin Mother of God. With fatherly care he watched over Jesus Christ your Son who was conceived by the power of the Holy Spirit."

St. Bernardine of Siena (early fifteenth century) said in a sermon: "What then is Joseph's position in the whole Church of Christ? Is he not a man chosen and set apart? Through him and, yes, under him Christ was fittingly and honorably introduced into the world."

According to the Jewish custom of the day, Jesus learned his prayers from Joseph. When he saw Joseph at work in his carpenter's shop, Jesus came to recognize the value and dignity of hard labor. Jesus experienced in Joseph the meaning of the beatitudes before he preached them; he saw Joseph as the man who was happy in being poor, in being meek, in being single-hearted. From Joseph he came to appreciate the importance of following the liturgical customs of his people.

Joseph was a dedicated father to Jesus. Jesus felt the warmth of Joseph's fatherly embrace after he had been lost in the temple for three days. Above all, the way he spoke to Joseph is the way he taught us to address God in prayer as "Abba," Father.

We Catholics have always prided ourselves on devotion to Mary, the Mother of God. I personally feel that she would be delighted to see us deepening our devotion to her husband. Jesus would be pleased more than anyone. St. Bernardine also said in his sermon: "Jesus does not now deny to Joseph the intimacy, reverence, and very high honor which he gave him on earth as a son to his father." With Jesus we owe honor to Joseph, and honored indeed would Joseph be if fathers were to accept him as their model.

New Year's Day, A

Solemnity of Mary, the Mother of God
Nb 6:22-27; Gal 4:4-7; Lk 2:16-21

Sometimes when you go to a buffet dinner and see all the offerings, your mouth may water but your brain tells you that there is just too much food even to get a sampling.

The Mass today is somewhat like a buffet. The featured offerings are that this is the Octave Day of Christmas, it is the Solemnity of Mary as the Mother of God, it is New Year's Day, and it is World Day of Prayer for Peace. Such rich realities should make our spiritual mouths water, and best of all we can get at a sampling of all these truths because, as a matter of fact, they fit together as one delicious dinner.

Christmas occurred just one week ago. That is what is meant by the octave day. It urges us not to forget about Christmas. Christmas is so important that the liturgy is trying to keep it before our minds. We can never comprehend the awesome truth that the eternal Son of God became human like us in all things but sin, that he was actually conceived in Mary's womb, born into our world, nursed at Mary's breast, and introduced to a full human life. This truth is so astounding that even some of our fellow Christians cannot bring themselves to acknowledge that Mary, a creature, a woman, could be called and actually *be* the Mother of God. But such she is, and the Church infallibly proclaimed this truth at the Council of Ephesus in the year 431. This octave day of Christmas rightly celebrates Mary as the Mother of God.

This is also New Year's Day. It reminds us that we count time back, not to the first day of creation when time began, or back to the founding of the city of Rome from which the ancient Romans counted time, but to the birth of Jesus Christ from whom time and life itself took on a new meaning.

In this new year of our Lord, we remember the meaning of the coming of Jesus. He entered our world to take away sins, to span the gap that separates us from God, to break down the barriers that isolate people, to reconcile us to one another in the family of the Church, and to unite us with God our Father. In other words he came to bring about peace.

When we fully accept Christ for who he is and for what he accomplished, we receive the gift of peace. This gift flows from a union with God and harmony with each other. Of course on this earth our peace is always incomplete and it can be interrupted by turmoil of various kinds. But when we pray for peace in our hearts, peace in our homes, and peace in the world we are praying that we will all embrace a true, active faith in Christ.

Many people have the practice of making resolutions on this day because it marks a new beginning, a chance to start over again. We as Catholics could make no better resolution than to pray for a practical and profound faith that will move us to make Christ the center and the heart of our lives. For nine months he lived in the womb of Mary, but he wants to live in our hearts forever, from this day forward until he invites us to enter his heavenly home where time will be no more but where, with life's goal finally achieved, we will indeed rest in peace.

Solemnity of the Epiphany, A

The Gift of the Magi

Is 60:1-6; Eph 3:2-3, 5-6; Mt 2:1-12

Christmas, with its liturgical and social forms of celebration, is for many people the happiest time of the year. Closely related to Christmas, but perhaps not as enthusiastically observed, is the Solemnity of the Epiphany.

The Epiphany celebrates the manifestation of the invisible God in visible, human nature for the salvation of the world. It rejoices in the truth that the son of Mary is the Son of God. That is its theological meaning, but what has captured the imagination of people for centuries is the coming of the Magi from the east, the astrologers whom we have dubbed the Wise Men. We think of them as three because of the three gifts they offered to Jesus, gold, frankincense, and myrrh.

The practice of giving gifts at this time of the year seems to have been derived from the action of these wise men. Most kids hate to get gifts which are practical or necessary. They want gifts which are fun. Actually the significance of gifts is not found in whether they are practical or fun, but in whether they have meaning.

The American author, O. Henry, wrote a short story which he called "The Gift of the Magi." It tells of a young married couple, Della and Jim, who were very poor but deeply in love. Della's greatest pride was her long, beautiful, dark hair. Her husband knew that she wanted a set of decorative combs to wear in her hair, and despite their poverty, he was determined to get them for her. Jim's greatest treasure was a gold pocket watch which had belonged first to his grandfather and then to his father. His wife saw a platinum watch chain which she thought would be perfect for his time piece, and despite their poverty, she was determined to get it for him.

Christmas eve came. He had the combs for her. She had the watch chain for him. But when they came to exchange gifts, they discovered that she had cut and sold her hair to a wig maker to buy the watch chain for him, and he had sold his watch to buy the combs for her. After their shock, they cried a little, then laughed a lot and fell into each other's arms. They realized that combs and watch chains mean nothing. It is love that counts. At Mass we stand with Christ before the Father to offer him a gift. In the Prayer over the Gifts we profess that our offering is not gold, frankincense and myrrh, but the sacrifice they symbolize: Jesus Christ himself. In the First Eucharistic Prayer we say to the Father, "From the many gifts you have given us we offer to you, God of glory and majesty, this holy and perfect sacrifice." That sacrifice is the perfect expression of love.

We could not have a more perfect or a more precious gift to offer to the Father than Christ himself, but a question remains. Does our offering have, not only value, but meaning? Does our sharing in the Mass signify that we are truly wise, that we are willing to sacrifice anything for God? Does deep love motivate us as it did Della and Jim in O. Henry's story?

O. Henry concluded by saying of the couple, "Of all who give and receive gifts, such as they are the wisest. They are the Magi." We too can be the Magi of our day.

Feast of the Baptism of the Lord, A

The Mark Is Upon Us
Is 42:1-4, 6-7; Ac 10:34-38; Mt 3:13-17

Most Catholics are dismayed when they learn that a priest has left the active ministry. Most too, I trust, realize that judgment belongs to God alone, not to us. Our dismay, however, reflects our realization that priesthood is not a career. It is a vocation. A career we choose; a vocation God chooses.

God's call to the priesthood is sealed by the Holy Spirit in the sacrament of holy orders. Being ordained is a once in a lifetime experience. It cannot be repeated since it grants a permanent effect, to be carried even into eternity, which is called the sacramental character. It is the mark of the Holy Spirit upon the soul of a priest. Once a priest, always a priest.

On this feast of the Lord's baptism, we do well to think of our own baptism. Just as the sacrament of ordination as a priest cannot be repeated, so baptism together with its completion in confirmation cannot be repeated. These sacraments too grant a permanent effect, to be carried into eternity, which is the sacramental character of Christian initiation. It is the mark of the Holy Spirit upon us.

Christian initiation is God's plan for us according to which "he chose us in Christ before the world began to holy and blameless in his sight, to be full of love… to be his adopted children" (Ephesians 1:3ff).

When we reflect on what a priest is, we probably think of someone who celebrates Mass. That is good thinking. Nothing distinguishes a priest more than his relationship to the Holy Eucharist. Presiding at Eucharist is not the only thing he does, but it is the most important. In fact, everything he does as a priest leads to the Eucharist and flows from it. When we reflect on what it means to be a Catholic, we should also think of the

Eucharist. The sacraments of baptism and confirmation actually bring about their full effect only when people receive their First Eucharist so that, to say it correctly, the sacraments of Christian initiation are baptism, confirmation, and the Eucharist. Celebrating the Eucharist, especially Sunday Eucharist, is not the only thing we do as Catholics, but it is what characterizes us as Catholics. The eucharistic celebration is the summit of our lives as Catholics.

While never passing judgment, we should be dismayed when fellow Catholics stop going to Mass. The mark of the Holy Spirit is upon them and constitutes them as a chosen race, a royal priesthood, a holy nation. They are a people consecrated to offer the Mass through the hands of the priest who bears the person of Christ the Priest who ceaselessly presents to his Father the one sacrifice of his body and blood in the name of all the members of his body, the Church. Catholics who do not go to Mass on Sunday are like violinists who never play the violin. They are like football players who sit on the bench during an entire game. They are like a husband and a wife who do not live together. All of this is said, not to judge others, but only to emphasize how central to our lives as Catholics is the celebration of the Eucharist. Both as priests and people we have the mark of the Holy Spirit upon us to lead us to the Eucharist.

The Season of Lent and Easter
Cycle A

"The season of Lent has a twofold character:
(1) it recalls baptism or prepares for it;
(2) it stresses a penitential spirit. By these means
especially, Lent readies the faithful
to celebrate the Paschal Mystery."
(*Constitution on the Liturgy*, 109)

First Sunday of Lent, A

Lent Prepares for the Paschal Mystery

Gn 2:7-9, 3:1-7; Rm 5:12-19; Mt 4:1-11

The First Sunday of Lent presents us with a startling and mysterious scene. The eternal Son of God, equal to the Father in all things, is led by the Spirit to be tempted by the devil. This is startling because any person of faith, upon reflection, should wonder how the devil could possibly enter into the mind of Jesus himself. It is mysterious because we cannot understand in what way the enticements offered by the devil could have been a real temptation for Jesus.

The Church is clear in her doctrine. Except for sin, Jesus was human like us in all things, including the need to resist temptations. Jesus' temptations were real and they were powerful. They were calculated to lure him away from the mission given him by his Father. Unlike Adam and Eve in the garden of Eden, Jesus came forth from the desert strengthened in his resolve to be faithful to his Father's will, and yet the mission upon which he embarked in his public ministry inevitably led him to a garden, that of Gethsemane, where he underwent a still further temptation. There he was tempted to forego the completion of his mission: his suffering and death on the cross. He was like a runner in a marathon who, exhausted by his prolonged exertion, is tempted to drop out of the race just a few paces from the finish line.

In the Gospel narrative which will be proclaimed on Palm Sunday we will hear Jesus cry out in the agony of anticipating his passion, "My Father, if it is possible, let this cup pass me by." Persevering in prayer Jesus received the strength to bow his head before his Father and say, "Still, let it be as you would have it, not as I."

Jesus accepted the Father's plan, the Paschal Mystery, the

astonishing truth that he would pass through the awesome, dark portals of death to the bright, wonderful reality of the resurrection. We call the death and resurrection of Jesus "paschal," because it is a passage through death to life. We acknowledge it as a "mystery" because the reason for its necessity is hidden in God's wisdom.

Our faith is that "Christ has died; Christ is risen." He experienced the Paschal Mystery, not for his own sake but for ours, not as a sinner but as the Savior of sinners. That is why we proclaim to Christ: "Dying you destroyed our death, rising you restored our life." The Paschal Mystery of the death and resurrection should be the guiding truth in all of our Lenten practices. The three traditional practices are prayer, fasting, and almsgiving. Formed by God's Word let our prayer be in union with Christ, our passover, a constant renewal of dedication: "Father, your will be done." Let our fasting or mortification be done in union with Christ's sufferings in his passion and death. Let our almsgiving be an imitation of the generosity of Jesus who, in his Paschal Mystery, thought not of himself but of us.

"Lent," the Church teaches us, "readies the faithful through closer attention to the Word of God and more ardent prayer to celebrate the Paschal Mystery" (*Constitution on the Liturgy*, 109).

Second Sunday of Lent, A

Violet for Lent, White for Easter
Gn 12:1-4; 2 Tm 1:8-10; Mt 17:1-9

Fashions are a big business in the United States. For many people in our country, clothes do more than protect from weather and maintain modesty. They express affluence. Fashion designers believe that clothes, although they do not make us who we are, do show something about us.

That thinking, even granting its materialistic basis, reflects a spiritual truth. The transfiguration of Jesus, about which we hear in this Sunday's Gospel, was an anticipation of the glory that would come to him in his resurrection from the dead. In describing the event, St. Mark tells us that Jesus' "clothes became dazzlingly white — whiter than the work of any bleacher could make them." The clothes, even of Jesus, showed something about him.

And yet God seems to love irony. The dazzling garments of the transfiguration were a prelude to that moment when Jesus would be stripped of all garments. The fulfillment of a glorious transfiguration came about only through an ignominious crucifixion. In the words of St. Paul, Jesus "humbled himself, obediently accepting even death, death on a cross; because of this God highly exalted him" (Philippians 2:6-11).

We see Jesus nailed to a cross. He wears no clothing to indicate who he is, not even the purple cloak placed upon him by the Roman soldiers in jest. But with the eyes of faith we see that in the moment of humiliation Jesus is actually exalted on a cross as our true Lord and Savior to the glory of God the Father. His resurrection confirms the words of the Father, "This is my Son, my beloved."

Those who are baptized are clothed in a white garment. It is the robe of God's children, and yet that robe of dignity may be placed upon people only when they have been stripped of the ugly garments of sin. In the Book of Revelation St. John says of God's children that "they have washed their robes and made them white in the blood of the Lamb" (7:14). As a visual image the expression, "washed white in the blood of the Lamb," is impossible, but as a spiritual reality it indicates that we are saved through the blood of the Lamb of God.

During the Easter Vigil the catechumens, then called the elect, are baptized and receive their white robes. They do so only after a long period, even years, of prayer, instruction, and the practice of virtue. The season of Lent which precedes their baptism is an intense period of scrutiny and prayer. For the rest of us Easter will be an opportunity to renew our baptism, but that renewal will have meaning in proportion to how well we spend Lent in union with the catechumens by deepening our prayer, by increasing our reading of the Scriptures, and by striving to be better disciples of the Lord.

One purpose of this Sunday's Gospel is to help us fix our eyes on the conclusion of Lent, to reflect on the reason for self-denial, and to understand the necessity of turning away from sin. God is eager to transform the penitential violet of Lent into the joyful white of Easter Sunday.

Third Sunday of Lent, A

Water Is a Reminder of Baptism
Ex 17:3-7; Rm 5:1-2, 5-8; Jn 4:5-42

When people are on a diet, it seems that everything makes them think of food. It can be maddening for them to walk by the golden arches and get a whiff of all the goodies which seem extra good because they are forbidden. They envy the little kids who are devouring hamburgers, French fries, and milk shakes enthusiastically without a concern in the world.

During the spiritual diet of Lent, the liturgy turns almost single-minded. Everything makes the liturgy think of the great sacrament of baptism, especially for the sake of the elect whom we accompany on their journey to Easter when they celebrate the sacraments of Christian initiation.

The liturgy today says, "Remember how God had Moses strike the rock in the desert so that water could flow forth for the people to drink? That should make us all think of the water of baptism." The liturgy then says to us, "St. Paul wrote to the Romans to remind them that they had been justified by faith and were at peace with God through the Lord Jesus Christ. We too have been justified by faith which is God's gift to us through our baptism."

The liturgy loves to reflect on the Gospel about the encounter between Jesus and the Samaritan woman. Jesus first directed her attention to the water she had come to draw. He said, "Everyone who drinks this water will be thirsty again." Jesus is single-minded. That ordinary water made him think of something greater, for he added, "Whoever drinks the water I give will never be thirsty; no, the water I give shall become a fountain within him, leaping up to provide eternal life." And the liturgy immediately thinks: "Baptism!" So should we.

The *Constitution on the Liturgy* states: "The Lenten season… recalls baptism or prepares for it." At the conclusion of Lent the elect will enter the Church through the sacraments of Christian initiation. These are baptism with its completion in confirmation and its celebration in First Eucharist. Those who participate in the full ceremonies of Easter night see those to be baptized coming forward enthusiastically, their cares and concerns put aside at least for this wonderful moment. This great sacrament of baptism the preachers of an earlier era often referred to as the door of the Church, like spiritual golden arches. Those who have already been baptized do not envy the child-like relish of those about to be initiated into the Church, not only because everyone is called to pray for and to support those to be baptized but because Easter is also a time for all members of the Church to renew their baptism, their becoming part of the body of Christ in the Church.

The *Constitution on the Liturgy* declared that "wider use is to be made of the baptismal features proper to the Lenten liturgy and elements which belonged to a now-lapsed tradition are to be restored" (109). This directive has been followed in the restored liturgy. One result is that on this Sunday and the two following the emphasis is on baptismal themes.

During these days of Lent our use of water, whether to quench our thirst or to cleanse our bodies, should make us think of baptism. Like Jesus and the liturgy, we need to become single-minded when it comes to the great gift of baptism.

Fourth Sunday of Lent, A

Faith, Like Love, Is the Way to See
1 S 16:1, 6-7, 10-13; Eph 5:8-14; Jn 9:1-41

We have a saying that "love is blind." You might hear this statement at a wedding from young men who wonder how a beautiful bride could possibly see anything in a groom who is, in their judgment, much less handsome than they. "What does she see in that guy?" they ask. Sometimes the situation is turned around and the young women ask, "What does he see in that girl?" With a shrug people respond, "Love is blind."

I believe it is a mistake to think that love is blind. I think that love, and love alone, can truly see all the wonderful qualities in a human person which those without love fail to perceive. Love gives a vision, a deeper way of seeing. Faith is something like that. Faith, and faith alone, can truly see all the wonders of God.

In the Gospel of this Sunday Jesus gives sight to a man who had been born blind. Jesus spat on the ground, made mud with his saliva and smeared the man's eyes with the mud. He then told him to wash in the pool of Siloam. After the man had washed his eyes, he was able to see.

The Pharisees who are part of this episode in the Gospel looked at Jesus and saw only a troublemaker who was overturning their customs. He was guilty, in their judgment, of violating the Sabbath rest. They objected to him and his actions even though he did only good and never evil. By contrast, the man who had been given his sight looked at Jesus and saw his Savior.

Jesus' miracle in today's Gospel is a symbol of the faith which comes to us when we are washed in the water of baptism. We were chosen like David in the first reading, and after our baptism we were anointed like him to share in the kingship of

Christ. We are extraordinary people. "There was a time," St. Paul reminds us in the second reading of this Sunday, "when we were in darkness, but now we are light in the Lord." This light in the Lord is the gift of faith which is given to us through the sacrament of baptism and strengthened in confirmation.

Those without faith look at a fellow human being and see only a rational animal. Those with faith see a child of God. Those without faith pick up a Bible and find only words. Those with faith discover the Word of God. Those without faith look at the Eucharist and see only bread and wine. Those with faith experience the reality of the Lord's body given up for us and his blood poured out for us. Those without faith look at suffering and see only tragedy. Those with faith believe that suffering is a sharing in the cross of Christ. Those without faith look at death and see separation and oblivion. Those with faith accept death as a step which leads to a new, fuller life through the resurrection of Christ.

Lent is a time to prepare for baptism or to renew its meaning. Baptism gives us a new life which makes us children of God and members of his family here on earth, the Church. Like newly born babies, members of this family open their eyes in the birth of baptism upon a new world. They can see the beauty of God's wonders because of the gift of faith. Faith, like love, is not blind. It is the only way to see.

Fifth Sunday of Lent, A

Baptism Is a New Life
Ezk 37:12-14; Rm 8:8-11; Jn 11:1-45

Lent is almost over and perhaps we feel we have not made the best use of this season. Whatever our feelings about all this may be, the Church earnestly wishes that before Easter arrives we focus our attention on the great sacrament of baptism. The Second Vatican Council teaches us that the Lenten season recalls baptism or prepares for it (*Constitution on the Liturgy*, 109). Those who are in the final stage of the *Rite of Christian Initiation of Adults* (RCIA) will climax the season of Lent by receiving baptism together with confirmation and their First Eucharist during the Easter Vigil.

All Catholics are called upon to accompany the catechumens during Lent by their prayers and support, and to renew their own baptism during the Easter Eucharist. Easter is the time for converts to begin a new life in Christ. It is also an opportunity for all Catholics to deepen their life in Christ.

The liturgy understands the story of Lazarus in this Sunday's Gospel as symbolic of baptism. Lazarus had died. Even from within the cave which was his tomb Lazarus heard the powerful words of Jesus who called him by name: "Lazarus, come out!" Lazarus responded and walked out of the tomb, bound hand and foot with linen strips. Jesus said to his sisters, Martha and Mary, "Untie him and let him go free."

Today's Gospel shows that Jesus was both human and divine. "As human he wept for Lazarus his friend. As the eternal God, he raised Lazarus from the dead" (from today's Preface). The sacraments are like Jesus, both human and divine. All of us at one time were buried in the tomb of sin. In baptism we heard the voice of Christ who pronounced our name and said,

"I baptize you in the name of the Father and of the Son and of the Holy Spirit."

Our human experience of baptism makes a difference because of its divine power through Christ. St. Paul states in his Letter to the Romans, "If Christ is in you, the body is indeed dead because of sin, while the spirit lives because of justice." Our spirit lives because baptism grants us the gift of the Holy Spirit. St. Paul continues: "If the Spirit of him who raised Jesus from the dead dwells in you, then he who raised Christ from the dead will bring your mortal bodies to life also through his Spirit dwelling in you." To each of us is extended the promise which the prophet Ezekiel made to the nation of Israel: "O my people, I will open your graves and have you rise from them."

Today we are in a position to put together the message of three Sundays of Lent. On the Third Sunday Jesus promised the woman at the well, "The water I give shall become a fountain... leaping up to provide eternal life." For us that water is the sacrament of baptism. On the Fourth Sunday Jesus cured the man who had been born blind. That miracle was a symbol of the light of faith which comes to us in baptism and enlightens us to see God and each other in a new way. And today the raising of Lazarus is a foreshadowing that, because of baptism, we will be raised from the dead for eternal life. Lent will soon end, but the grace of baptism will lead us to everlasting life.

Passion or Palm Sunday, A

We Celebrate a Single Reality
Is 50:4-7; Ph 2:6-11; Mt 26:14-27:66

This Sunday we enter upon a time which is known as Holy Week or the Great Week. It begins with Palm Sunday and the triumphant procession of Jesus into the city of Jerusalem. This entrance is a prelude to those events which God planned whereby he would exalt Jesus as King and unite him with the people of his kingdom.

On Holy Thursday evening we see Jesus institute the sacrament of the Eucharist. We should view Holy Thursday as the eve of Good Friday. In the reckoning which Jesus followed, Friday began with the setting of the sun on Thursday. He gave us the Eucharist on that evening in order to perpetuate for all time the reality which would be carried out in the daytime of Friday, his sacrificial death on the cross.

Our Holy Thursday Mass is actually the Mass of Good Friday as a Saturday evening Mass is the Mass of Sunday. This means that we should not look upon the events of the Last Supper in isolation from the sacrifice of the cross. In the daylight hours of Good Friday we recall the details of the suffering and death of Jesus, the substance of which is a reality in the celebration of the Eucharist. But there is even more to the Eucharist than the death of Jesus, as the subsequent events reveal.

When darkness falls after the burial of Jesus, the liturgy retreats in silence during the night and throughout the day of the Sabbath. The only prayer of the Church is the muted offering of the Liturgy of the Hours. There is a hushed air of expectancy, like the counting of the conductor before the downbeat when orchestra and chorus join in a jubilant sound.

The Easter Vigil introduces this jubilation. The Vigil begins in darkness to emphasize that Christ is the Light of the world and that his resurrection is a blazing forth of God's truth and love. Through the sacrament of baptism during the vigil the Church, the body of Christ, incorporates new members to illustrate that people form the kingdom of the glorified and risen King. The penitential spirit is transformed into the joy of a new "Alleluia" and the Mass of the Resurrection is celebrated.

The reality of Easter reveals that the Eucharist is the celebration of the resurrection as well as the death of Jesus. The two go together. Although the events of the first great, Holy Week unfolded in a sequence of time, and although we separate them in our liturgical observances, they are so intimately connected that they form but a single reality. This reality is known as the Paschal Mystery.

Christ's death and resurrection are somewhat like the two sides of a coin. Heads and tails are different and yet they form a single coin. People who participate in all the liturgy of Holy Week should step back and view the events as coming together as a whole, which is the Paschal Mystery. Those who are present only for Sunday Mass should realize that the resurrection is the outcome of the death of Jesus, that Easter flows from Good Friday. All of us should see the death and resurrection of Christ, the Paschal Mystery, as the great, holy reality of this great, Holy Week, of which the Eucharist is the sacrament.

Passion or Palm Sunday, A (alternate)

Easter Is a Trinity
Is 50:4-7; Ph 2:6-11; Mt 26:14-27:66

When we hear the word, "Trinity," we readily think of the Father, Son, and Holy Spirit. Another important trinity consists of the three days known as the Easter Triduum. They are Good Friday, Holy Saturday, and Easter Sunday when we celebrate the trinity of Jesus' death, burial, and resurrection.

Good Friday and Easter Sunday call to our minds the awesome reality of the Paschal Mystery. It is why Jesus became human, why he was born and lived among us. Lost between these two momentous days, like an orphan to whom scarcely any attention is given, is Holy Saturday. It is the day of Jesus in the tomb. As the Father rested on the seventh day from the work of creation, so Jesus rested on the seventh day from the work of salvation.

Saturday is the link between Friday and Sunday not only chronologically but theologically. The tomb is the sign that Jesus was really dead. His death on the cross was not an illusion, not some kind of pretense by divinity in the guise of humanity, not a mere interval between this life and the next. Jesus, the eternal Son of God, having opened his arms freely on the cross, and having offered his spirit to the Father, died. The burial of Jesus tells us that he was really dead.

But the tomb is also the sign of the resurrection. Those who came to the tomb early on Sunday morning found it to be empty. The resurrection of Jesus did not consist in his being restored to some spiritual life only. Nor can he be considered to have been raised to new life only in the sense that he now lives in the minds and hearts of his people. The empty tomb declares that Jesus was raised in the fullness of his humanity because Jesus was beloved by his Father not only in soul but in body, not only in his spirit but in his flesh.

Holy Saturday is the day of the tomb, the memorial of the burial of Jesus. The only liturgical prayer on Holy Saturday is the Liturgy of the Hours, the divine office. Those who do not offer the prayer of the Church may nonetheless capture something of its spirit by joining in some of the psalms which are assigned to this day, especially psalms 4, 16, 27, and 143.

Ideally all of Saturday should be spent in quiet and recollection. It is a day for silence. Of course this ideal is difficult to achieve when duties call people to activity: some people have to go to their jobs, others have to shop for Easter dinner, and some will want to do some Easter cleaning. But everyone can find at least an hour or so to spend with Jesus in the tomb by recalling his death and awaiting his resurrection. An appropriate practice is visiting a cemetery to pray for loved ones who have gone before us in faith and for all the dead "whose faith is known to God alone."

Once a year we celebrate the Sacred Triduum of the death, burial, and resurrection of Jesus. The celebration begins on Holy Thursday evening because Jesus at that time instituted the Holy Eucharist, the sacrament which makes his death, burial and resurrection a reality among us in every Mass. At this time God offers us the grace to grow in our understanding and appreciation of the Paschal Mystery.

Solemnity of Easter, A (Saturday night)

The Easter Story
Ex 14:15-15:1; Rm 6:3-11; Mt 28:1-10

Easter is our great celebration because it is the story of our salvation in Christ. Every story has a beginning, a middle, and an end, and so does ours. In a typical plot boy and girl meet to begin the story. They fall in love. In the middle of the story obstacles arise and conflicts develop which either separate the lovers or bring about a misunderstanding between them. When love triumphs over all, they come back together and live happily ever after. But if loves fails, the story ends in tragedy.

In a story we all know well, it was love at first sight for Romeo and Juliet. But there was an obstacle. Their families, the Montagues and the Capulets, were mortal enemies and neither would hear of a marriage. Even the great love between Romeo and Juliet was not strong enough to overcome the hatred between the families, and the story ended in the tragic suicides of the lovers.

When Jesus came into our world, it was love at first sight. At the time of his birth the shepherds came and worshipped him and the Magi offered him precious gifts. It was no wonder. He was attractive as a baby and offered no challenge. When he grew up and began to preach, matters started to change.

Jesus proclaimed paradoxical doctrines: the poor were blessed, the humble would be exalted, those who serve are really first. He declared that to be his disciple meant taking up the cross every day. He prophesied that even he would suffer and die but would be raised up on the third day.

Enmities developed. Hatred hatched a plot against him. He was crucified. It seemed to be a tragedy, a victory of hatred over love. But we know that is not the truth. We see that the resurrection was a triumph over sin and death. Love was the conqueror after all.

The resurrection, in a sense, is the end of the story for Jesus. He is living happily ever after with his Father in heaven. But at which point are we in the story? Some of us, newly baptized this night, are at the beginning when love is strong and affection is fervent. Most of us are somewhere in the middle of the story; it is a crucial time.

Some are returning to Mass at Easter after a separation from the Church. They must now persevere so that what had been a separation may not become a divorce from God. Some have made a good confession after recognizing their growing indifference to God like a husband and wife who have taken each other for granted. They must now deepen their appreciation for our faith. Some may have realized that they are standing pat in their religion, despite the lack of any serious sins. They must be determined to grow in their love for God and all his children.

Our relationship with God through his Church is a love story. It can end in either triumph or tragedy. The brilliant light of a joyful Easter filled with jubilant Alleluias is God's offer of the grace we need to turn any tragedy into triumph. The end of our story can be, "And they lived happily ever after."

Solemnity of the Resurrection, A

Easter Is a Story Without Suspense
Ac 10:34, 37-43; Col 3:1-4 or 1 Cor 5:6-8; Jn 20:1-9

The Easter story is the great event of our salvation in Christ. Like every story, it has a beginning, a middle, and an end. An element which makes a story interesting is suspense. Whether it is a novel or a short story, the narrative gains impetus as we read on toward the climax. If you are just at the beginning of a story and someone tells you how it turns out, you probably will not bother to continue with the book. Knowing the conclusion eliminates suspense and destroys your interest.

Imagine you had never heard the story of our salvation in Christ. You pick up the Gospels and begin to read about the conception and birth of Jesus. Right away there is some indication of how the story will turn out because Herod threatens the life of Jesus shortly after his birth. Is this some indication of his fate? You are not sure and so there is some suspense.

You read into the middle of the story. Slowly suspense begins to disappear. It seems obvious that Jesus, though innocent, will be put to death. In fact, three times Jesus himself predicts that he will go up to Jerusalem there to suffer and to die. When you get to the part about his passion and death, you are not surprised. You go back and check the three predictions of his death and you notice something you missed the first time: Jesus not only said that he would die but that he would also be raised up on the third day. You return to where you were in the text and read on, and there it is. The climax of the story goes beyond his death to his resurrection. There was little or no suspense in the story. What Jesus had predicted came true in the end. The resurrection of Jesus is not, however, the actual end of the story. It goes on to include us because all that Jesus did was for our salvation.

Our story had its beginning the day we were baptized. We were born again of water and the Holy Spirit. We became children of God, part of his family, the Church, and heirs of the kingdom of heaven. Easter is a reminder of the beginning because during our celebration of this great feast people are initiated into the Church through baptism, confirmation, and First Eucharist, and all of us are invited to renew our baptismal commitment.

After baptism we enter the middle of the story. If there is to be suspense, it begins now. Such suspense is of our own doing and does not depend on God. We have freedom to make our own choice. How will our story end? That is up to us. We can color the middle of the story with uncertainty which causes tension and anxiety, or we can flavor it with an expectation which gives a joyful hope. There was no suspense for Jesus because he was following the plan of his Father. Jesus declared, "I have come to do the will of him who sent me." Jesus has taught us to pray to the Father, "Thy will be done," and he urges us to follow his example. In real life, as opposed to a story about life, suspense is not needed for interest. In fact, we gain serenity and peace when we know how our story will end. A life which begins through Christ and is lived with Christ will end in Christ and the glory of his resurrection.

Second Sunday of Easter, A

An Absent Thomas Is a Doubting Thomas
Ac 2:42-47; 1 P 1:3-9; Jn 20:19-31

One aspect of this Sunday's Gospel is so powerful that it has given an expression to our language. Everyone knows what it means to say that a person is a "doubting Thomas." Thomas the Apostle insisted on seeing the Lord Jesus before he would give up his doubt that Jesus truly had been raised from the dead.

On the evening of the Sunday of the resurrection, Jesus came and stood before his disciples. By showing them his hands and side, he made clear to them that he was the one who had been crucified and who was now raised from the dead. Thomas missed out because, so to speak, he did not come to church that Sunday. The room where the disciples were staying did not constitute the Church. The place was incidental. The people who were Jesus' disciples formed the Church which had been born from his side when he was dying on the cross. Now Jesus had come to confirm and strengthen their faith through the gift of the Holy Spirit.

Thomas may have had a good excuse for not being at church that eventful Sunday. Whatever the problem was, he corrected it the following Sunday. He was with the disciples, the assembly of the Church. Jesus revealed himself to Thomas because Thomas had once again joined his spiritual brothers and sisters.

These men and women, the first to believe in Christ, were instructed that they were a new people, the family of God "who in his great mercy had given them a new birth, a birth unto hope which draws its life from the resurrection of Jesus Christ from the dead" (second reading). They learned what they had to do on all the Sundays following the resurrection. The first reading today informs us that they "devoted themselves to the apostles' teaching and the communal life, to the breaking of bread and the prayers."

We follow their example. We come together on Sunday as a local expression of the universal Church. We listen to the apostles' teaching in the scripture readings of the day. We offer our prayers together, and we celebrate the breaking of the bread, the New Testament code word for the Holy Eucharist, which is the source of our communal life as children of one heavenly Father.

From this assembly we do not absent ourselves as Thomas did from the first gathering of disciples. We see the necessity of uniting with our sisters and brothers in prayer. We want to acknowledge that Jesus comes to us as we are gathered in his name.

The church building is not a place of convenience to house a number of people so that Mass will not have to be celebrated an excessive number of times on Sunday. The physical structure represents a great truth which is strongly stressed by the Second Vatican Council: "It has pleased God to save us and make us holy, not merely as individuals without any mutual bonds, but by forming us into a single people, a people who worship him in truth and who serve him in holiness" (*Constitution on the Church*, 9). We should not be a doubting Thomas; nor should we be an absent Thomas.

Third Sunday of Easter, A

The Church Is Our Emmaus
Ac 2:14, 22-28; 1 P 1:17-21; Lk 24:13-35

By the time St. Luke came to write his Gospel around the year 75 A.D., the first Christians had already laid the foundation for our tradition of coming together on Sundays to hear the story of Jesus and to celebrate the Eucharist.

In the beginning, before the New Testament was composed, the stories were told as people remembered them. The four evangelists, inspired by the Holy Spirit, committed these narratives to writing so that they would not be lost. Now many centuries later we are blessed on Sunday to hear proclaimed to us from the sacred text these wonderful narratives.

As we hear the Gospel, we note that the evangelist never begins by saying, "Once upon a time...." One obvious reason is that the Gospel is not a fairy tale, a fiction. Another very important reason is that the introduction to a fairy tale invites us to drift into the fanciful past through our imagination. The purpose of the Gospel may seem less romantic. It is to make us aware of present reality. Our faith is that we see what God has done in order to understand what God is doing. We listen to what God has said so that we may grasp what God is saying. God's words and actions of the past are present among us, especially during the celebration of the sacred liturgy.

This Sunday we hear the touching story of how two disciples encountered Jesus on the night of his resurrection but at first failed to recognize him. As Jesus spoke to them on the road to their home in Emmaus and explained the Scriptures to them, their hearts were burning inside them. When Jesus sat down to eat with them, he took bread, pronounced the blessing, broke the bread and began to distribute it to them. Then they recognized him.

St. Luke preserved this story, not so that we could look back and see how blessed these two disciples were, but so that we could believe that what Jesus had done for them he continues to do for us. When we follow our sacred tradition of coming together for Mass on Sunday, the church becomes our Emmaus. Jesus speaks to us through the Sacred Scriptures. We may at times not be particularly stirred by what we hear, but when we open ourselves to the grace of the Holy Spirit, the author of the Scriptures, the words have the power to penetrate our being. Then we will realize that it really is Jesus who speaks to us.

As we look to the altar during the eucharistic prayer we see the actions of Jesus and hear his words as surely as did the two disciples in their home: "He took bread, pronounced the blessing, then broke the bread and began to distribute it."

St. Luke notes that the name of one of the disciples was Cleopas. He does not tell us the name of the other one. We are that disciple, all of us who gather on Sundays to fulfill our sacred tradition of hearing the word of God and celebrating the Holy Eucharist together in our church which is for us a real, and not a fanciful, Emmaus.

Fourth Sunday of Easter, A

Being in Love with Priesthood
Ac 2:14, 36-41; 1 P 2:20-25; Jn 10:1-10

I love being a priest. I can think of a number of things I could have done and would have enjoyed if I had not been a priest, so it is not as if I had no alternative.

I would have liked being a professor of literature, to smoke a pipe and wear one of those tweed coats with leather patches on the elbows, and teach about dead poets. But I prefer to preach about Jesus who is alive and who brings greater beauty to life than the poets of all times, dead or alive. It is a joy to wear, not a tweed jacket but vestments, since vestments symbolize my being clothed in Christ who is the one priest of our religion.

My favorite sport is baseball. I realize that I would never have been wealthy enough to have been an owner or talented enough to have been a player, but maybe I could have been a scout. It would have been satisfying to search for youngsters who seemed to show the ability to become a professional and to follow them up through the levels of baseball to the major leagues. But I am happier searching for lost sheep and gathering the flock around Christ, the Good Shepherd.

I confess that I could have been quite content to have married a beautiful woman who was not only a great cook but also fabulously wealthy, and who never tired of spoiling me. But to tell the truth, I think that God has spoiled me with the beautiful and fulfilling grace of a vocation to share in the ordained priesthood of his Son.

But the joy of proclaiming Christ is lacking when people are not eager to learn the great truths of our faith. It is frustrating to gather people together as one in the Church, especially for the celebration of the sacred liturgy, when they seem intent on going their own way, complaining about everything in the parish and of being satisfied with nothing. It is heroic virtue to continue to be thrilled about being a priest when people insist on turning their own beauty into ugliness through pettiness and gossip, and who resist participating fully and actively in the eucharistic banquet.

I say these things so that Catholics may realize that priests are ordained for them, not for themselves, and that priests do not fulfill their mission unless people are eager to cooperate with them. I know that some Catholics feel that they have been given an incompetent priest. All of us are disappointed when priests betray their calling and violate the trust which people place in them. But let's think about the ordinary, good priests who are trying their best with God's grace to live and act in accord with their vocation as priests. Such priests need people who are trying their best to live and act in accord with their vocation as Catholics.

The Pope has designated the Fourth Sunday of Easter as world day of prayer for vocations to the priesthood. Pray we must, but living as good Catholics will encourage priests to persevere generously in their calling and move others to join them in what can and should be a joyful, satisfying, and beautiful life.

[See the following homily as an alternate for this Sunday.]

Fourth Sunday of Easter, A (alternate)

The Shepherd and His Flock
Ac 2:14, 36-41; 1 P 2:20-25; Jn 10:1-10

One of the most endearing, as well as enduring, images of Jesus is that of the Good Shepherd. It was and remains a favorite of Christian artists going back as far as the time of the catacombs in Rome. We are far removed from a society in which shepherding was a common and almost indispensable occupation, and yet we continue to find in the Good Shepherd a picture which gives us a sense of warmth and security. The shepherd cared for his flock. He provided for their nourishment and protection, and he remained faithful to his sheep.

When Christians pray Psalm 23, the "Good Shepherd" psalm, they almost always think of Jesus, even though the psalm is really about God the Father. The truth of our saying, "Like father, like son," applies in this instance. Going a step further in our doctrine of the Trinity, we see that God the Father, the eternal Good Shepherd, and his Son who came into our world as the living image of his Father, are imbued with a spirit of love, the Holy Spirit, who is the bond of their union and the expression of their devotion to one another.

When Jesus came to our earth, he brought with him the faithful love which is the family life of God in the blessedness of a Trinitarian life. He wants his Church to be a family, a reflection of the Trinity, in which a spirit of unselfish love prevails, where mutual care, nourishment, and protection are the manifest gift of the Spirit of love.

To lead and inspire the people of his Church, Christ has given us shepherds whom we call "pastors," the Latin word for shepherd. This Sunday, Good Shepherd Sunday, the Pope has designated as world day of prayer for vocations to the priesthood. Pray we must for good, faithful priests, especially now when many Catholics are shocked and disillusioned by the scandalous behavior of some priests. But we must do even more than pray. We must become flocks who are worthy of good shepherds.

Jesus came from heaven, from the divine family of which he is a part in eternity. Priests come from the Church here on earth, from among the people who form God's human family. Priests who have made serious, scandalous mistakes get the newspaper headlines and a prime place in the evening news. For them we ought to pray without passing judgment, and then we must focus our attention upon the many faithful priests, who day after day are zealous in their ministry, who try to be available to the seemingly ceaseless demands of their people, who offer devout celebrations of the liturgy despite their weariness from hard work, and who struggle to find time and energy to prepare helpful homilies according to the model of Jesus even when they scarcely have a moment for the reflective prayer which good preaching demands.

To these priests, our good shepherds, Catholics must respond energetically and enthusiastically by becoming the reflection here on earth of God's family. From the divine family came forth Jesus, and from Catholics who reflect that family will come the good shepherds whom we need in the Church today.

Fifth Sunday of Easter, A

The Way, The Truth, and The Life
Ac 6:1-7; 1 P 2:4-9; Jn 14:1-12

Michael Jordan is perhaps the best basketball player of all time. Young players look to him to show them the way to play basketball, but Michael Jordan has never said to anyone who wants to imitate him, "Follow me; I am the way." Albert Einstein was a great genius. From him the whole world learned deep truths about science, but Einstein never said, "I am the truth." Jonas Salk and other outstanding medical people like him have done much to safeguard human life, but not one of them dared to proclaim, "I am the life."

Jesus at the Last Supper in his final testament said what no human person could: "*I am the Way, the Truth, and the Life.*" The reason Jesus could make such a statement is that he is different from every human person. He is so different in fact that there never has been nor ever will be anyone like him. Jesus is unique. He is of human nature like us in all things except sin, but he is a divine person, equal to his Father in everything.

A guide tells us, "That is the way; follow it." Jesus says, "I am the way." A teacher tells us, "This is the truth, accept it." But Jesus says, "I am the truth." Parents tell their children, "We gave you life; appreciate it." But Jesus says, "I am the life."

Only because he is a divine person can Jesus rightly declare, "I am the Way, the Truth, and the Life."

We cannot do without Jesus. Without the way there is no going. Without the truth there is no knowing. Without the life there is no living. Where, then, do we find this divine person? We find him primarily in the celebration of the Mass.

At Mass Jesus is our great high priest. That means that he is the Way to the Father. He leads us in our worship of the Father, but not by pointing out the proper way to worship; rather he joins us to himself as members of his body, his mystical body, the Church. Through Christ we worship the Father in the best possible way.

At Mass Jesus speaks to us in the words of Sacred Scripture. He is the very Truth of God. He reveals himself to us, and in doing so he reveals his Father to us also since he and the Father are one. When we are with Christ at Mass we can be sure that we hear the truth.

At Mass in the Holy Eucharist Jesus is our Life. He never allows us to be neglected in the distribution of this sacred food and drink. By his almighty divine power he changes bread into his body given up for us and wine into his blood poured out for us. His body and blood become our spiritual nourishment, strengthening and increasing his gift of supernatural life within us. We became so united with Christ that we no longer live alone; we live in him.

Our worship is through, with, and in Christ. Through him because he is the Way. With him because he is the Truth. In him because he is the Life.

Sixth Sunday of Easter, A

The Power of the Spirit

Ac 8:5-8, 14-17; 1 P 3:15-18; Jn 14:15-21

Late at night a car goes out of control and bangs into a power pole. The driver is unhurt but electricity is cut off in the neighborhood. Those who are still awake light candles and find their flashlights. People are frustrated because their TV show is interrupted. A man goes into his bathroom and by habit flips the light switch. Of course the light does not go on. His wife begins to worry about whether the food in the refrigerator will spoil, and upstairs the young computer whiz is like a person whose hands have been severed.

Electricity is an unseen, awesome power but we usually do not appreciate it until we lose it, even for a short time. The Holy Spirit is somewhat like spiritual electricity. He is the power within the Church who is unseen and perhaps unappreciated.

On the night before he died Jesus had the Spirit on his mind. He knew that when he left this world, his disciples would continue to be his followers in his Church, but he understood that they and all of us would need the power of the Holy Spirit. That is why at the Last Supper, as recorded in this Sunday's Gospel, he made a solemn promise: "I will ask the Father and he will give you another Paraclete to be with you always: the Spirit of truth."

The Paraclete is our advocate (such is the literal meaning), the divine helper at our side. Jesus warned that the world neither sees nor accepts the Holy Spirit, but we, equally without seeing, must be open to the movement, the power of the Holy Spirit.

Reflect on what happened after Jesus sent the Spirit from his Father upon the Church at Pentecost. The apostles went forth to preach the good news and win people to the Church.

From a tiny band of dedicated disciples, the Church spread from Jerusalem throughout Judea and Samaria and even to the ends of the earth. The Church today is truly catholic, a universal Church which embraces people of every nation and ethnic origin. The power of the Holy Spirit accomplished this marvel.

Philip was one of the early dedicated preachers who went to Samaria. He baptized many converts. When the apostles, Peter and John, arrived they immediately were concerned that these neophytes should be fully incorporated into the Church. They prayed and imposed hands on them so that they might receive the Holy Spirit.

For us the sacrament of confirmation completes baptism. The bishop (or priest) prays, imposes hands, and anoints the baptized person with chrism on the forehead in the form of a cross, and says, "Be sealed with the Gift of the Holy Spirit."

Confirmation gives us both the right and the duty to call upon the Holy Spirit so that we may be faithful, active Catholics. St. Peter (second reading today) warns that we must be ever ready to reply should anyone ask of us the reason for our hope. To put it another way, we must give witness to our faith not only by words but by actions. People should know that we are Catholics by the way in which we live with such a veneration of Christ that Christ and his Church shape our values and our lives.

The power of the Spirit, like electricity, is real though unseen. Christ, unlike a power pole which can be knocked over, is with us always in the Church to grant us the gift of the Spirit.

Seventh Sunday of Easter, A
[unless Ascension is observed today]

Waiting for Pentecost
Ac 1:12-14; 1 P 4:13-16; Jn 17:1-11

Sometimes important things go unnoticed for a while. When Jesus died on the cross, his death seemed just another in a long line of executions in a distant and unimportant province of the Roman Empire. Even when Jesus rose from the dead, he made himself known to only a few, and the truth of the resurrection was cherished by a small number of disciples. These disciples pondered the meaning of these extraordinary events but without understanding them.

On this Sunday we await the great Solemnity of Pentecost. On the first Pentecost day the Holy Spirit made sure that the most important events of all of history would not go unnoticed. The Spirit, like a brilliant light, illuminated the cross and the tomb so that people of faith could begin to see their meaning. The disciples, filled with wisdom, were moved to penetrate the deep mystery of the death and resurrection of the Lord Jesus. They came to recognize that Jesus by his cross and resurrection had set us free from sin and death, and that by dying he had destroyed our death and by rising had restored our life.

In the Preface of our Second Eucharistic Prayer, we acknowledge that Jesus by his death and resurrection fulfilled his Father's will and won for him a holy people. We, the Church, are those people. The life which Jesus offered to his Father in sacrifice on the cross was restored to him in a glorious manner in his resurrection. From the cross the life which was manifested in the resurrection flowed into the Church, the people of God. The Church, born from the side of Christ as he was dying on the cross, was brought to light on the day of Pentecost. Pentecost is an epiphany, a manifestation of the Church to the world.

We celebrate Pentecost every year fifty days after Easter. During this celebration we must remember that within the twentieth century a monumental event took place which has rightly been called a new Pentecost. It was the Second Vatican Council, the twenty-first ecumenical council in the twenty-century history of the Church. Vatican II was a council by the Church about the Church.

From this event we take a renewed understanding of the Church. Vatican II declared: "By her relationship with Christ, the Church is a kind of sacrament or sign of intimate union with God, and of the unity of all people. She is also an instrument for the achieving of such union and unity." The will of God is that our relationship with him be lived out through our relationships within the Church. In fact, "it has pleased God to save us and to make us holy, not merely as individuals without any mutual bonds, but by forming us into a single people, a people who worship him in truth and who serve him in holiness."

The Church is not a club or a convenience. To understand the death of Jesus is to see that he opened his arms on the cross to embrace in unity and love all of God's people and to form them into his body, the Church. God's will is that we stand before him, not as isolated individuals, but as a united people, the universal Church. This week the Church prays for a renewal of Pentecost which will bring an ever deeper understand of the Church.

Solemnity of the Ascension

Forty Days and the Ascension
Ac 1:1-11; Eph 1:17-23; Mt 28:16-20

St. Luke in the Acts of the Apostles tells us that Jesus after his death and resurrection appeared to the apostles over a period of forty days and then ascended into heaven. In the Bible "forty" does not designate a mathematical sum. It is not to be taken literally. That would be reading the Bible as if it were contemporary literature. The number "forty" throughout the Bible does not refer to a specific numerical value. We ourselves may say that something happened two or three years ago, by which we mean an indefinite time. "Forty" in the Bible is something like that.

More importantly "forty" in the Bible indicates a period of time in which God accomplishes his work. There are sixteen references in the New Testament to forty days or forty years, and over seventy such references in the Old Testament. Two examples are the fasting of Jesus in the desert for forty days, and the wandering of the Israelites in the desert for forty years.

Our attention is now focused on the forty days after Easter, following which Jesus ascended into heaven. Forty in that instance, we must remember, has a meaning beyond a numerical figure. It points to the final acts of Jesus on this earth. Jesus was about to ascend to heaven. All was in readiness for that. He made his solemn promise that, despite the fact that he was to leave this world in bodily form, he would be with his Church always until the end of time. Jesus in union with his Father would send his Spirit, the Holy Spirit, upon the Church.

The Solemnity of the Ascension calls us to celebrate the truth that Jesus, after his death and resurrection, faithfully completed his mission on this earth and prepared the Church for the great event of Pentecost. The point is that when Jesus rose from the dead, he did not return to the form of life which he had lived on this earth from the moment of his conception in Mary's womb until his death on the cross. Jesus rose from the dead as Lord and Christ, the Savior of the world and the Head of his mystical body, the Church. His was now a glorified life. That is the theological meaning of our statement in the Creed: "He rose from the dead, ascended into heaven, and sits at the right hand of the Father."

We should recognize that Jesus did his part to fulfill the Father's plan. Now it is up to us. We need to be a people who take responsibility for the mission of the Church. We will know what to do and we will receive the strength to do it by being open to the movement of the Holy Spirit in our lives, the Spirit who was the gift to the Church on Pentecost, and who will come to us again in our liturgical celebration of Pentecost.

More than anything else the work of the Spirit is to form us into one body, the mystical body of Christ, the Church. Being Catholics does not mean that we stand in an individual relationship with God, isolated from other people. Being a Catholic means being part of the one body of Christ. Because we are one body in Christ we are as responsible for the well-being of each other as much as we are responsible for the well-being of the parts of our own human body. We express that responsibility in the Prayer of the Faithful, the General Intercessions. From these intercessions we must take the resolve to turn prayer into action which manifests the love we have for all the people of the Church, the body of Christ. However long we live, we should be able to put "forty" at the end in the sense that during our lives we have accomplished God's work on this earth.

Solemnity of Pentecost, A

The Christian and Catholic Church
Ac 2:1-11; 1 Cor 12:3-7, 12-13; Jn 20:19-23

After Jesus ascended into heaven, his disciples were alone and confused. They were not quite sure what they should do or even what it meant to be a disciple of Jesus. Were they another Jewish sect such as the Pharisees, or the Zealots, or the Essenes? They needed the Holy Spirit to enlighten them.

On the day of Pentecost the apostles remembered Jesus' parting words to them: "You will receive power when the Holy Spirit comes upon you; then you are to be my witnesses in Jerusalem, throughout Judea and Samaria, yes, even to the ends of the earth." Things became clearer. They were to move beyond Jerusalem and Judea into Samaria, Gentile territory. The realization that Gentiles were called as well as Jews made them realize that Jesus had done something new. Antioch in Syria beyond the boundaries of Judea and Israel became the center for a large number of disciples, and it was in Antioch that the disciples were called Christians for the first time (Acts 11:26).

Only after much discussion, debate, and at times very heated arguments did the Christians come to see that Jesus had founded a Church for all people of all times and all places. Then St. Ignatius, the bishop of Antioch, around the year 100 A.D. used the term "Catholic" for the first time to refer to his Christian community. The word, of course, means "Universal." It is most appropriate for the Church of Jesus Christ, and the name eventually became permanent and official. We now express our belief in the "one, holy, *catholic*, and apostolic Church."

Catholic we must be not only in name but in reality. The Church is not Italian or Irish or Polish. It is not Mexican or American or Canadian. It is universal. The Second Vatican Council was a striking witness to the catholicity of the Church.

At the First Vatican Council in 1869 there were bishops from all over the world but they were not indigenous bishops. For the most part they were European, even those who came from the United States. At Vatican II the bishops were not only *from* all the countries in the world, they were *of* all the countries in the world.

Paradoxically the Church to be fully Catholic must be freed from a single culture in order to embrace all cultures. The change from Latin with its European roots to the vernaculars of the world was more than a way of facilitating full, active participation in the liturgy; it was an expression of a deeper understanding of the Church as Catholic.

Latin, or any single language is not the means for oneness in the Church. Sharing in the same Holy Eucharist is the means for the Church to be both one and holy. The many vernacular languages manifest that the Church has been truly apostolic in proclaiming the good news to all the world, and these languages are a sign that the Church is now truly Catholic or universal.

Pope John Paul II declared in his book, *Crossing the Threshold of Hope*, that the Second Vatican Council was like a new Pentecost for the Church. In celebrating the liturgical observance of Pentecost we give thanks and praise to God for calling us into the Church which is one, holy, catholic, and apostolic.

Solemnity of the Trinity

God Is Family
Ex 34:4-6, 8-9; 2 Cor 13:11-13; Jn 3:16-18

Our names are very important to us. Our first name indicates who we are. Our last name indicates the family to which we belong. We are not only Jane or James; we are also the child of our parents and the sibling of our brothers and sisters. We are an individual and we are part of our family.

Even more important to us than our own names is the name of Jesus. It is the sacred name, given to Jesus by the angel before he was conceived. That name is precious to us, but it does not actually indicate Jesus' identity; rather it designates his mission. The name "Jesus" means "God saves."

The family name of Jesus, the name which is his from all eternity, is Son of God. Being the Son of God is the actual identity of our Savior. When Jesus asked the apostles, "Who do you say that I am?" Peter responded, "You are the Messiah, the Son of the living God." Jesus commended Peter: "Blessed are you, Simon son of Jonah, for flesh and blood have not revealed this to you, but my heavenly Father" (Matthew 16:16ff.). The true identity of Jesus was not apparent even to the apostles. To know it required a revelation from God the Father who declared of Jesus, "This is my beloved Son" (Matthew 3:17).

Father and Son from all eternity, that is the great revelation which has been granted to us. Jesus is not only an individual; he is part of a divine family. And yet the New Testament by itself did not speak of this relationship in terms precise enough for a clear definition of this doctrine. The Church pondered the revelation for three centuries before it was ready to formulate our faith by means of the first two ecumenical councils, that of Nicea in the year 325 and that of Constantinople in 381 (Vatican II was the twenty-first such council).

We will never comprehend the Trinity, not even in heaven, but the statement of our faith is clear. In God there are three persons, all equal and yet distinct. The Father is the first person who begets his Son, the second person in eternity, and they are bound by an everlasting love, the Holy Spirit, the third person. God is Father, God is Son, God is Spirit. These are the personal names of God, and they indicate that God is relationships. God is not alone, some mighty potentate living in isolated and solitary splendor. God rejoices in the warmth of intimacy and the richness of relationships. God is family.

The truth of God is not abstract and without significance for us. God is eager to share his richness with us, to draw us into the intimacy which is the divine life. "Those whom God foreknew he also predestined to be conformed to the image of his Son so that the Son might be the firstborn among many brothers and sisters" (Romans 8:29). Through baptism we have been born into God's family. We have become children in God's child, his eternal Son who became human to lift us up to the divine.

Jesus is Son forever and we will enjoy being one with him in the Trinity forever and ever. To which we must add a fervent and grateful, "Amen."

Solemnity of the Trinity, A (alternate)

Getting to Know (and Love) God
Ex 34:4-6, 8-9; 2 Cor 13:11-13; Jn 3:16-18

Getting to know a person can be a fascinating experience which changes one's life. Two people are attracted to each other. They begin to date. Next they are engaged. Then they marry. From what they learned about each other they decided that they want to live as one in the sacrament of marriage for the rest of their lives.

Everyone in the human family attempts in various ways to know God, whether everyone realizes that or not. The human mind is compelled to search for ultimates. In the fourth century before Christ in Greece great philosophers were engaged in a profound search for truth, in particular Socrates, Plato, and Aristotle. St. Thomas Aquinas was so impressed by Aristotle's philosophy that he made it the basis of his theology.

Aristotle simply by using his intellect arrived at a conviction that there had to be a supreme being. He understood this supreme being as the uncaused cause, the unmoved mover. If Aristotle were alive today he would say to his students, "Lay out all the components of an automobile on a huge sheet. Throw all of them into the air. Will they assemble themselves into an automobile? Of course not. There has to be someone who puts all the parts together. That is the ultimate cause, the supreme being." Later St. Paul would write in his Letter to the Romans, "God's eternal power and divinity have become visible, recognized through the things he has made" (1:20).

The philosophical approach to God is impressive but pretty impersonal. Brilliant though he was, Aristotle was unaware that fully fifteen centuries before his time God had revealed himself to a wandering Aramean to whom God himself gave the name, Abraham. God saved Abraham's offspring from slavery in Egypt and led them into a promised land. Later God revealed through Moses that he is "a merciful and gracious God, slow to anger and rich in kindness and fidelity." Through the prophets God solemnly testified, "I will be your God and you will be my people." God manifested that he is a loving God. Abraham and the revelation granted to him are so important to us as Catholics that the liturgy calls Abraham our father in faith.

And yet it took Jesus Christ and his Church to reveal that this personal, loving God is actually a family, that God is Father, Son, and Spirit.

God did not become a Father. He *is* a Father from all eternity. Without beginning or end he pours out the gift of his life to his Son. Fatherhood is who he is as a person. The second person did not become a Son. He is not later in time than his Father. Rather with the Father he is eternal. Being a Son is who the second person is. The Holy Spirit did not come into being after the Son. The Spirit too is eternal. The Spirit is the personified love between Father and Son, uniting them in an eternal embrace of family devotion.

Who God is as the Trinity is of ultimate importance to us. We are more than creatures of God. Through baptism we have become God's children, like the Son, united in love by the Holy Spirit. God is more than a mystery to be contemplated. God is the great reality of life and love, and we are part of his family.

Solemnity of the Lord's Body and Blood, A (*Corpus Christi*)

A Blessed Procession
Dt 8:2-3, 14-16; 1 Cor 10:16-17; Jn 6:51-58

Some of the fondest religious recollections of older Catholics center around the Corpus Christi procession. They fondly remember the long, winding lines of people, accompanied by the subtly moving melodies of the Gregorian Chant and the arcane Latin syllables of ancient hymns, always crowned by the magnificence of the *Pange Lingua* and its familiar conclusion, the *Tantum Ergo*. Some of us miss those old time processions.

The truth is that every Sunday during the communion of the Mass we have the opportunity of sharing in a Blessed Sacrament procession, accompanied by hymns and songs. The meaning of this procession is different from those of earlier times and actually goes back to the youth of the Church. This procession reflects the beautiful doctrine that we have been freed by the death of Christ from the slavery of sin, and we have risen with him to a new life in his Church. The purpose of the communion procession during Mass is to celebrate the Holy Eucharist as the great sacrament of the death and resurrection of Christ, the sacred means of our unity in his body, the Church.

The doctrine which teaches us that the Blessed Sacrament is a sacrament of unity is not new. It is just about as old as can be. St. Paul has left us in his First Letter to the Corinthians the most ancient written presentation of the Blessed Sacrament. In the tenth chapter he wrote, "Is not the bread we break a sharing in the body of Christ? Because the loaf is one, we, many though we are, are one body, for we all partake of the one loaf."

Singing together is the sign of our joyful union with each other in Christ, and yet many parishes experience difficulty in getting people to sing during the procession to the communion station. Some liturgical observers believe that the problem lies in a failure to understand, or to accept, the truth that the Eucharist is a sacrament of unity. Those of us who grew up in the 1930's certainly did not receive any instruction about the Eucharist as the "effective sign of the unity of the Church." Communion was a matter between the individual and the Lord. People were clearly taught the beautiful truth that Jesus himself comes to us in Holy Communion, but that teaching is quite incomplete without adding that Jesus in the Eucharist unites all of us through himself with each other.

The communion song begins as soon as the priest receives the body of the Lord. It should be simple and easy to sing. If necessary, people should carry the hymn book with them during the procession. Sometimes a cantor or choir sings the verse of a song and the people join in a refrain which can be sung without the aid of a book. Singing by the people is an integral part of the communion procession.

On the night before he died, Jesus prayed that we all might be one as he and his Father are one. Then he gave us the gift of the Holy Eucharist, the sacrament of our oneness with him and each other. The Church believes that this wonderful reality is something worth singing about together on our way to receive the body and the blood of the Lord.

Solemnity of the Body and Blood of Christ, A (alternate)

The Eucharist Is Our Great Tradition
Dt 8:2-3, 14-16; 1 Cor 10:16-17; Jn 6:51-58

This homily is drawn from the writings of an important person from our Catholic past. His first name is Justin but he does not have a last name. He died as a martyr at Rome in the year 165. We are blessed to have some of his writings. Of particular interest is his description of the celebration of the Sunday Eucharist at a time which was very close to the era of Christ and his apostles. This is what St. Justin wrote:

"On Sunday we have a common assembly of all our members. The recollections of the apostles or the writings of the prophets are read. When the reader has finished, the president of the assembly speaks to us; he urges everyone to imitate the examples of virtue we have heard in the readings. Then we all stand up together and pray.

"At the conclusion of our prayer, bread and wine and water are brought forward. The president offers prayers and gives thanks to the best of his ability, and the people give their assent by saying, 'Amen.' The Eucharist is distributed, everyone present communicates, and the deacons take it to those who are absent.

"The wealthy may make a contribution, and they themselves decide the amount. The collection is placed in the custody of the president who uses it to help the orphans and widows and all who are for any reason in distress, whether they are sick, in prison, or away from home. In a word, he takes care of all who are in need.

"We hold our common assembly on Sunday because it is the first day of the week, the day on which God put darkness and chaos to flight and created the world, and because on that same day our savior Jesus Christ rose from the dead. For he was crucified on Friday and on Sunday he appeared to his apostles and disciples and taught them the things which we have passed on for your consideration.

"No one may share the Eucharist with us unless he believes that what we teach is true, unless he is washed in the regenerating waters of baptism for the remission of his sins, and unless he lives in accordance with the principles given us by Christ. We do not consume the eucharistic bread and wine as if it were ordinary food and drink, for we have been taught that as Jesus Christ our Savior became a man of flesh and blood by the power of the Word of God, so also the food that our flesh and blood assimilates for its nourishment becomes the flesh and blood of the incarnate Jesus by the power of his own words contained in the prayer of thanksgiving.

"The apostles in their recollections which are called Gospels handed down to us what Jesus commanded them to do. They tell us that he took bread, gave thanks and said: 'Do this in memory of me. This is my body.' In the same way he took the cup, he gave thanks and said: 'This is my blood.' Ever since then we have constantly reminded one another of these things."

And ever since then Catholics throughout the centuries have been faithful to the command of Christ, "Do this in memory of me." St. Justin would readily recognize the Mass as the liturgy which he experienced. The Catholic Church never has and never will deviate from this sacred tradition.

The Season of the Year
Cycle A

"Recalling the mysteries of redemption,
the Church opens to the faithful the riches of the
Lord's powers and merits, so that these are in some
way made present at all times, and the faithful
are enabled to lay hold of them and
become filled with saving grace."
(*Constitution on the Liturgy*, 102)

Second Sunday of the Year, A

Behold the Lamb of God!
Is 49:3, 5-6; 1 Cor 1:1-3; Jn 1:29-34

Playing word association can be fun. One person says a word and you answer what comes to your mind. I say "small" and you say "big." I say "football" and you say "Super Bowl." John the Baptist says "Lamb of God" and we probably say "What?"

In pointing Jesus out, would not John have done better to have exclaimed, "Look, there is the Lord" or "There is the Savior" or "There is the Christ"? All of these titles seem more impressive than "Lamb of God."

Actually for the Jews to whom John preached, the expression "Lamb of God" called to mind the entire doctrine of their faith as the People of God. They immediately thought, not of the smallness of a lamb, but of the bigness of God's power and mercy toward them since it was through the blood of the lamb that they had been saved from slavery in Egypt and brought to freedom and a new life in the promised land. Every year on the feast of the passover they remembered and celebrated their salvation by partaking of the passover supper.

In the Mass, the celebration of our salvation in Christ, we look upon the body and the blood of the Lord and we recognize him by acknowledging the words of the priest: "This is the Lamb of God who takes away the sins of the world." When we hear these words before Holy Communion, we are invited to remember what Jesus means to us as our paschal lamb. We express that meaning in the eucharistic acclamations. Remembering that the paschal lamb was slain in sacrifice, we are invited to reflect on the culmination of the coming of our Lord and Savior into this world: "Christ has died; Christ is risen; Christ will come again."

Thinking of the freedom granted to our ancestors in faith,

we are invited to reflect upon our freedom from sin: "Lord, by your cross and resurrection you have set us free. You are the Savior of the world." Thinking of the new life of our spiritual ancestors in the promised land, we are invited to reflect on our new life in Christ: "Dying you destroyed our death; rising you restored our life." Thinking of how our ancestors commemorated their salvation by partaking of the passover supper, we are invited to reflect on how we celebrate our salvation in the eucharistic banquet: "When we eat this bread and drink this cup, we proclaim your death, Lord Jesus, until you come in glory."

In his invitation to Holy Communion, the priest adds: "Happy are those who are called to his supper." Or another version is, "Blessed are those called to the banquet of the Lamb." The supper or banquet referred to is not the Last Supper but the wedding feast of the Lamb of God in heaven where all of God's faithful people celebrate God's covenant of love and fidelity (see Revelation 19:9). That magnificent, eternal banquet is our destiny because we are one with the Lamb of God in heaven.

No single word is sufficient as a response when we hear "Lamb of God," but a reflection on the richness of this title will help us to know Jesus better and lead us to fuller participation in the eucharistic banquet of the Lamb of God.

Third Sunday of the Year, A

Christ Calls Us by Name in Baptism
Is 8:23-9:3; 1 Cor 1:10-13, 17; Mt 4:12-23

St. Matthew today tells us how Jesus called some of the apostles. He could have told the story in a general way, simply informing us that Jesus gathered some special disciples around himself. Instead he made it a point to give us the names of those who were the first to be called by Jesus. They were Simon (later named Peter) and his brother, Andrew, and James and his brother, John. There is something special about our names.

A TV show ("Cheers") in its theme song expressed the sentiment that it's nice to go where everybody knows your name. How thrilled those four fishermen must have been when they heard Jesus calling them by name to be his followers! They were so deeply moved that they abandoned their former way of life on the spot and went off to follow Jesus. They saw something in Jesus which they had never witnessed before. The light of faith helped these men to begin to see Jesus for who he truly is, the Son of God. But at first the light was not the marvelous revelations which Isaiah prophesied when he wrote, "The people who walked in darkness have seen a great light." It was but a dim light, a light which allowed them at times to doubt Jesus and even to deny or abandon him at the time of his passion. But the light never went out. Rather it gradually grew and with the coming of the Holy Spirit at Pentecost it became like a bright, warming fire. Dedication replaced doubts.

Much the same happened to us. Through the Church at the time of our baptism Christ called us each by name. Speaking through the voice of the priest, he said: "Ann (or Andrew), Bridget (or Barry), (or whatever is our name), I baptize you in the name of the Father and the Son and the Holy Spirit." We were given a lighted candle, the symbol of faith. Whether we were infants or adults at the time, we received the light of faith. At first that light was a little dim but with the sacrament of confirmation, which completes baptism, that light was brightened.

With faith we see Jesus as truly the Son of God whom the Father has sent into this world, conceived as he was in the womb of Mary by the power of the Holy Spirit. We believe that Jesus went about preaching the good news of the kingdom of God, a good news which we continue to hear through the Scriptures and the other teachings of the Church. We know that Jesus' ministry led him to Jerusalem where he suffered, died and rose for our salvation. Our faith teaches that through our participation in the Holy Eucharist, we share in the marvel of the death and resurrection of God's Son.

We follow Christ by being part of his body, his mystical body, the Church. We can make our own the sentiments of Psalm 27: "The Lord is my light and my salvation; whom should I fear? The Lord is my life's refuge; of whom should I be afraid?"

The psalm continues, "One thing I ask of the Lord; this I seek: to dwell in the house of the Lord all the days of my life." We must always remain faithful to the call of our baptism, to remain in the Lord's house which is his Church, and never doubt or abandon Jesus Christ who has called us by name to be his followers.

Fourth Sunday of the Year, A

Happy People Live the Beatitudes
Zp 2:3, 3:12-13; 1 Cor 1:26-31; Mt 5:1-12

It is only natural to want to be happy, but happiness is elusive. It slips from our hands like a wet bar of soap in the shower. We all try to be happy, but we do not always agree on what happiness is. It is like having different tastes in music and food. We even differ on whether we should spend our money now on what we think will make us happy or whether we should save for a "rainy day" in the future.

Whatever people may think about happiness, Jesus stands alone in his teaching about what happiness is and how and when we can achieve it. We have all heard his teaching but perhaps we have failed to grasp the unique character of what Jesus proclaims.

We call his teaching the beatitudes, from the Latin word *beatus* which simply means "happy." We notice first that the beatitudes are not commandments nor are they even advice. They are declarations. The only thing which Jesus today tells us to do is "Be glad and rejoice." Other than that he is concerned with indicating in what happiness consists. He states directly that people are happy who are poor, sorrowful, lowly, and hungry. Equally he insists that they are happy who show mercy, who are peacemakers, and who suffer persecution. It is not really a list of things we would choose for ourselves. If we had received poverty, sorrow, and hunger as Christmas gifts, we would have thought that Santa Claus had become Scrooge indeed.

But Jesus is no Scrooge even though he says, "Humbug," to what a lot of people think constitutes happiness. The key to Jesus' teaching is found in the sixth beatitude which tells us, "Blessed are the single-hearted, for they shall see God."

The single-hearted are people who, like the saints, center

their entire lives on God. In their poverty they realize that real riches are found only in God. In their sorrow they discover that true joy is experienced only in God. In their lowliness they understand that only God can lift up a person. In their hunger and thirst they value the Eucharist because the body and the blood of the Lord will lead us to the great banquet in heaven. They show mercy, and not vengeance; they work for peace, and not hatred, because they know that God is the source of all mercy and peace. They are even willing to be persecuted because they feel privileged to suffer and even to die as a witness to the truth.

Because the single-hearted are centered on God they come to the realization that Jesus practiced what he preached. Jesus is the poor man who endured the sorrow of his passion and who became as lowly as a criminal on the cross. They see that Jesus underwent hunger and thirst in the desert to prepare for his mission, and that he transformed his emptiness into a yearning to fill us with his life and his love. Jesus showed mercy to the sinners, and he offered everyone the gift of his peace.

Although not one of the beatitudes is a commandment, we do well to tell ourselves, "Become like Jesus. Become single-hearted. Center your whole life on God." That would be good advice to give ourselves. In following it we will be able to fulfill the one thing which today Jesus tells us to do: "Be glad and rejoice for your reward in heaven is great."

Fifth Sunday of the Year, A

Shining Our Light On the Needy
Is 58:7-10; 1 Cor 2:1-5; Mt 5:13-16

A reporter during an interview with Pope John Paul II asked him, "For whom and for what do you pray?" The Pope answered by quoting the opening sentence of Vatican II's *Constitution on the Church in the Modern World*. That sentence is: "The joys and hopes, the sorrows and the anxieties of the people of this age, especially those who are poor or in any way afflicted are the joys and hopes, the sorrows and the anxieties of the followers of Christ" (from *Crossing the Threshold of Hope*, page 20).

Actually the Pope answered the question not only as he is the Pope but also as he is a Catholic, a follower of Christ, just like us. The direction of his prayer should be ours as well. Prayer of concern must lead, of course, to action of concern for others.

Turning prayer into action is the teaching of Isaiah the prophet in today's Mass: "Share your bread with the hungry, shelter the oppressed and the homeless. Clothe the naked when you see them, and do not turn your back on your own." These touching words were addressed to the Jewish exiles who were returning from slavery in Babylon. They found a land inhabited by a people not their own, a people who did not share their religion or their moral convictions. They felt like a minority in a somewhat hostile environment.

We are not unlike them in our own society. Catholics are not only a minority, but a growing number of people around us seem to be hardening their hearts against those who are in need, such as the hungry, the immigrants, the homeless, and welfare recipients. The needy are readily dismissed as unworthy and undeserving. In some places a mean spirit has replaced compassion. We Catholics are not immune to these influences. Sometimes the effects are so subtle that we are unaware of them.

Some people today would like the poor and the needy to huddle in some dark corner where they do not have to be seen. But Jesus teaches us that we must shine the light of our goodness on those in need so that they cannot be ignored. The prophet Isaiah helps us to understand what Jesus means by telling us: "If you remove from your midst oppression, false accusation and malicious speech, if you bestow your bread on the hungry and satisfy the afflicted, then light shall rise for you in the darkness."

We may need to call ourselves back to thinking like Catholics and to acting as followers of Christ, for whom the joys and sorrows, the needs and the anxieties of the people of this age, especially the poor or those who are afflicted are our concerns.

Actually all of us are in great need, no matter what our economic status may be. We are in need of God and his grace. God does not turn aside from us. He sees us and he is generous in his response to us, especially during the celebration of the Mass. He calls us away from the homelessness of the secular world into his home, the Church. Here he welcomes us as his beloved children, speaks to us gently and lovingly in the words of Sacred Scripture, and nourishes us with the body and the blood of his Son. Are we worthy of all this? Do we deserve it? Surely God's gracious generosity toward us should move us to follow the Pope's lead and to make the needs of others truly our own.

Sixth Sunday of the Year, A

Do Not Be Afraid to Climb the Ladder
Si 15:15-20; 1 Cor 2:6-10; Mt 5:17-37

A young boy was flying his kite when it became tangled in a tree. He rushed into the house and asked his father to get his kite for him. The father took him by the hand and said, "Come with me." They went into the garage where the father picked up a ladder, went out into the yard, and placed the ladder against the tree. He said to his young child, "Climb the ladder and get the kite for yourself." But the child was afraid and protested, "No, I will fall." The father insisted, "Climb the ladder; I will be here to catch you if you fall." Trembling but now determined, the boy went slowly up the ladder and retrieved his kite. He came down safely and with a big smile he embraced his father and said, "I did it!"

Jesus today is inviting us to climb a ladder. Today's Gospel is part of his Sermon on the Mount. In his sermon he urges us to work to achieve high ideals, not to be satisfied with the minimum, the lowest rung of the ladder, in our relationship with God and each other. Above all he does not want us to leave it to others, the saints, to follow the ideals he taught and exemplified.

In a moment of anger we might say, "I could murder that person," but of course we do not mean that. And yet the anger which underlies our outburst violates the ideal Jesus wants us to follow. We can rightly be aghast when we hear of domestic violence, but Jesus tells us that we must avoid even abusive language. We may lament the ludicrous ease with which TV and movies show people casually entering into adulterous relationships, but Jesus warns us that even lustful wishes are contrary to what he expects of us.

Somewhat shocking is Jesus' insistence that if a brother

or sister has anything against us, we must leave our gift at the altar and go and be reconciled. Do we dare to take him literally? Would most of us have to leave Mass to go and find a person whom we have offended so that we may seek reconciliation? A start is to pray for reconciliation and to resolve to seek forgiveness.

When we listen carefully to the words of Jesus in today's excerpt from his sermon, we should be able to conclude that Jesus teaches us that love for God cannot be separated from love for our neighbor. It is a serious error to act as if our relationship with God is personal and private and has nothing to do with people. When we acknowledge God as Father we must embrace in our love all of his children.

Ideals can scare us. Just looking at them can make us afraid. The child who wanted to rescue his kite had to change his way of thinking. It did not occur to him to try to get his kite on his own until his father taught him how. Even then he was afraid of falling. Today in his sermon Jesus has pointed out to us the way we are to follow as his disciples. We must believe that when we try to go higher, he will be with us to catch us if we fall and to put us back safely on our feet so that we may try again. Here at Mass he gives us the strength we need through the spiritual nourishment of his body and blood in the Holy Eucharist.

We must never ask, "What is the least I must do to avoid sin?" We should heed the voice of Jesus who is telling us, "Climb the ladder."

Seventh Sunday of the Year, A

Have We Made Any Progress?
Lv 19:1-2, 17-18; 1 Cor 3:16-23; Mt 5:38-48

The human race has made remarkable progress in recent history. Think of the contrast between a "horseless carriage" and a modern automobile, or the difference between that first flight at Kitty Hawk, North Carolina in 1903 and modern air travel. No one a hundred years ago even imagined that people would one day sit in front of a box, called television, and see images and hear sounds.

Our advances are astounding, and yet the question remains whether we are more moral and civilized than people who lived a century ago or even thirty centuries ago. Jesus in the Gospel alludes to the Book of Exodus which gives the account of incidents which took place roughly 1400 years before he was born. From that context he quotes the aphorism, "An eye for an eye and a tooth for a tooth." The meaning is *only* an eye for an eye and *only* a tooth for a tooth. In other words, this is a plea for a precise justice at a time when a potentate could without hesitation have put someone to death for having stolen a single grape from the royal table. Recall that even in Jesus' day, so many years after this plea for moderation, King Herod did not hesitate to cut off the head of John the Baptist because this petty monarch had made a foolish promise to a lewd dancing girl.

Jesus looks for a high morality in his followers. In a picturesque image he demands that we not insist on strict justice. That is the meaning of the injunction to turn the other cheek. Jesus goes *further*. He declares that it is not enough to love our countrymen. He gives the command to love even our enemies and to pray for our persecutors. Cynics sneer at these teachings. They think that Jesus is naive and that his teachings are impractical ideals. Of course Jesus is not naive; he is infinitely wise.

The ideals he proposes are not unattainable goals. At least we as people of faith must hear and accept his challenge: "You must become perfect as your heavenly Father is perfect." Jesus expects that the axiom, "Like Father, like Son," will be realized not only by himself but by us as well. To fill this tall order we begin by reflecting on our resources.

St. Paul asks us, "Are you not aware that you are the temple of God, and that the Spirit of God dwells in you?" False modesty should never move us to forget our dignity. We judge a church to be holy because it is the house of God. In the same way we must acknowledge our holiness as temples of God. God's Holy Spirit lives within us, transforming us into God's children, conformed to the image of God's Son, Jesus himself. Does that not tell us that we must be different, that we must not delude ourselves by thinking in a worldly way? We are called to act according to God's standards, not those of our contemporary society.

When we come to Mass we first hear the Word of God, the Scriptures which propose to us ideals and challenges. Then we participate in the Liturgy of the Eucharist and we receive the body and the blood of the Lord. The Eucharist is the strength God gives us to follow the ideals of the Scriptures and to accept their challenges. There will be no real progress in morality unless we are willing to try as hard as we can to heed the call of Jesus: "You must become perfect as your heavenly Father is perfect."

Eighth Sunday of the Year, A

Concern Yes, Worry No
Is 49:14-15; 1 Cor 4:1-5; Mt 6:24-34

People who have serious responsibilities toward others may well think that Jesus' teaching today is beautiful but not realistic. It seems impossible, for example, to tell parents that they should not worry about how they are going to feed, clothe, and educate their children. The words of Jesus may be suitable to a hermit who lives in the wild by himself, but they do not seem to have an application to the vast majority of us.

And yet we cannot readily dismiss the words of Jesus. In fact, we cannot afford to ignore them if, for no other reason, we profess as Catholics to be his disciples. Perhaps the key to Jesus' teaching is found in one word: "worry."

There is a difference between worry and concern. Jesus does not say that we should not be concerned. He says only that we should not worry. Concern is the mature response of those who recognize their duty toward others, as well as toward themselves. Worry is the troubled fretting of those who are filled with uncertainties. Worry is painful. Concern can be fulfilling. Concern is the flower that grows on the tree of responsibility. Worry is the spoiled fruit of anxiety.

Worried people think that they have to do everything by themselves. Responsibility is a heavy burden which they fret about because they doubt that they can carry such a weight by themselves. They may either forget about God's help or they may have despaired of receiving any assistance from God. They are like the people who were addressed in the first reading.

These people were in exile far from their beloved homeland and the temple in Jerusalem which had been the center of their lives. Now the temple lay in ruins and they felt their lives were devastated. They were existing as slaves rather than living the life of the free people of God. They worried that God had abandoned them. They lamented: "The Lord has forsaken me; my Lord has forgotten me." If their fears had been true, they would indeed have had good cause for worry. But to them the prophet addressed beautifully consoling words: "Can a mother forget her infant, or be without tenderness for the child of her womb? Even should she forget, I will never forget you."

Nor does God forget us. But we must not forget him either. Prayer, confident prayer, is essential. Following the Our Father at Mass, the priest prays in the name of us all: "Protect us from all anxiety as we wait in joyful hope for the coming of our Savior, Jesus Christ." That coming of our Savior need not be only his return at the end of time. We may rightly understand by this prayer the truth that the Lord comes to help us in all our needs when we remember to rely on him and to turn to him in earnest prayer. Especially at Mass he comes to us in Holy Communion. When we receive the body and the blood of the Lord, we ought to turn our lives over to him. In prayer tell the Lord that you need him, that you rely on him, that you trust him. And that even though you are concerned about many things, you promise not to worry.

Ninth Sunday of the Year, A

Prayer Should Not Be Cheap Words
Dt 11:18, 26-28; Rm 3:21-25, 28; Mt 7:21-27

It has often been said that words are cheap. They are easy to say, but to live in accord with them is another matter. At a wedding spouses say to each other, "I take you for better or for worse, for richer or for poorer, in sickness and in health, until death." Those words, which are pronounced in an instant, require devotion and fidelity for a lifetime.

Our words spoken to God, which we call prayer, also require devotion and fidelity for a lifetime. We should not be surprised that Jesus insists that our prayer, whether liturgical or private, must lead us to action. In fact, he teaches us that the authenticity of our prayer can be measured by how devoted we are to God's will.

All of this does not mean that we should demean the importance of words. To the Israelites some of the most precious words in their tradition were those of the great commandment: "Hear, O Israel! the LORD is our God, the LORD alone! Therefore, you shall love the LORD your God with all your heart and with all your soul, and with all your strength." These words were so important that Moses instructed the people, "Take these words of mine into your heart and soul." Then he directed them, "Bind them to your wrist as a sign, and let them be a pendant on your forehead." It became, then, the custom for devout Jews to follow this directive by writing out the great commandment on parchment, folding it and placing it inside a small leather case, called a phylactery, which is sometimes attached to the wrist, sometimes suspended over the forehead.

Of course the wearing of a phylactery expresses true devotion only when the wearer actually practices the great commandment. Although we Catholics do not wear phylacteries, some of us do wear medals or small crosses, usually beneath our clothing. When a medal or a cross is suspended from our neck by a chain, it lies close to our heart. It is to be a reminder that religion is a matter, not merely of words, but of the heart.

If we were to write out certain words to be put into a case like a phylactery, what would those words be? It would be fitting for us to take the Old Testament words of the great commandment, but I suspect that after some reflection, we could come up with other ideas to express our Catholic faith. I want to suggest some words which we hear every time we celebrate Mass. Those words are the words of Jesus who says over the bread, "This is my body," and who says over the wine, "This is the cup of my blood." The consecration, the heart of the eucharistic prayer, makes present and real for us the great sacrifice of Christ. The bread truly becomes his body given up for us; the wine truly becomes his blood poured out for us. The Eucharist fulfills the words of Jesus: "Greater love than this no one has...."

Keeping the love of Christ before our minds should motivate us in our lives as Catholics. Figuratively attaching the words of the consecration to our wrists should move us to want to act and do things only in accord with God's will. We should never hesitate to cry out, "Lord, Lord," but we must make sure that our words lead to devotion and fidelity for a lifetime.

Tenth Sunday of the Year, A

Optimism and Pessimism
Ho 6:3-6; Rm 4:18-25; Mt 9:9-13

It is difficult to maintain a balance between optimism and pessimism. This is true even in our relationship with God. On the one hand, should we be so confident of God's mercy that we may always expect him to forgive our sins? On the other hand, should we perhaps be so cautious that we may not presume upon God's mercy?

Balance is the right approach but balance is not always easily achieved. Some people have scrupulous consciences and some have lax ones. Some people have a positive image of God, and others have a negative one. Taking to heart today's Scriptures can help achieve the balance we need.

Matthew was looked upon as a sinner simply because he was a hated tax collector for the despised Romans. Why would Jesus want to accept an invitation to dinner from such a man? And why would he actually go into Matthew's home when it became obvious that many tax collectors and those known as sinners had come to the dinner? The Pharisees could not comprehend the reason for Jesus' action, and so they complained about what he was doing. They were shocked that he would associate with sinners, but they were positively dismayed by his explanation: "I have come to call not the self-righteous, but sinners."

The Pharisees in the Gospel were self-righteous. The emphasis is on the word, "self." They were so satisfied with themselves that they thought they did not need God. Because they were so centered on themselves, they had only contempt for those whom they judged to be sinners. They failed to understand the vision of God who looks upon all of his people with love and who wants everyone to be saved and to come to the knowledge of the truth. The Pharisees could not even begin to suspect that God's love would be so great that he would "hand over his Son to death for our sins and would raise him up for our justification" (see the second reading).

We should not be negative as were the Pharisees. We have great cause for optimism in our relationship with God. On the other hand, we must not presume too much from God. That is the lesson of the first reading today from the prophet Hosea. In effect the people were saying to each other, "Don't worry about God. Just as the sun comes up every morning and the rain falls in springtime, so God will come to us." But through the prophet God warned, "Your piety is like the morning dew that early passes away. It is love that I desire and not your sacrifices." The people were not faithful in their love for God, and so they were not pleasing to him.

The starting point for us is that we are all sinners and we need the saving grace of Jesus Christ. Would Jesus accept an invitation to dinner from us? We need not answer that question because the truth is that he invites us every Sunday to his dinner, the great eucharistic banquet. Here we celebrate his death and resurrection, the sign of God's great love for us which moved him to grant us forgiveness. Our participation in the Mass, however, must be an expression of authentic love which guides and directs us in our lives. We can be optimistic about God's mercy provided we are humble enough to know that we need God and loving enough to want to be faithful to him always.

Eleventh Sunday of the Year, A

God Is Always Close to Us
Ex 19:2-6; Rm 5:6-11; Mt 9:36-10:8

Sometimes God seems far away. We do not see him and we do not hear him. After all, we may think, he must be very busy since he is the creator of the universe and is responsible for its care. Could he really be concerned about this tiny speck in the vastness of all of his creation which we call earth? Does he have any reason to value us, poor petty and sinful humans, when he has countless hosts of angels to stand before his throne in heaven to praise him night and day?

Maybe we are not alone in the universe. There may be another solar system with a sun and its planet more magnificent than our own. Perhaps there are many other planets, populated with creatures who are far superior to us and who have always remained faithful to God. About these matters we do not know. But what we do know is of enormous significance to us. We are aware of the incomprehensible truth that the Son of God has come into our world, not merely to live here, but to suffer here for us who are mere mortals, even to die for us who are a sinful people.

St. Matthew today paints a picture of Jesus which reveals his compassion. He writes that "at the sight of the crowds, the heart of Jesus was moved with pity." Jesus was so moved because the people "were lying prostrate from exhaustion, like sheep without a shepherd." That is the expression of a human heart which is filled with divine love.

Jesus is our Good Shepherd who laid down his life for his sheep. St. Paul was amazed as he reflected on the death of Jesus for our salvation. He expressed his astonishment to the Romans: "It is rare that anyone should lay down his life for a just man, though it is barely possible that for a good man someone may have the courage to die. It is precisely in this that God proves his love for us: that while we were still sinners, Christ died for us." The death of Jesus is so central to our understanding and appreciation of God's loving care for us that we celebrate it in every Eucharist. We are invited to cry out: "When we eat this bread and drink this cup, we proclaim your death, Lord Jesus, until you come in glory."

The saving death of Jesus which becomes a reality for us through our celebration of the Eucharist is neither distant nor impersonal. Jesus did not die for us as if we were an anonymous flock of sheep. He knows each one of us intimately. He called us by name at our baptism just as surely as he called the twelve by name to be his apostles. That is why we must enter into the Mass knowingly, actively, and fruitfully (see the *Constitution on the Liturgy*, 11).

We do not know what has gone on throughout the universe, but we do know that the Son of God has come to our world and has died for our salvation. We do not know what is happening at this moment in some distant galaxy, but we do know that on the altar the death and the resurrection of Jesus becomes a reality for us to share. Never should we think that our God is far away. Even if we do not see him or hear him, we experience his divine love in the eucharistic celebration of his Son's death and resurrection.

Twelfth Sunday of the Year, A

Intimidation Begets Fear
Jr 20:10-13; Rm 5:12-15; Mt 10:26-33

Fear can paralyze us. It can freeze us and make us immobile. It can prevent us from both thinking and acting according to our Catholic convictions.

A particularly detrimental form of fear comes from intimidation. It is that kind of fear which is the concern of Jesus in today's Gospel. When Jesus said, "Do not let men intimidate you," he was perhaps thinking of the great prophet, Jeremiah. This man of God refused to be intimidated by attacks upon his character and plots against his life, and so he was not afraid to speak out in the name of the Lord.

Jeremiah accused his people of sins against their covenant with God and warned of God's judgment upon them. He insisted that their crimes against each other were crimes against God. He condemned reliance on military pacts rather than on God, and he predicted the destruction of Jerusalem (which occurred in 587 B.C.).

Jeremiah was forced into exile in Egypt by his enemies. According to one tradition he was murdered there by some of his own countrymen. These evil men are no longer remembered, but Jeremiah is. He lives not only in the pages of Sacred Scripture but with Jesus in heaven, the Messiah whom he never knew on this earth but to whom he was faithful without realizing it.

Others after Jeremiah, knowing and loving Jesus, have also reached great heights of heroic action born of deep convictions. In the twentieth century alone there are many examples. Archbishop Oscar Romero of El Salvador was a martyr for the sake of social justice. He was murdered by unscrupulous men who saw the Archbishop's defense of the poor as a threat to their greed. During the Second World War St. Maximilian Kolbe, the Polish priest who refused to be intimidated by the Nazis, offered his life in exchange for a prisoner, a husband and father, whom the commandant of the concentration camp had singled out for execution.

A young girl in Italy refused to be intimidated by a man who threatened to kill her because she refused his sexual advances. And kill her he did on July 6, 1902. Maria Goretti was declared a saint by Pope Pius XII in 1950. Her mother and Alexander Serenelli, the man who killed her, were present at her canonization.

These dedicated people, and countless other men and women like them throughout history, believed the words of Jesus: "Whoever acknowledges me before men I will acknowledge before my Father in heaven."

These days we are in danger of being intimidated by movements in our society. Pro-choice advocates would make us feel that we violate women's rights when we insist that abortion is an unspeakable crime. Corrosive individualism militates against our concern for the poor, the homeless, and the hungry. Xenophobia and greed would bring wrath upon the immigrants whom the Church insists have human rights.

Jesus says to us gathered in worship: "I see you here in church as the People of God. I will continue to acknowledge you before my Father in heaven as long as you continue to follow my teachings and not those of the people who oppose the Gospel. Do not let them intimidate you."

Thirteenth Sunday of the Year, A

Hospitality and the Son of God
2 K 4:8-11, 14-16; Rm 6:3-4, 8-11; Mt 10:37-42

Hospitality is a beautiful form of kindness which sometimes comes from surprising sources and which produces unexpected results. In the first reading the woman of Shunem was not an Israelite. Although as a Shunemite she would usually despise any Israelite as a foreigner, she recognized in the prophet Elisha a holy man. She prevailed upon her husband to offer hospitality to this man of God, who accepted the hospitality from a surprising source. The woman's unexpected reward was that within a year she gave birth to a son for whom she had yearned for a long time.

This episode anticipated the teaching of Jesus in the Gospel: "He who welcomes a prophet because he bears the name of prophet receives a prophet's reward." The Shunemite woman's reward was a son, a child of her own flesh and blood. Jesus says to all his people: "Whoever welcomes you welcomes me." When we are hospitable to one another, we too receive a son, but not a son of our flesh and blood. We receive the eternal Son of God the Father. When we reach out to others, we reach out to Christ himself.

St. Martin of Tours is an example. He is generally considered the first person to be honored as a saint who was not a martyr. He was born in France when the terrible persecutions were coming to an end. Previously those men and women were honored as saints in the early Church who died like Christ and for Christ. Now the emphasis began to shift to living for Christ and to loving Christ.

An episode in the life of Martin highlights the truth that love for others is actually love for Christ. While Martin was a catechumen and serving in the military, he was on guard duty on a bitterly cold winter night when a poor man, shivering and clothed only in tatters, stood before him. Martin whipped off his cloak, drew his sword, cut the cloak in two pieces and gave one to the beggar. That night in a dream Martin saw Christ clothed in the part of the cloak he had given away. He heard Christ say, "Martin, still a catechumen, has clothed me in this garment."

This episode illustrates an essential part of our faith about Christ. As Catholics we believe that Christ is present in the word of Scripture and that he speaks to us when the word is proclaimed during the liturgy. We believe that Christ is present in the Eucharist and that on the altar we celebrate his death and resurrection. Equally and with the same conviction we must believe that Christ is present in people, that in serving others we are serving him, and that in ignoring others we are ignoring him. We must have a consistent faith in the reality of Christ in the word, in the Eucharist, and in people. Liturgy is not a private devotion, an individual relationship between God and one person. It is the expression of the Church which is one body, one Spirit in Christ. That unity in Christ must motivate the way we live.

When we come across homeless, hungry people, we must recognize Christ in them. When we notice young, single mothers who are pregnant again and who are on welfare, we must see Christ in them. When we are aware of aliens, documented or otherwise, among us, we must acknowledge that it is Christ who is the foreigner. And we must act accordingly. We must always welcome Christ and not turn him aside. Catholics should not be a surprising source of hospitality. Kindness should be a true expression of our faith.

Fourteenth Sunday of the Year, A

How Humble Is Our God
Zc 9:9-10; Rm 8:9, 11-13; Mt 11:25-30

Every religion of the world requires its followers to humble themselves before its god, but ours is the only religion in which the Divine Son of God has humbled himself before his people.

God the Father lives with his Son in the eternal embrace of the Holy Spirit. Theirs is a life of glory and perfection, and yet in the fullness of time God sent his Son to be our Savior, human like us in all things but sin. A prayer of the Church says to Jesus: "When you became man to set us free, you did not spurn the Virgin's womb" (the *Te Deum*). The Incarnation is the great act of humility.

Some people say that if we could see Jesus in the Blessed Sacrament in all the splendor of his divinity we would fall down in abject worship, afraid even to raise our eyes to look upon his splendid countenance. But that is not the relationship Jesus wants us to have with him. Jesus offers us a warm invitation to embrace him in trust and love without fear. He could not be more explicit. He says, "I am gentle and humble of heart."

Since we are not to fear Jesus, but to embrace him, we need never hesitate to bring to him our burdens so that he may lift them. Jesus spoke of his yoke. A yoke was a heavy wooden beam which was fixed across the necks of a pair of oxen to harness them together. Perhaps as a youth Jesus had seen Joseph the carpenter fashioning such yokes and struggling with their massiveness and weight. Jesus resolved to teach that his religion is not like those heavy, restricting beams of wood. That is why he said, "My yoke is easy and my burden is light."

The prophet Zechariah, inspired by the Holy Spirit, saw an image of the Messiah to come. He declared to the people, "See your king comes to you." And yet this king was not to come robed in royal splendor and riding on a regal stallion. Rather he would be meek, and riding on an ass, on a colt, the foal of an ass. He was to come not on a horse upon which a mighty king would ride into battle, but on a lowly beast which a farmer would use to till the soil.

Jesus fulfilled this image by his entry into the city of Jerusalem on Palm Sunday. There he underwent the greatest act of humility: his passion and his death on the cross for our salvation. The idea of such a humble God is not one which the human imagination could create. Only God's revelation to us makes the thought possible and his love for us makes that thought a reality in our lives.

In every Mass we should hear within our hearts the invitation of Jesus: "Come to me, all you who are weary and find life burdensome, and I will refresh you." And go to Jesus we do in our communion procession toward the minister who, acting for Jesus, will present to us his sacred body and his precious blood, our spiritual food and drink, our divine refreshment. We go to Jesus because he is gentle and humble of heart. In him our souls find rest for his yoke is easy and his burden is light.

Fifteenth Sunday of the Year, A

The Treasures Are Open
Is 55:10-11; Rm 8:18-23; Mt 13:1-23

No farmer who is interested in a profit would be as lavish in spreading seed as the farmer in today's Gospel. A discreet farmer is careful to sow only in places which are sure to produce results. But the farmer in the Gospel is lavish with the seed since he represents God who is always generous with his gifts.

The seed represents the Word of God which is found in the inspired pages of Sacred Scripture. There are forty-six books in the Old Testament and twenty-seven in the New. God sows his seed in our minds and in our hearts primarily by means of the Liturgy of the Word within the celebration of the Mass.

In the previous liturgy the same readings were used every year so that it was impossible to get a representative sampling of the richness of the Bible. One result of this arrangement was that some magnificent passages were never heard by Catholics on Sundays. The parable of the Prodigal Son was not part of any Sunday liturgy; neither was the story of the Good Samaritan. Epistles supplied the first reading but a long list of what was omitted could be compiled. The Acts of the Apostles, the story of the early Church, was chosen only once a year on Pentecost Sunday. Nothing from the Old Testament or the Book of Revelation was read at Sunday Mass.

The Second Vatican Council, using the image of riches, decreed that "the treasures of the Bible are to be opened up more lavishly so that richer fare may be provided for the faithful" (*Constitution on the Liturgy*, 51). The revised Liturgy has fulfilled this decree by selecting biblical passages over a three-year period on Sundays rather than one, and by supplying two readings rather than one, before the Gospel.

This current year, known as Cycle A, features the Gospel

according to St. Matthew. Cycle B presents the Gospel according to St. Mark, and Cycle C that according to St. Luke. The Gospel according to St. John is used primarily on the Sundays of the A cycle during Lent, during the Easter Season, and to fill out the B cycle. Throughout the Easter Season the first reading is from the Acts of the Apostles; otherwise, the first reading is from the Old Testament. The second reading is always from New Testament writings other than the Gospels. The Book of Revelation is the second reading during the Easter season in Cycle C.

To appreciate these generous presentations of the treasures of the Bible we must all make sure that we are prompt in coming to Mass. In fact, we ought to see to it that we get to church in plenty of time to settle down so that we may pay close attention to the readings. We are to listen in faith that it is Christ who speaks to us when the Scriptures are proclaimed (see the *Constitution on the Liturgy*, 56-57).

Granting the importance of the Word, what about Holy Communion? One way to view communion is to see that the sacrament of the body and the blood of the Lord is like the rain and the snow which come down from heaven to make the earth fruitful. Holy Communion gives us the means we need to turn the Scriptures we hear into the truth which guides and directs our lives according to God's will. The Holy Spirit has not only inspired the pages of the Bible; the Holy Spirit has blessed us through the work of the Second Vatican Council.

Sixteenth Sunday of the Year, A

God Is Patient with Weeds
Ws 12:13, 16-19; Rm 8:26-27; Mt 13:24-43

Sometimes it seems that God should swoop down upon earth and with his scythe cut down all the evil weeds in our society. It would seem to be a great blessing if God were to eliminate from our midst the abortionists, the child molesters, the drug lords, the gang leaders, the serial killers, the terrorists, the white collar crooks, the bigots, and all who abuse human goodness and dignity. But it is not happening. Why not? The Book of Wisdom tells us that God gives people grounds for hope that he will permit repentance for sins. In other words, God is patient. God respects our freedom. He considers freedom to be such a precious gift that he tolerates evil, at least until the day of judgment. God will not force anyone to avoid evil and do good, but he does want to give all of us enough time to repent and change our lives.

The type of wheat which was used in Palestine was in its early stages indistinguishable from weeds. That fact is behind the caution, "Pull up the weeds and you might take the wheat along with them." The English translation of the parable uses words which help to exemplify its meaning. Listening to the English it is very difficult to distinguish the word "wheat" from "weed."

We may be too quick to judge someone or something as so evil that tolerance is not acceptable in our view. That can be a serious mistake. The truth is that it is not ours to judge the guilt of anyone. That right belongs to God alone. Abortion is a grave evil, which the Vatican Council calls "an unspeakable crime." And yet a person who has had an abortion may have been so confused or so coerced that guilt is significantly diminished. Although our society has been poisoned by a plague which refuses to acknowledge responsibility and proposes excuses for every kind of wickedness, we do not have the right to condemn a person, only the evil action.

The reality is complicated. Even in the Church, which by definition is holy, we experience scandals. There are weeds in the field of the Church. We are distressed when we hear of scandals in the Church, but such evil should not surprise us since among the twelve apostles chosen by Jesus, one was a traitor. Jesus could have eliminated Judas while the act of treachery was still only an evil thought in his mind, but he did not pull up the weed, which was Judas, from among the wheat, the other apostles.

A political or military leader will eliminate an enemy as soon as he is aware of him. But not God. Rather God's way was expressed in our responsorial psalm: "Lord, you are good and forgiving." We ourselves are fortunate that God is good and forgiving. Who in this world is sinless? Who is pure wheat with no admixture of weeds? Do we want God to take us away from this world to face him in judgment when the field of our lives still contains weeds? Do we not realize that the invitation to receive Holy Communion is a sign of God's patience with us? He does not require us to be perfect before receiving the body and blood of his Son. Communion, we should understand, is not a reward for having been good, but a means for becoming good.

God is patient with each one of us in our struggles, and he is patient with everyone in the world. Only at the end of time will he tell his angels to collect and burn the weeds and to gather the wheat into his barn.

Seventeenth Sunday of the Year, A

Wisdom Is a Great Gift from God

1 K 3:5, 7-12; Rm 8:28-30; Mt 13:44-52

When we think of wisdom, we may picture an elderly man with a long white beard, corn cob pipe in his mouth, rocking back and forth in his chair, and uttering wise sayings such as "A penny saved is a penny earned." But that is not the biblical meaning of wisdom. In the Bible wisdom is not theoretical or abstract. It is practical. It has to do with the right, the wise, way to live.

King Solomon prayed for wisdom, not so that he could sit comfortably in his palace and ponder the verities of the universe. He asked God to give him wisdom, an understanding heart, so that he could govern his people properly.

We need to ask God to grant us this gift, or more precisely to increase it within us, because we received wisdom, a gift of the Holy Spirit, when we were confirmed. Wisdom guides us in fulfilling our responsibilities. Parents have the grave duty of rearing children. They are the first and primary educators of their children, even in the matter of religion. Next we may think of priests, teachers, doctors, police, and all the many professions which serve people, and yet we all have responsibilities toward others since we live in the same society. Although we may not think of it often, we also have responsibilities toward ourselves.

Perhaps the wisest way to consider our responsibilities is to ponder what the practical values are in our lives. What are our goals? What are our ambitions? What do we really want in life?

In 1849 many people thought they knew what they wanted in life. Gold had been discovered in California. Ranchers and farmers made a frenzied dash on horses and in wagons across the continent in an effort to be among the first to harvest a crop of yellow metal.

A wheat farmer in Kansas, not content with the golden grain he harvested year after year, could think of almost nothing other than leaving farm and family in search of fortune. His wife was frantic. She had four small children to care for and she doubted that the venture her husband ardently yearned for could be successful. Reluctantly the farmer stayed home. One night in a dream he saw himself in a room filled with gold. After gleefully running the nuggets through his hands, he realized he was hungry. When he looked for something to eat, he found only gold. He called for his wife, hoping to be comforted by the warmth of her love, but there was only the coldness of yellow metal. He longed to look into the sparkling eyes of his children, but the only sparkle he saw was that of his lifeless riches. He woke with a start. In a moment's reflection he realized what his true values were. Through a dream he became a wise man, a person who knew and accepted his responsibilities.

Responsibilities, even for a wise person, can be a heavy burden. St. Paul, surely one of the wisest of people, wrote: "We know that God makes all things work together for the good of those who love him." It is a vital part of wisdom to rely on God, to place ourselves in his hands, to pray for his help, to acknowledge that all good gifts come from God. These should be our sentiments when we join with Christ in offering the eucharistic sacrifice to God our Father. Our devout sharing in the Eucharist is a sure sign that we know what the true values in life are, that we are acting in accord with the great gift of wisdom.

Eighteenth Sunday of the Year, A

The Mass Is What We Do as Catholics
Is 55:1-2; Rm 8:35, 37-39; Mt 14:13-21

A baseball announcer sees his team in the ninth inning about to blow a lead and lose the game just as they have done on several previous occasions. He sighs and says, "It's *déjà vu*," and then as if to add a note of humor he adds, "all over again." Actually the expression does not mean seeing something happen again; rather, it refers to an illusion, a misconception, that one has previously had an experience which is actually new.

A Catholic hearing today's Gospel about the feeding of the five thousand might be tempted to say, "*déjà vu*," in the correct sense of the expression. We celebrate the Eucharist every Sunday. In today's Gospel we see actions, and we hear words, which are part of every Mass. When St. Matthew wrote his Gospel, the Christian community was already in the practice of celebrating the Eucharist every Sunday, just as we do today. He expected his listeners to relate what Jesus did in a deserted place to what they were doing in their assembly.

St. Matthew wrote: "Jesus took the five loaves and two fish and, looking up to heaven, blessed and broke them and gave the loaves to his disciples, who in turn gave them to the people." Does that not sound like what the priest says and does at Mass, even to giving the Eucharist to ministers to distribute Holy Communion to the people?

Of course what Jesus did in that deserted place was not the Eucharist since he did not institute the Eucharist until the night before he died. What Jesus did at the Last Supper with his disciples gathered around him was much greater than what he did in feeding the five thousand. Equally we are much more blessed than were those people who were favored by a wonderful miracle. The Eucharist is a marvelous gift to us as Catholics. Its value cannot be measured. Never must we take this gift for granted. We can avoid that mistake, and actually grow in our appreciation, by allowing many aspects of life to remind us of the Eucharist as does today's Gospel.

When we wake hungry and thirsty, we should think not only about our next meal but also about our next Eucharist. When we are enjoying a dinner with family or friends, we should allow the festivities to turn our minds to the celebration of the Eucharist. When we buy a loaf of bread or a bottle of wine, we should remember how Jesus takes the elements of bread and wine and transforms them during the Mass into his body and his blood. When we read about balanced diets, we should realize that Jesus gives us the perfect nourishment for our spiritual lives in the Holy Eucharist.

The Eucharist is so valuable to us that it is invaluable. In other words, its worth cannot be measured. We should, then, heed the invitation of the prophet Isaiah: "You who have no money, come, receive grain and eat." This was an invitation to the people returning from exile to participate in God's love. Often the Old Testament uses the image of eating and drinking together as a sign of God's covenant, the testament of his love.

We enjoy the great sacrament of the Eucharist, Jesus' body given up for us and his blood of the new and everlasting covenant. The Lord Jesus is our spiritual food and drink. The Eucharist is not *déjà vu* all over again. It is the great reality of our Catholic faith.

Nineteenth Sunday of the Year, A

Stay in the Boat

1 K 19:9, 11-13; Rm 9:1-5; Mt 14:22-33

Water covers about two thirds of the earth's surface. We know that we cannot live without it, but sometimes we cannot live with it. Water is a powerful, mysterious force which can mean life *or* death.

The apostles understood water very well. From it as fishermen they derived their livelihood. For them water usually meant life. But one night in particular, with the wind howling above them and the water roaring beneath their boat, they knew that water could mean death. How astounded they must have been when they saw Jesus walking toward them safely and unperturbed on the lake! When they realized it was really Jesus and not a ghost, they began to calm their fears, but impetuous Peter was not satisfied. He desired something more than what he saw. He expected Jesus to act in a still more extraordinary manner: he actually wanted Jesus to empower him to walk on the water.

"Tell me to come to you across the water," Peter demanded. Surprisingly Jesus said, "Come." But it didn't work. Peter began to sink because of his lack of faith. Perhaps Jesus acceded to Peter's untoward demand because he wanted to teach Peter, and all of us, a lesson: be satisfied with the way the Lord acts and do not require that he do things our way.

It was a lesson even the great prophet Elijah had to learn. Elijah had just witnessed the spectacular power of God who, in response to his prayer, had brought down fire from heaven to consume a young bull as a sacrifice. This was after the prayer of the prophets of the pagan gods proved useless. Queen Jezebel, Elijah's mortal enemy, furious at his success, swore that she would kill him. Elijah fled for his life. We find him in today's reading taking refuge in a cave. There apparently he expected further extraordinary manifestations of God in a strong and heavy wind, next in an earthquake, and then in fire, but the Lord was in none of these phenomena. But Elijah did find God in a tiny, whispering sound. Elijah learned that we must be content with the way God chooses to act.

We may want God to act on our behalf in unusual ways, to allow us, so to speak, to walk to him across the water. But we are to remain in the boat, the boat which symbolizes the Church. The Church will not sink even in the most tumultuous waves which cause great scandals in the Church and confound us. The Church will not be tossed upside down even by the most powerful winds which threaten to upset our faith and disturb us. Whatever may be the approach others may take, we know where we will always find God.

Within the Church God acts in his own way. We no doubt would be thrilled to see the Lord in some brilliant flash of light like the fire which consumed the holocaust offered by Elijah, but Jesus' way is simple, like that of a tiny whisper. He chooses to speak to us, not in the tumult of a strong wind, but in the ordinary sounds of human words through the Sacred Scripture. He chooses to come to us, not in the rumbling of a mighty earthquake, but under the simple appearances of bread and wine.

In every circumstance, throughout every need of life, we will find the Lord, but we are to remain in the boat, to be faithful disciples in the one, holy, *catholic* and apostolic Church.

Twentieth Sunday of the Year, A

Christ Leaves No One Outside
Is 56:1, 6-7; Rm 11:13-15, 29-32; Mt 15:21-28

Sometimes it seems that this must be the age of the greatest disputes within the Church. Catholics argue about many things with each other, and the media would like the world to believe that in the United States we rebel against everything the Pope says. When disputes end in hatred and disunity, we know that they are serious.

The fact is that nothing in our contemporary Church can compare in seriousness, and bitterness as well, with the dispute in the early Church between Jewish and Gentile converts to the faith. Jewish Christians, who came to be called Judaizers, believed that for the Gentiles to become disciples of Jesus, they had to be circumcised and follow the law of Moses. In other words, they had to become Jewish. The Gentiles insisted that Jesus had done something new. He had extended an invitation to everyone without distinction to embrace the God of Israel, the one true God.

His invitation was prefigured in the book of Isaiah the prophet. The reading for this Sunday is taken from the third part of Isaiah. It was composed for those Jews who had returned from exile in Babylon only to find their homeland occupied by foreigners whom they deeply resented. The returning Jews could either attempt to expel the foreigners or they could follow the teaching of Isaiah who proclaimed that the foreigners who joined themselves to the Lord should be accepted. The Lord said through the prophet, "My house shall be called a house of prayer for all peoples."

This universalism was a hard lesson for the Jews to learn. That is why at the time of Jesus and even afterwards there was a bitter dispute about the place of the Gentiles. The Canaanite woman in today's Gospel was not Jewish; she was a Gentile. Jesus' disciples wanted him to have nothing to do with her, to send her away. When the woman persisted in asking Jesus to heal her daughter, Jesus said, "It is not right to take the food of sons and daughters and throw it to the dogs." How could Jesus say such a harsh and mean thing? Actually his words are an echo of the Judaizers who wanted nothing to do with Gentiles and looked upon them as dogs. St. Matthew who wrote the Gospel story hoped that hearing these harsh, cruel words on the lips of Jesus would shock his readers into realizing how improper it was to reject the Gentiles. The woman by her faith won the favor of Jesus.

Today we do not think that people have to become Jewish in order to become Catholics. But maybe we practice other forms of exclusiveness. In some instances roles have become reversed; the anti-Semitism of today has replaced the "anti-Gentilism" of the first Christian century. Racism is a serious problem in our society. Hatred for immigrants, many of whom are fellow Catholics, has given meaning to that strange word, "xenophobia."

The word we should concentrate on is "Catholic." It reminds us that ours is a universal, world-wide Church, which embraces everyone. Every Catholic church is a house of prayer for all peoples. Here the Lord offers to all of us, not the scraps from the table, but the precious body and blood of the Lord. The Lord who comes to us in Holy Communion is the Lord of all. To be faithful to him is to accept all peoples without exception.

Twenty-first Sunday of the Year, A

Who Do You Say Jesus Is?
Is 22:15, 19-23; Rm 11:33-36; Mt 16:13-20

When the President of the United States calls a press conference, reporters show up in great numbers. Almost everything the President has to say is newsworthy, not because his words are always profound or will change the course of world events, but simply because of who he is. Once he is out of office, he retains only minimal interest for the media.

Who a person is makes all the difference. That is why Jesus' question about himself was of great importance as he turned to his disciples and asked, "Who do you say that I am?" Peter, acting as spokesman for all the disciples, did not make the mistake of some of the people who thought Jesus was John the Baptist or one of the former prophets who had returned to earth. Peter solemnly declared: "You are the Messiah, the Son of the living God."

Peter's declaration was in two parts. First he acknowledged that Jesus is the Messiah. This answer gratified the disciples. The hope for a Messiah became sharp and clear during the reign of the great King David, especially through the prophet Nathan in the tenth century B.C. That hope had grown so strong at the time of Jesus that some people expected the Messiah to appear at any time. The hope of the disciples now focused on Jesus.

But there was a second part to Peter's declaration. To the amazement of everyone concerned, Peter proclaimed that Jesus is the Son of the living God. It was clear to Peter that Jesus is the Son of God, not in the sense which can be affirmed of every person of faith, but in a unique way which can apply only to Jesus. Jesus insisted that no mere man had revealed this truth to Peter, but he was not satisfied in saying simply that "God" had revealed it. He emphatically stated: "My heavenly Father has revealed this."

This type of language amazed the disciples. Jesus was laying the foundation for the awesome truth that God is his Father, that he is truly God's Son, not in a loose or analogical way, but in a meaning which transcends all human understanding.

In response to Peter's expression of faith, Jesus spoke the famous words: "You are Rock and on this Rock I will build my Church." The connection between the truth of Jesus as the Son of God and the Church as founded on rock is not coincidental. Rather it became the firm mission of the Church to clarify, to teach, and to live according to the truth that Jesus is the Son of God.

By means of its earliest ecumenical councils (of which Vatican II was the twenty-first) the Church clarified the identity of Jesus as Son of God. Throughout the centuries the Church has continued to teach each new generation of Catholics to make Peter's profession of faith their own, as we must do ourselves. We believe that Jesus is the Messiah, but we also believe that he is more than that since the Messiah was understood to be a representative of God. Jesus is truly the unique Son of God, equal to the Father in all things. This true identity of Jesus is what makes his words so precious to us and his actions so invaluable. This true identity of Jesus is also what makes everything he did pleasing to his Father and effective for our salvation. Everything about Jesus flows from his true identity. How deep are the wisdom and knowledge of God which have revealed to us the identity of Jesus. This is the truth made firm on earth and held bound in heaven for all eternity.

Twenty-second Sunday of the Year, A

Read the Contract Carefully

Jr 20:7-9; Rm 12:1-2; Mt 16:21-27

Everyone who has ever bought an insurance policy or signed a contract knows that you have to read all the conditions, even those contained in the fine print. God has entered into a contract with us, except that we call it a covenant.

Today the liturgy urges us to read all the conditions of the contract, but there is no fine print. The Scriptures, relating the teachings of Christ, set before us in bold print what we need to know about our covenant with God. We should also note the difference between a contract and covenant: a contract is binding by law; a covenant is binding by love.

A legal marriage is a contract. A sacramental marriage is a covenant. A contract is binding by law. A covenant is binding by love. In the covenant which is the Church the binding force is God's love, to which we are expected to respond with our love. A contract, indicating the duties of both parties, is printed on paper, signed and sealed. Our covenant is expressed in a person. That person is Jesus Christ. Within him is God's love through his divinity. Also within him in his humanity is our love. This means that to understand the covenant we must in the first place look to the person of Jesus Christ.

Today in the Gospel Jesus indicates his part of the covenant. He will go up to Jerusalem. There he will die for us. He will seal the covenant, not in print, but in his own blood. Then he indicates the part of God the Father in the covenant. Accepting the love expressed in the death of his Son, God the Father will raise him to new life.

What is our part in the covenant? Jesus states it this way: "Those who wish to come after me must deny their very selves, take up their cross, and begin to follow in my footsteps." This may seem a strange kind of love, to have to take up the cross in order to come to the fullness of life, but it is God's wisdom, his plan. We call his plan the Paschal Mystery.

Even the great prophet Jeremiah struggled to understand God's wisdom. He did not hesitate to complain: "You duped me, O Lord, and I let myself be duped." Only at God's insistence did Jeremiah accept the role of prophet, and then when he spoke the truth all it brought him was ridicule and persecution.

St. Paul, blessed with a fuller revelation, had a better grasp of the Paschal Mystery. He urged the Romans to present their bodies as "a living sacrifice, holy and acceptable to God." We ourselves are invited to follow that urging by our participation in Mass. During the eucharistic prayer, and especially at the time of the consecration, we are to join Christ our priest in offering ourselves to God the Father just as Jesus offered himself on the cross. That will be our way of saying that we want to follow God's will in our lives, whatever that may entail. It will be our way of confirming our covenant with the Father, a covenant sealed in the blood of Christ, the blood of the new and everlasting covenant.

We must continue to reflect on the terms of the covenant. With faith and God's grace we can accept the terms gladly because by doing so we unite ourselves with Jesus Christ, the Son of God who will lead us to the fullness of love which is the real meaning of our covenant with God.

Twenty-third Sunday of the Year, A

We Are Watchmen for One Another

Ezk 33:7-9; Rm 13:8-10; Mt 18:15-20

The weather service is charged with giving advance warning to people about possibly dangerous conditions, such as hurricanes and flash floods. Officials of the weather service are not excused from their duty on the presumption that people do not listen to warnings anyway, or that the warnings upset them and make them angry, or that bringing bad news makes them feel uncomfortable.

The liturgy of this Sunday makes us aware that we have responsibilities toward each other. Storms arise in the lives of the people whom we know and love. The weather service cannot prevent floods and hurricanes; it can only give warnings which are early enough for people to get out of the way. Unlike the weather service, we can actually turn some personal storms aside, especially when we are early enough in our warning.

We must accept the fact that God has appointed us as watchmen for each other as he appointed the prophet Ezekiel. We must recognize that the debt that binds us to love one another includes the courage to warn each other of danger or impending disaster.

Many teenagers get upset with parents and teachers who warn them about cigarettes, alcohol, drugs, and sex. They think that their elders are "out of it," that they are not "cool." They really wish they would treat them like adults and talk about something else. The pressure on those who are responsible for young people is great, but only regret follows upon the failure to give proper warnings.

Adults know very well that it is not only the young who make mistakes. So often it happens that when a marriage breaks up, a friend says, "I'm not surprised. I could see that coming."

Someone should shake that friend by the shoulders and demand, "Why didn't you do or say something about it?"

A man or a woman loses a job because he or she has slowly sunk into the abyss of uncontrolled drinking. That does not happen all of a sudden, nor does it usually go unnoticed by a spouse, a friend, or a co-worker. It is a shame that no one has the courage to stand up and say, "You need help. Come with me to an AA meeting."

People of different ages can gradually slip away from the Church. They become irregular in going to Mass. Soon they go only at Christmas and Easter, and then not at all. They lose a sense of direction and purpose in life. Can it be that there was no one to invite them warmly to stay with the Church or to urge them to return to the practice of their Catholic faith?

It is never easy to warn others that they are about to trip and fall. But like the prophet Ezekiel we have been made watchmen for each other. The debt we owe which binds us to love one another includes the obligation to warn each other about spiritual dangers in our lives. Excuses do not relieve us of our obligations. We cannot get by through presuming that the person in question will not listen to us anyway, or that he or she will get upset and angry, or that we are just not very good at this sort of thing.

At Mass we join our voices in prayer for each other. This prayer should lead us to do the right thing. We know that the right thing is to accept responsibility for each other.

Twenty-fourth Sunday of the Year, A

God Is Our Best Judge
Si 27:30-28:7; Rm 14:7-9; Mt 18:21-35

Let's imagine that the day has come. You have died. Your entire life has passed before your eyes. It is the moment of judgment. You see before you figures of your spouse, your kids, your boss, your best friend, your parents. You realize that, if you wish, you may choose one of these persons to be your judge.

At first you think, "Of course, my spouse; we really loved each other." But then you remember some of the arguments and fights you had which you fear may not really have been forgotten. Your kids? They may think you were too hard on them. Your best friend? Your friend, you fear, knows too much about you.

You are about to select your parents when the figures fade. In their place you see St. Francis de Sales who was known for his kindness and compassion. Not a bad choice. Then you see St. Vincent de Paul. A more charitable person has hardly ever walked the earth. He would be good too, you think. Other saints flash before you. Then above them all you see the Blessed Virgin Mary. "Of course," you think, "I will choose to be judged by the kind, tender, loving woman who is my spiritual mother."

Before you can say anything, Mary places your hand in that of her Son. Jesus leads you before a throne and points to the person seated there whom you are moved by grace to recognize as God the Father. Jesus says simply, "Here is your judge; choose no other."

Of course Jesus is right. We naturally hope that the people we have been close to during life would be merciful to us in judgment. We may well believe that Mary is surely profoundly compassionate. But Mary and all the saints only share in the mercy and compassion which God does not merely possess in an infinite degree, but which God actually is. God is mercy and compassion.

The king in Jesus' parable is his Father. When an official begged the king to be patient with him to give him time to pay what he owed, the king wrote off the debt. He wiped it out. He canceled it. Of course no human king would do such a thing because humans are limited. You can be certain that your credit card company is not going to cancel your debt no matter how much you beg and plead. But we cannot paint a picture of God according to our human experience. We come to know God's mercy through his Son.

In order to wipe out the debt of sin God the Father gave his Son up to death for us and for our salvation. We must never forget this act of enormous generosity. Listen attentively to the words of consecration over the wine. Speaking through the priest Jesus says to us in every Mass: "This is the cup of my blood… It will be shed for you and for all so that sins may be forgiven." And forgiven are our sins, wiped out, canceled when we fulfill God's condition, which is to strive to be as forgiving toward each other as he is to us. We boldly say, "Forgive us our trespasses *as* we forgive those who trespass against us." This disposition must be in our hearts when we make an act of contrition, when we ask forgiveness during the Eucharist, when we celebrate the sacrament of penance. The Book of Wisdom reminds us: "Remember your last day, set enmity aside; remember death and cease from sin." But the profundity of wisdom is to rejoice that God, and no one else, will be our judge.

Twenty-fifth Sunday of the Year, A

God Is Generous
Is 55:6-9; Ph 1:20-24, 27; Mt 20:1-16

These days there is a great insistence that all workers, whether male or female, who do the same work with the same qualifications should receive the same pay. That is only just. It seems, at least at first glance, that the owner of the estate in Jesus' parable who paid all the workers the same wage had it only half right. You pay all the workers the same wage provided they all work the same amount of time.

One way of explaining that the strange action of the owner was not unjust is to point out that all the workers, from start to finish, agreed to accept the usual daily wage. No injustice was done to the first workers since they received exactly what they agreed to. And yet most of us still feel uncomfortable about the parable. We have not yet gotten to the bottom of it.

Another step is to recognize how we fit into the parable. There is no reason for us to think that we are the ones who have worked so long and so zealously for the Lord that we are represented by the first workers who, as they said, "worked a full day in the scorching heat." What really have we done for the Lord, especially if we compare ourselves with all the great saints over the centuries? And so we surely should have no complaint about the parable.

Still there seems to be more meaning to the parable than what we can in humility and honesty apply to ourselves. That meaning is revealed in the words of the owner of the estate. When the first workers complained to him, he replied by insisting, "I do you no injustice," and then he added a rhetorical question, "I am free to do as I please with my money, am I not?" To this question the workers had to answer in the affirmative.

But the owner had one more thing to say which reveals the heart of the parable: "Are you envious because I am generous?"

In one word the parable is about generosity, God's generosity. Actually all the workers, except the last ones, do not represent any group of people. Jesus included the early workers in his parable only so that he could emphasize that God is always just but more importantly he is generous. God is so generous to every human person that the last workers to go into the vineyard represent all of us.

God offers his grace to every person. We need not try to understand why some people seem to reject God's grace. Our effort should be put into recognizing God's gracious generosity toward us. He has given us life, our families, this world to live in, and he has given us our Catholic faith. All is a grace, a gift from God. There is simply nothing that we can do to earn God's blessings.

God's generosity is manifested during the celebration of the Holy Eucharist. He nourishes us with the body and the blood of his divine Son. We admit quite correctly, "Lord, I am not worthy to receive you." The greatest saints were not worthy of the Eucharist; even they did not earn such a wonderful sacrament. And yet after we admit our unworthiness, Jesus invites us to come to him and to receive his body and blood in faith.

And faith it is that should make us never complain to God as did the first workers, but always to give thanks and praise to our God who beyond our imagining is generous to us.

Twenty-sixth Sunday of the Year, A

Death Leads to Life in God's Plan
Ezk 18:25-28; Ph 2:1-11; Mt 21:28-32

A student spends long hours at night and the early morning preparing for an examination which will qualify her to enter graduate school. A violinist practices for months in order to play Mendelssohn's melodious and masterful First Violin Concerto. An athlete runs long distances every day, gradually working up to a point at which he can participate in a marathon.

Is God like that? Did he have to practice before he got creation right? Is he now building his stamina to bring the universe to a harmonious conclusion? Is God growing and developing into something more powerful than he is now? Of course not. God is perfect. He cannot grow and he cannot change — that is, in his divinity. But with the Incarnation the situation is different.

The Son of God, eternal and equal to his Father in all things, did not hesitate to become human. While still remaining divine, he became like us in all things but sin. The words which St. Paul boldly uses to describe the Incarnation are as remarkable as the event itself. Jesus "emptied himself and took the form of a slave, being born in the likeness of men." Jesus became human in response to the will of his Father in order to carry out the plan of his Father for our salvation. Jesus, like the older son in his parable, said "Yes" when the Father asked him to go into the vineyard of the world to work for our salvation, and like the younger son Jesus actually went. That meant that he became lovingly obedient even to accepting death, death on a cross. The Father responded to this extraordinary act by raising his Son to life in the resurrection. The Father did not want his Son to undergo death in such a way as to enter into oblivion, even if that were only in his human nature. No, he wanted to exalt his Son and to bestow upon him a name above every other name. But the condition for this exaltation — more correctly, the *cause* of this exaltation — was an obedient death. St. Paul emphatically states: Jesus accepted death and because of this God highly exalted him. We should hear that word, BECAUSE, as written in capital letters.

It is not that Jesus died and came to life somewhat like the foolish person who beat himself on the head because it felt so good when he stopped. The truth is so profound that we call it a mystery, the Paschal Mystery, the plan of the Father whereby sorrow would become the way to joy, humility would be turned into exaltation, and death would be transformed into eternal life.

The Paschal Mystery is the Lord's way, not only for Jesus, but for us as well. We came into contact with the Paschal Mystery in baptism whereby we died to sin and rose to a new life of holiness in Christ. We celebrate the Paschal Mystery in every Eucharist: we proclaim "Christ has died; Christ is risen; Christ will come again." From the Eucharist we draw the strength to live in accord with the meaning of baptism. Like Christ we must be obedient to the will of God in all things, even to the point of death. In a way we are preparing for a final exam, we are practicing to share in the rich harmonies of heaven, and we are struggling to grow more and more like Christ himself. God's way, the Paschal Mystery, may seem strange to some, or even unfair, but God led his own Son through the Paschal Mystery. We should see the wisdom and the joy of sharing the Paschal Mystery with Christ.

Twenty-seventh Sunday of the Year, A

Jesus Is Still with Us

Is 5:1-7; Ph 4:6-9; Mt 21:33-43

If Jesus were to return to earth in the manner in which he first came, what kind of reception do you think he would get? Would the reception be different today in our own country from what it was centuries ago in Judea?

Jesus came into the world after a long line of prophets in the era of the Old Testament had been rather generally rejected or ignored by the people of their own time. They were treated like the slaves in the parable which Jesus tells in today's Gospel. These slaves, whom the property owner sent to collect what was rightly his from the tenant farmers, were treated shamefully. In frustration the owner sent his own son because he expected that they would respect him. But his son they killed.

We need no imagination at all to recognize that the son in the parable represents Jesus himself. What about today? Would Jesus coming anew into our world suffer the same fate which he endured twenty centuries ago?

We need, not imagination, but faith to answer the question. The truth is, according to our Catholic faith, that Jesus is constantly coming among us, especially in the unwanted, the despised, and the destitute members of our society.

Jesus comes in the person of every child in the womb. He is trying to be born again into our world, but the abortion movement is rejecting him by destroying him in what should be the safest sanctuary on this earth, the womb. Is God the Father still saying, with the property owner, "Surely they will respect my son"?

Historically Jesus was born in Bethlehem. Just the sound of the name of that city recalls a beautiful story of our religion. And yet within the tender story of Bethlehem is a tragic admission about the holy family: "There was no room for them in the inn." Actually Mary and Joseph were immigrants. They were from Nazareth, far to north. Even though Jesus was born in his ancestral city of Bethlehem, he was treated like a foreigner. Was the inn really crowded, or was the truth simply that they were not welcome? "There was no room for them."

Still today Jesus tries to be welcomed by us in the person of immigrants to our country, those children of God who are rejected as foreigners even though they have come to a land, which like all the earth, belongs to God their Father.

Jesus' public life was filled with controversy because of his teaching and preaching. His compassion for the poor and the sick aroused indignation because he did good deeds on the Sabbath. His promise of the Eucharist required his listeners to accept or reject him. Many turned and walked away. Rejection turned to hatred and hatred built to a frenzy: Jesus they crucified as a criminal.

Is it too much of a leap of faith for us to see Christ in a criminal? If so, can we not at least remember that Jesus forgave the repentant thief and excused those who crucified him by saying, "They do not know what they are doing"? Do we know what we are doing when we favor capital punishment and countenance an act which reduces us to barbarism?

A parable Jesus told long ago has meaning for us today if we are humble enough to let it challenge us to question whether, like many in our country, we fail to find Christ in others.

Twenty-eighth Sunday of the Year, A

Come to the Wedding Banquet
Is 25:6-10; Ph 4:12-14, 19-20; Mt 22:1-14

Jesus, it seems, never refused an invitation to dinner, no matter who the host was or who the guests were. At times that got him into trouble with the self-righteous people of his day who were shocked that "he welcomed sinners and ate with them." Maybe Jesus accepted invitations to dinner because he was an itinerant preacher who, as he himself admitted, on some occasions did not have even a stone upon which to lay his head. He welcomed a good meal.

More profoundly Jesus saw in the human experience of dining a symbol of our final union with himself and his Father in heaven, united as we will be by the Holy Spirit, the bond of love. That is why he referred to heaven as a wedding banquet. The joy and camaraderie, the feasting and the celebrating, which characterize a dinner in honor of a couple newly joined in matrimony are an image, however faint, of the wonders of heaven.

Why then did the desired guests in the parable refuse the invitation to dinner, an invitation from no less than a king? The parable was addressed to those people who opposed Jesus, the very ones who were shocked that he would welcome tax collectors and sinners. In their deluded self-satisfaction, they wanted no part of Jesus as their savior. Eventually they plotted his death and stood at the foot of the cross only to jeer at him.

Little did they know that Jesus' love was so great that he died for them as well as for his mother and his disciples. Jesus opened his arms on the cross in welcome to everyone who would come to him in faith and humility. Actually in the cross everything symbolized by the wedding banquet was fulfilled.

The cross is the means of our reconciliation with God. In

a way the human race was like a wife who abandoned her husband to go her own way, forgetting the love with which they began their life together. Divorce confirmed the separation. Jesus intervened in our sad plight. He was sent by his Father to seek out his bride. Jesus by his death tore up the decree of divorce, and in his own blood he wrote and signed a certificate of the new and everlasting covenant, which sealed the marital union between God and his people. [*The allusion is to the prophet Hosea which accounts for casting God in the role of a husband and the people in that of the wife.*]

This new and everlasting marriage covenant is celebrated in a great wedding banquet, that of the Holy Eucharist. A wedding banquet is celebrated only once, immediately after the marriage takes place. But our union with God is so important that we celebrate it every time we come to church for Mass. We are here because we have accepted, and not rejected, God's invitation.

Let us make no mistake. We should understand that in our search for love and happiness we are looking for God. During the celebration of the Eucharist we should rejoice and be glad that Jesus has saved us, that he has reached out his hand to place our hand in that of his Father. When our time on earth is ended, Jesus will lead us to live in the house of his Father all the days of our lives. There we will continue the great wedding supper, the everlasting banquet of our union of love with God in heaven. [*It seems better to use the short form of the Gospel since many scholars say that the story of the man without a wedding garment was originally a separate parable.*]

Twenty-ninth Sunday of the Year, A

Give to God What Is God's
Is 45:1, 4-6; 1 Th 1:1-5; Mt 22:15-21

If Jesus had to take an examination in school today, he would not pass. He never answers a question, at least not directly. Some people are like that. You ask them, "How are you?" and they answer, "Thank you for asking." That is not an answer.

In today's Gospel Jesus was asked whether it was lawful to pay tax to the emperor or not. A simple yes or no would have answered the question. Instead Jesus made his adversaries show him a Roman coin and then demanded that they reach their own conclusion. Of course Jesus had a good reason in this incident for not giving a direct answer since his questioners were not sincere; they were trying to trap him in his speech. If he were to answer, "Yes, it is lawful to pay the tax," the Pharisees would have accused him of betraying his own Jewish countrymen. On the other hand to answer "No," could have exposed him to arrest by the Romans.

The surprise is not that Jesus, from the lesson of the coin, told them that they should give to Caesar what is Caesar's. Rather the surprise, or even the shock, is that Jesus added, "But give to God what is God's." It was like telling a fervent football fan, "Don't forget to watch some games on TV and if somebody gives you a ticket to a game, make sure you go." That kind of advice to a football fan is superfluous. And as far as the Pharisees were concerned, telling them to give God what belonged to him was not only superfluous; it was downright insulting.

Jesus' intention was not to insult them, but to challenge them. There was no doubt that they would pay taxes to the emperor. The Romans would see to that, by force if necessary. But God does not force us to do anything. He looks for service which is freely given. Above all he asks for a love which is genuine and unselfish, like his own toward us. The people who were trying to trap Jesus in his speech believed that religion was little more than external observance. They thought it was like building a wall: put the bricks together and the wall will rise. What they did not realize was that their satisfaction with mere externals was putting a wall between themselves and God together with his people. They were successfully isolating themselves from any real demands upon their generosity either in their worship of God or in their service to his people who were in need.

What is the challenge to us? Do we give to God what belongs to God? Can we be worthy of St. Paul's commendation of the Thessalonians: "We constantly are mindful... of the way you are proving your faith, and laboring in love, and showing constancy in hope in our Lord Jesus Christ"? Proving our faith: that could mean living in such a way that people know we are Catholics who take our religion seriously and are willing to be different. Laboring in love: that could be realized in us when we go out of our way to be kind to one another, when we volunteer to visit the sick or to go shopping for shut-ins. Showing constancy in hope in Christ: that challenge is to live in such a way that our lives would not make sense if God did not exist because we obviously are motivated by eternal and not merely temporary values.

Jesus felt no necessity of answering the question of the Pharisees, but we should be eager and willing to respond with a fervent "Yes" when he asks, "Will you give to God what is God's?"

Thirtieth Sunday of the Year, A

When Two Equal One
Ex 22:20-26; 1 Th 1:5-10; Mt 22:34-40

If a poll were taken to determine people's opinion as to who was the greatest football player of all time, or the greatest actor, or the greatest musician, there would be many opinions. For Jesus' contemporaries, the question "Which commandment of the law is the greatest?" had but a single answer which was obvious to any devout Jew. Even though the commandments of the law were many, it was no surprise when Jesus answered, "You shall love the Lord your God with your whole heart, with your whole soul, and with all your mind." What *was* surprising is that Jesus insisted on adding, "You shall love your neighbor as yourself." To the question, "What is the greatest commandment?" there should be only one answer, but Jesus gave two.

The first answer is a quotation from the book of Deuteronomy (6:5) and the second, from the book of Leviticus (19:18). Jesus was saying nothing new. His unique contribution was to combine two commandments, separated into distinct books of the Bible, and make them one. His insistence was that there can be no true love of God without love of neighbor, and there can be no proper love of neighbor without love of God.

For most people of good will it is usually easier, or less demanding, to love God than it is to love people. After all, we know that God is perfect. If ever we feel that God is not doing right by us, we know that the fault lies in our failure to understand and not in God himself. The same cannot be said of our relationships with people.

Even people we love can annoy us at the time we are looking for a little peace and quiet, interrupt us while we are speaking, and flip through all the TV channels when we want to watch a particular program. Political rhetoric can turn us against unwed mothers who are on welfare, self-satisfied people can influence us to hold in contempt the jobless and the homeless, and public opinion can move us to favor fundamental disregard for human life through abortion, euthanasia, and capital punishment.

If our religion consisted of nothing more than coming to church to thank God for his favors and to pray for his help, it would almost always be a pleasant and easy experience. But even during Mass we are called to express our love for our fellow human beings.

After the homily we voice petitions which are intended to be generous and outgoing. We pray usually for the needs of the Church, for public authorities and the salvation of the world, for those oppressed by any need, and for our local community. This prayer, which is an integral part of our worship of God, helps us to fulfill the commandment to love our neighbor. We offer each other a sign of peace, which is actually a prayer that we may all achieve the unity and peace with each other which Jesus in the Eucharist intends for us.

The temptation is to separate love for God from love for neighbor. Jesus will hear none of that. The commandment to love God and the commandment to love our neighbor are presented in separate books of the Bible, but they must not be separated in our hearts or in our actions.

Thirty-first Sunday of the Year, A

Give God's Place to No One

Ml 1:14-2:2, 8-10; 1 Th 2:7-9, 13; Mt 23:1-12

Children call their male parent "father" even though Jesus said, "Do not call anyone on earth your father." Instructors in school accept the title "teacher" even though Jesus said, "Avoid being called teachers." It would be absurd to maintain that these practices contradict Jesus' directives. Obviously their meaning is not literal. And yet, through these rather strong imperatives, Jesus did want to teach us an important lesson. He wanted to instruct us that we may give to no one the place in our lives which belongs to God.

We are all children of our parents. Some of us have been blessed in the parents we have, and quite honestly some have not. Ultimately, however, we must look to heaven to find the perfect parent, that unimaginably wonderful person who is the Father of our Lord Jesus Christ and who has become our Father too. We cannot allow anyone to take God's place in our lives.

We all have had to have teachers from the moment we were born, during all our years in school, when we got a job, and really throughout our entire lives. And yet the one person who can teach us the most essential truths about life, both here and hereafter, is Jesus Christ. We cannot allow anyone other than Jesus to be our teacher about the values of life.

God, speaking through the voice of Malachi his prophet in the first reading of this Sunday, proclaims, "A great King am I." Can any person of faith deny that? And yet God demands an answer to his question: "Do you accept that you must not put anyone in my place as your sovereign Lord?" We must answer, "Amen!"

Perhaps, however, our circumstances are not very much

different from those of the people to whom Malachi preached his message. They had returned from exile in Babylon only to find their homeland populated by a people who did not share their religion or their values. The situation was a challenge to the faith of both the priests and the people. That is why Malachi preached to them with such great urgency.

And it is why the Gospel of this Sunday has great meaning for us. We live in a country which is motivated primarily by individualism, materialism, and consumerism, not by the values of religion. Most people may say that they believe in God but the temptation in our country is to live as if God did not exist. That temptation is real for us, however subtle or distant it may seem as we sit in church.

And yet the church should be and is our haven, our spiritual home here in earth. Here we pay heed to Jesus, our teacher, as we listen to his words proclaimed in Sacred Scripture. We follow his teaching by praying to God as "Our Father," not only in the Lord's Prayer but throughout the Mass. We join him in his sacrifice to acknowledge that God is our Creator, our great King, to whom we offer thanks and praise.

Here too we should find people with whom we share the same values in life, people who support us in our faith and people whom we are willing to help in their time of need. The Jews returned to a land which seemed foreign to them. We should never feel out of place in a Catholic church. We should find in each other dedicated people who want to live according to the values which Jesus, the Son of God the Father, has given us.

Thirty-second Sunday of the Year, A

Keep Your Eyes Open
Ws 6:12-16; 1 Th 4:13-17; Mt 25:1-13

Jesus seems to have been very fond of weddings. He worked his first miracle at the wedding feast at Cana and he enjoyed referring to weddings and wedding banquets as symbols of heaven. The caricature of a contemporary wedding is that the bride is late and leaves everyone waiting for her at the church, but in Jesus' parable it is the groom who is late. There is some little humor in this since we can readily see that the groom represents Jesus himself. The groom is so late that half of the bridesmaids use up the oil in their lamps and drift off to sleep. We do not know what they were thinking, but it seems that they lost patience with the groom. They were foolish. The other bridesmaids not only stayed awake; they had also brought a sufficient supply of oil with them. We can surmise that they were willing to wait for the groom as long as it took. They were wise.

This Gospel, like many parables, is complex in its meaning. As we approach the end of this Church year, which will conclude in two weeks, the liturgy favors the interpretation that the Gospel is about the end of the world when Christ will come again in glory. That day no one knows. Every wise generation of Christians, from those to whom St. Paul wrote in Thessalonica, to the present has waited for Jesus' return with patience. We ourselves in every Mass profess after the "Our Father" that "we wait in joyful hope for the coming of our Savior, Jesus Christ."

Just before Holy Communion, we hear the declaration by the priest: "Happy are those who are called to his supper." This does not refer to the Last Supper in the past but to the heavenly supper in the future. The quotation is from the Book of

Revelation (19:9). St. John had a vision of a great wedding supper in heaven. An angel said to him, "Write this down: Happy are those who have been invited to the wedding supper of the Lamb." Waiting patiently for that supper is very wise. And we are called to be wise, to wait in patience for the coming of the Lord. The end of the world seems far off. Maybe it is and maybe it isn't. If he does not come sooner, the Lord will come in the moment of our death. It is a moment which actually we should look forward to in joyful hope. From a human standpoint that is a difficult recipe to follow. We naturally fear death and cling to life. Unlike the bridesmaids we are in no hurry for the groom to come. "Heaven can wait" is probably our sentiment. And yet we must heed the point of the Gospel: be alert, wide awake, and ready to meet the Lord whenever he comes.

The Church in her prayer book (the Liturgy of the Hours) urges us to prepare for death every night before we fall asleep. Sleep is a symbol of death. As we are about to go to sleep the Church suggests that we have the sentiment which Jesus had as he was about to die: "Father, into your hands I commend my spirit."

Holy Communion is a preparation for death. A Catholic who is about to die is entitled to, and directed to receive, communion as "viaticum," the food for the journey from this life to the next. Even when we receive communion at Mass we should be mindful of death, but always with faith in our resurrection from the dead. Standing to receive communion is a sign of that faith. The moral is "Keep your eyes open, for you know not the day or the hour."

Thirty-third Sunday of the Year, A

Do What God Wants
Pr 31:10-13, 19-20, 30-31; 1 Th 5:1-6; Mt 25:14-30

With only a few seconds left in a football game, the coach called for a running play to get the ball into the middle of the field where, after the team's final time out, they could kick a game-winning field goal. The quarterback changed the play, threw a long pass to the end zone which was intercepted, and lost any chance to win the game. A professor in a history class assigned a paper of no more than five hundred words on the meaning of the battle of Hastings in the year 1066. One student decided to write a thousand words, missed the point, and got an "F."

It is better to do what is right than to do what we want. From the Gospel today we can learn that we should want to do what is right in God's eyes. That means that we should not want to do great things for God; we should want to do whatever God asks of us. If God wills that we should become a great person in the Church, canonized shortly after our death, and venerated by Catholics around the world, that is like being the person in the Gospel who was given five thousand silver pieces.

On the other hand, perhaps our lives are not spectacular. It may be that to all external appearances we are little different from the people with whom we work or the people with whom we stand in line at the supermarket. The important thing is that we are trying to live in accord with God's will, to honor the commitments which our calling in life entails, and to be faithful and devout in our religion. We are like the person in the Gospel who was given, not five, but only two thousand silver pieces.

A woman whose life is like that of the one in the first reading today, the worthy wife, will never be featured on the TV show, "Sixty Minutes." The man who as a faithful husband entrusts his heart to his wife will never be featured in *People* magazine. Does it really matter, as long as these people are known intimately by God and loved deeply by him? The Gospel suggests that God was equally pleased with the servant who earned two thousand silver pieces as he was with the one who earned five thousand.

The mistake is to live like the person in the Gospel who received a thousand silver pieces but buried them in the ground. He protested that he was afraid of his master. Fear should have induced him to do something, almost anything, in order to placate the one whom he thought of as a harsh master. The master, we may surmise, would have been tolerant of failure, but he could not countenance the fact that the servant made no effort at all.

The master obviously did not need the thousand silver pieces. In the end he gave them to the man who had earned five thousand. The truth is that God does not need us. He can work his will in an instant if he so chooses. What God has chosen is to give us his grace. We must understand that everything is a grace from God: our life, our family, our faith, our talents, even our desire to love and serve God. All things are a gift, but they are a gift to be used in accord with God's will, for his glory, and for the good of his people.

Actually in a sense we are all called to do great things for God because whenever we do anything in accord with God will, no matter how small or insignificant it may appear in human eyes, that something is very great indeed.

Solemnity of Christ the King, A

We Are Part of a Great Movement

Ezk 34:11-12, 15-17; 1 Cor 15:20-26, 28; Mt 25:31-46

On the first day of September in 1939 Adolf Hitler invaded Poland and set into motion the Second World War. We now recognize that act of barbarism as the act of a masterful maniac, but at the time he had convinced many people in his nation that he would lead them to greatness.

Powerful instincts reside within the human heart. One of these instincts produces a yearning to be part of something great, to be involved in a movement that will change history, to become immortal through sharing in a grand enterprise of worldwide proportions.

Throughout history unscrupulous men have taken advantage of this strong instinct. Adolf Hitler is a prime example of how an egomaniac who possesses what today is called "charisma" can scoop almost an entire nation into the palm of his hand. From our vantage point in time we may look back and wonder that rational and responsible human beings were so easily duped until we realize how passionate the hunger to be significant can become. Because he understood this passion, Hitler based his oratory on the principle that if the lie you tell is big enough, people will believe it. In effect he demanded that his people turn over to him their entire being so that the goals of a master race could be achieved.

The greatest sin of Adolf Hitler was not the terrible atrocities which brought about the execution of millions, horrible though that was. Nor was it the fact that he plunged this planet into the Second World War, tragic though that was. His ultimate sin was a blasphemy, the fact that he wished to enthrone himself within the human heart in the place which belongs to Christ alone. Hitler, and demagogues like him, are worse than false prophets. They are the abominable and destructive presence standing in the holy place.

Christ as our King claims dominion over all creation. He alone deserves to receive a throne within our hearts. Powerful though he is, he does not win our hearts by force of conquest. Rather he invites us to be the people of his eternal and universal kingdom. He does not play upon our instinct to be part of greatness; he fulfills it.

His is a kingdom, not of deceit and destruction, but of truth and life. It is a kingdom, not of evil and conceit, but of holiness and grace. It is a kingdom, not of exploitation, hatred, and violence, but of justice, love, and peace. As members of the Church we are called to be a sacrament of this kingdom, a sign to the world of what the kingdom of God really is.

The kingdom is already present and yet to come. It is present among us in imperfect form, but the way in which we live as faithful people will help to bring it to perfection when Christ will come again in glory.

We need not be unimportant people whose lives are absorbed by a petty living out of an inconsequential routine which inevitably leads to a meaningless death. Life is not absurd. It is a sharing in the one really great movement of history as faithful followers of Christ the King.

A PLEDGE OF ALLEGIANCE TO CHRIST THE KING

This Sunday is an appropriate time to pledge our allegiance to Christ the King. The following suggested form, which is based on the Preface of the Eucharistic Prayer for this Solemnity, may be used at Mass by having the people repeat the lines of the pledge after the priest or other minister.

> We pledge allegiance to Christ the King.
> We embrace his eternal and universal kingdom.
> We acknowledge his kingdom to be one of truth and life,
> of holiness and grace.
> We wish to do what we can through prayer and action
> to bring to the world his kingdom
> of justice, love, and peace.

The B Cycle of Readings

*"This is the Gospel of Jesus Christ,
the Son of God."*
(Mk 1:1)

The Season of Advent and Christmas
Cycle B

"Next to the yearly celebration of the
Paschal Mystery, the Church holds most sacred the
memorial of Christ's birth and early manifestation.
This is the purpose of the Christmas season."
(*General Norms for the Liturgical Year*, 32)

First Sunday of Advent, B

Growing in Hope During Advent
Is 63:16-17, 19; 64:2-7; 1 Cor 1:3-9; Mk 13:33-37

The season of Advent is four weeks long — but only approximately. When Christmas falls on a Monday, we have an Advent of only twenty-two days. When Christmas falls on a Sunday, we have an Advent of a full four weeks.

Most of us seem to love Advent and that is one reason for wanting it to be as long as possible. There is a distinct pleasure in looking forward to Christmas. Advent, however, is a season of expectation not only for the celebration of the birth of Christ but also for his return at the end of time. Then Christ will turn the universal kingdom over to his Father for his honor and glory. The Church has already waited a long while for that return, and so a lengthy Advent seems appropriate.

Sometimes we may have a vague feeling that the period of the Old Testament was much longer than the time of the New Testament. The fact is that the era from the time of the birth of Christ until the present is now longer than the era from the call of Abraham in the Old Testament until the first Christmas.

But just where are we in the history of the Church and the world? Are we almost at its end? Will we see far past the year 2000 or will Christ come in glory before a new century turns old? Are we actually still only at the beginning of our history so that possibly Catholics living in the year 6000 will say of us living at this time, "How blessed they were to have lived so close to the time of Christ and his apostles"? Who knows?

Jesus himself said, "As for the exact day or hour, no one knows, neither the angels in heaven nor the Son, but the Father only" (Matthew 24:38). Despite this clear teaching, every now and then a religious fanatic proclaims that the end is near, and somehow manages to enlist a following. Such proclamations tend to bring ridicule on the concept of the second coming of Christ.

And yet the truth that Christ will come again is part of our faith. The first part of Advent is an anticipation of the second coming, but throughout the entire year in every Mass we pray to the Father: "Protect us from all anxiety as we wait in joyful hope for the coming of our Savior Jesus Christ."

The reason for joyful hope is explained by the Vatican Council: "As deformed by sin the shape of this world will pass away. But we are taught that God is preparing a new dwelling place and a new earth where justice will abide, and whose blessedness will answer and surpass all the longings for peace which spring up in the human heart. Then with death overcome, the children of God will be raised up in Christ" (*Constitution on the Church in the Modern World*, 39).

It is right that we look forward to the fulfillment of justice and peace. We ought to yearn for the day of the general resurrection when Christ will hand over the kingdom to his Father (see 1 Corinthians 15:24). During Advent we should pray for the virtue of hope, a confident trust that at the second coming all wrongs will be righted, justice will be done, and peace will prevail — all to the greater honor and glory of God.

Second Sunday of Advent, B

Let The Real Santa Claus Stand Up
Is 40:1-5, 9-11; 2 P 3:8-14; Mk 1:1-8

The liturgy on this Second Sunday of Advent features St. John the Baptist. For many people, however, the saint who is most closely connected with Christmas, after Mary and Joseph, is not John the Baptist. It is St. Nicholas.

Jolly St. Nick in his bright red suit presents quite a contrast with the austerity of the Baptist who was clothed in camel's hair and wore a leather belt around his waist. Even so, St. Nicholas can serve as part of our Advent reflections. He was a fourth century bishop of Myra in Lycia (which is now part of Turkey). A popular story about him revolves around a poor man who could not provide dowries for his three daughters. As each girl reached marriageable age, Nicholas secretly left a bag of gold for the father so that he could arrange the weddings. Over the centuries Nicholas became a symbol of the gift-giving which is part of the celebration of Christmas.

This bishop's name is Greek ("Nikelaos"). The first part of his name, "*Nike*," means "victory." It is the name that was given to the Greek goddess of victory. Our government has employed it to designate a missile, and a sporting goods company has used it for its products. We should associate it with Christ.

Some representations of Christ the King place this word, "*Nike*," beneath his feet to remind us that Christ has won the victory over the selfishness of sin and the finality of death, and has been exalted as King of the universe. There is a second part to the name; it is "*laos*" which means "people" (it is the Greek word from which we have derived our word for the baptized, the "lay" people). This meaning should help us recognize that the great victory of Christ was for the benefit of his people. He won for us the victory over sin and death by means of the greatest act of generous giving the world has ever known.

The legends about the goodness and gift-giving of St. Nicholas have been symbolized in the Dutch version of his name, Santa Claus. This name represents some of the most delightful experiences of childhood, but even for adults it suggests jolliness and good-natured generosity and a man clothed in a bright red suit rather than camel's hair.

But Santa Claus does not push the Baptist aside during Advent. By his preaching John hoped to move people away from the basis of sin, which is self-centeredness. Santa Claus symbolizes unselfishness. He represents what the Baptist intended to accomplish. He is the gift giver who never receives a gift.

Behind all the legends of the good St. Nick is a yearning for a manifestation in a human person of the unselfish goodness which the eternal Son of God brought to our world. Even people who have no faith of any kind instinctively long for a sign of the generous love which Jesus both proclaimed and lived. That's why they love Santa Claus.

Preparing for Christmas means trying to become what Santa Claus represents, a personification of the kingdom of Christ. We are imbued with the Christmas spirit when indifference is turned into justice, when hatred is overcome by love, and when violence gives way to peace. Is there a Santa Claus? Of course. He is found in every person who shares in Christ's victory over sin.

Third Sunday of Advent, B

Christmas Happens Every Year
Is 61:1-2, 10-11; 1 Th 5:16-24; Jn 1:6-8, 19-28

Time is a reality which we all experience, but which is very difficult to define. An English Bishop of the last century, Cardinal Henry Edward Manning, observed that "God so values time that he gives it to us only moment by moment, and he never gives us a moment without taking the last away."

We say that time does any number of things. It provides us with experience, strengthens us in good resolves, and heals many wounds. But as the same Bishop pointed out, time does nothing. And yet it is the condition of all things which God accomplishes within our universe. Time is precious because it is the circumstance in which we live out our lives.

We say that time is of the essence when something important must be accomplished within a stated period, but time is a measure for all created realities without which they do not exist. Only God is outside the limits of time since he lives in an eternity without past or future.

Time is of concern to the Church, and it is consecrated by the celebration of the liturgical year, because God is working out our salvation within its framework. In the instant of creation time became a reality. With the call of Abraham on a particular date in time our salvation history began. Because of promises made to Abraham, the eternal Son of God was born into time as our Savior. "John the Baptist was his herald and made him known when at last he came."

Time is moving toward a point of consummation in God's plan when Christ will come again to bring the kingdom of God to fulfillment. Some call this the omega point (from the last letter of the Greek alphabet). Meanwhile time seems to be moving in a circle as similar events are repeated in an annual cycle.

Last year December 25th was Christmas and this year December 25th will be Christmas all over again. The Church celebrates each year as a cycle because the liturgy is the living re-presentation of the events of the past so that we may participate in them. The *Constitution on the Liturgy* (102) of Vatican II expressed it this way: "Within the cycle of a year the Church unfolds the whole mystery of Christ from his Incarnation and birth to the day of Pentecost. Recalling thus the mysteries of redemption, the Church opens to the faithful the riches of the Lord's powers and merits, so that these are in some way made present for all time, and the faithful are enabled to lay hold of them and become filled with saving grace."

Are all the wonderful events of which we read in Sacred Scripture buried in the past? By no means. The liturgy is a channel which allows us to enter into that timeless realm wherein the events of the life, death, and the resurrection of Christ are held by God in his eternal memory. Remembering is an essential element in all liturgy. While living out our days in time, the liturgy allows us to share in eternity.

One day time will end. At that moment we will indeed be a joyful people if we have used time well. We will be especially blessed if through the gift of time and its annual liturgical cycle we have entered prayerfully and devoutly into the mysteries of Christ our Savior.

Fourth Sunday of Advent, B

A Baby Transforms Lives
2 S 7:1-5, 8-11, 16; Rm 16:25-27; Lk 1:26-38

When a woman conceives a child, her whole life changes. When she goes to see a doctor, he urges her to stay healthy. She must maintain a proper diet and avoid smoking and drinking. All of this is not only for herself but also for the sake of her baby.

On this Sunday we hear about a woman who conceived a child. It was such an extraordinary event that an angel announced the fact to Mary, an angel whose name, "Gabriel," means "the strength or power of God." Through the power of the Holy Spirit God himself conceived this child without a human father because this child is unique: no one was ever like him before or since. This child is God's Son from all eternity, and in time he became the Son of Mary.

God had seen to Mary's spiritual health by granting her the favor of having been conceived in the womb of Ann, her mother, without sin. We call that truth her immaculate conception. God also willed her continued spiritual health by preserving her from sin for her entire life.

During her pregnancy Mary must have glowed with a special light because of her awareness that Jesus was living within her. St. Luke, who tells us this wonderful story in today's liturgy, observed of Mary after Jesus' birth that "Mary treasured all these things and reflected on them in her heart" (Luke 2:19).

We too should treasure the marvelous events of the conception and birth of Jesus. Upon reflecting on them in our heart, as did Mary, we ought to come to see that they are not far-off events which happened on the other side of the world only to and for Mary. These marvels are ours as well by the gracious design of God.

Jesus comes to us in the sacrament of baptism. He truly

lives within us since we as the Church are his body, his mystical body. He nourishes and intensifies his life within us through the sacrament of the Holy Eucharist. This reality should transform our lives. We should wish to maintain a healthy spiritual life for the sake of keeping Jesus within us. We should be motivated to be filled with faith, strengthened in hope, and moved to love because we take Jesus wherever we go.

The saints have all understood and acted in accord with this truth. One in particular is a Vincentian priest who was martyred in China in 1840 and who was canonized by Pope John Paul II on June 2, 1996. St. John Gabriel Perboyre (pronounced "Per-bwáhr") composed a prayer which expresses an ideal which Mary fulfilled and for which we should strive:

"O my divine Savior, transform me into yourself. May my hands be the hands of Jesus. May my tongue be the tongue of Jesus. Grant that every faculty of my body may serve only to glorify you. Above all transform my soul and all its powers that my memory, my will, and my affections may be the memory, the will, and the affections of Jesus. I pray you to destroy in me all that is not of you. Grant that I may live but in you and by you and for you, and that I may truly say with St. Paul, 'I live, now not I, but Christ lives in me.'"

The sentiments of this prayer, if not the exact words, are appropriate after Holy Communion. The conception and birth of Jesus are a grace with which God wishes to fill our minds, our hearts, and our souls.

Solemnity of Christmas, B (night or midnight)

Faith Gives Meaning to Christmas
Is 9:1-6; Tt 2:11-14; Lk 2:1-14

For people of faith the crib is the center of our Christmas celebration. Many families put up the crib early in Advent, but it is empty. Gradually they add the figures: first Mary and Joseph, then the shepherds, then the animals, and last of all on Christmas eve night they reverently place the baby Jesus in the manger.

The crib has meaning because of faith. Imagine what Christmas would be without faith. We would not know God and his great love. Without faith the first figure to go from the crib would be Jesus himself. Why should we be concerned about a Jewish baby born in poverty almost twenty centuries ago?

Next to go would be Mary. To us without faith Mary would be an unknown Jewish girl who lived and died like all the other girls in her village. We would not know and love her as the Mother of God and our Mother. Of course Joseph would go too since without faith we would not cherish his relationship to Mary and to Jesus. We would not care about the shepherds; they themselves would take their sheep back to the fields, and the animals would wander away to look for a warm place for the night. We would be the last to go. Without faith a great darkness would come over our lives, and we would be no better off than the vicious King Herod who attempted to kill the infant Jesus.

Without faith our entire lives would be different. The crucifixion would look like a failure, and all the sayings of Jesus would have no more meaning than the reflections of a forgotten rabbi or an unrecognized prophet. Without faith we would have no Church, no Eucharist, and no hope for eternal life.

But the truth is that Jesus has cured us of spiritual blindness. He has given us the gift of faith. That is why our Christmas is so surrounded by lights, the symbol of faith. Multiple candles adorn the altar in church and they enhance our Christmas decorations at home. The ornaments on our Christmas tree come alive in the reflection of the lights strung throughout the tree.

When Isaiah wrote of the future age which is ours to enjoy, he put a strong emphasis on vision and light. In the first reading of Midnight Mass he declares that "the people who walked in darkness have seen a great light." We are those people. At baptism the priest gave us a candle and said, "Receive the light of Christ." That light is the gift of faith, and it is faith which makes all the difference. Even nature cooperates since from the time of Christmas the days gradually grow longer and the hours of light slowly increase. Light, much light of every kind, is the most important accompaniment to our Christmas celebration since light is the symbol of faith.

Our custom of gift-giving at Christmas follows the example of God the Father who gave the first Christmas gift, his only begotten Son. And yet his Son is not his first gift since something is needed for us to embrace Jesus with understanding, love and gratitude. That something is the gift of faith which puts Jesus back in the crib and which puts meaning and purpose into our lives.

Solemnity of Christmas, B

Bethlehem Is Everywhere
Is 62:11-12; Tt 3:4-7; Lk 2:15-20

Christmas is a wonderful day. It is favored with some of the most beautiful music ever composed. The marvelous carols we hear during this season help to stir up within us the Christmas spirit. Christmas trees, decorations, lights, cards, and gifts — all add to the festive mood of hope and vitality.

But a funny thing happens on December 26th. We awaken to the same old world. Trees and decorations suddenly appear limp. The only cards we receive are from people who were late because, to their embarrassment, they had forgotten all about us until they received our card. Abruptly all the carols come to an end, and usually so does the Christmas spirit.

Even on Christmas day itself some people sense a touch of melancholy because the passing of each second means that we are inescapably moving away from an event which contains a special meaning. We know that we will have to return to business as usual, and there is a sadness that the joy and good will of Christmas cannot somehow last throughout the year. Is there another day which is filled with more emotion for a greater number of people than Christmas?

Christmas is so significant to us that few cities hold as much meaning for us as that of Bethlehem. The name does not recall the reality of a town on the other side of the earth where peace is shattered and promises are broken. When we hear the word, "Bethlehem," we are lifted above our world of sin to one of goodness and love.

Father John W. Lynch wrote in his poem, *A Woman Wrapped in Silence*, that "Bethlehem is a name which drifts to us from out remembered years, and holds within the sound and lilt of it a sweetness that we may not drone away; its syllables are stars, and songs, the good simplicity of shepherds, and the word is linked to all the innocence we've saved."

The greatest significance of the name of this little town is found in its literal meaning. "Bethlehem" in Hebrew means "House of Bread." Among many ancient people bread was a symbol of all the good things needed to sustain life since it was the fundamental source of nourishment. That is why Jesus taught us to pray for our daily bread. We even speak of a person who earns a living for the family as the "bread-winner." A "house of bread" is a home where a person can be fed, and warmed, and comforted.

Jesus chose bread together with wine to be the elements of the Holy Eucharist. Having taken human nature from his mother and been nourished at her breast, he wished to nourish us by transforming bread and wine into his body and blood. The Eucharist sustains our spiritual lives. It helps us to grow more like the giver, Christ himself. It repairs the wounds of sin. It gives joy to the heart of believers.

The beauty and meaning of Christmas need not end on December 26th. During every celebration of the Mass the church becomes a house of bread where we are fed, warmed and comforted. Bethlehem is not far away. It can be found in every Catholic church.

Feast of the Holy Family

Human Life Is Made Holy
Si 3:2-6, 12-14; Col 3:12-21; Lk 2:22-40

The marvel of Christmas is to acknowledge with the eyes of faith that the baby born in Bethlehem is the eternal Son of God.

Yes, a baby! God could have sent his Son into our world as a fully grown adult. After all, the mission of Jesus was accomplished within the span of some three years after he had reached the rabbinic age of thirty. Why did God wish his Son to go through conception, birth, infancy, and adolescence? Why did he ask his Son to begin his life on earth within a human family and to live a full, human life? One reason is that God the Father wanted to give a new sanctity to human existence. The Second Vatican Council explains this truth in its *Constitution on the Church in the Modern World* (22): "By his Incarnation the Son of God has united himself in some fashion with every human person. He worked with human hands, thought with a human mind, acted by human choice, and loved with a human heart. Born of the Virgin Mary, he has truly been made one of us, like us in all things except sin.... He showed us the way, and if we follow it, life and death are made holy and take on a new meaning."

Human life is holy because it is the creation of God, but it has taken on a deeper sacredness because Jesus Christ lived our human life. We apply this truth of the Incarnation when, with the mind of God, we honor family life, and when we respect, defend, and foster human life in all its forms from conception to death. Part of the Christmas story is that of the Holy Innocents, the little children who were exterminated by King Herod. They direct our attention to the unborn children who are exterminated daily by abortion, an act which the Second Vatican

Council in the same Constitution branded as "an unspeakable crime" (51).

The Council teaches that "God, the Lord of life, has conferred on the human race the surpassing ministry of safeguarding life, and so from the moment of conception life must be guarded with the greatest care" (*ibid.*).

We need laws to safeguard human life before birth for the same reason that we have laws to safeguard human life after birth. And yet law will not alter people's minds or change their hearts. We must embrace an ethic which not only abhors abortion but which also rejects any violation of human dignity at any age and in any circumstance.

Conscientious Catholics follow a consistent ethic. We respect children in the womb because Jesus began his human existence in the womb of Mary. We respect the family because Jesus led a family life at Nazareth. We respect aliens because Jesus himself was an alien in Egypt. We respect the poor because Jesus lived as a poor person "who had no place to lay his head." We respect the life even of criminals because Jesus, though innocent, died as a criminal. We do not pick and choose among these human issues because God did not assign to his Son only one aspect of human existence. In one of the prefaces of this Christmas season we proclaim to the Father our motive for our ethic: "Father, your eternal Son has taken upon himself our human weakness, giving our mortal nature immortal value." By becoming human Jesus has given all humans a high dignity.

New Year's Day, B

A Chance for a New Beginning

A rabbi, the story goes, was told that the Messiah had arrived. The rabbi went to the window, looked out, and returned shaking his head in the negative. "No," he said. "I see no change in anything."

We believe that everything has changed with the coming of Jesus Christ, the Messiah. And yet in a sense the rabbi was right. This New Year's Day, when we celebrate Mary as the Mother of God, is dedicated to peace. Where is that peace? Has anything really changed for the better in our world? We are still plagued with war, hatred, violence, racism, murders, greed, selfishness (need I continue?). The problem is, as Father Yves Congar, the French Dominican theologian, expressed it: "We would like to have the kingdom and, if I may put it this way, all we get is the king!" What about the kingdom?

The kingdom was inaugurated by Jesus. It is present among us, and yet it is still to come. Back on the Solemnity of Christ the King, when we were about to begin the season of Advent to prepare for Christmas, the liturgy directed our attention to the end times when Christ will return in glory to bring his kingdom to perfection. The kingdom, like Jesus himself, was born as an infant and perhaps we are loathe to admit that it has not grown much since the awesome day of the death of its founder. It seems that the day of completion, the second coming of Christ, is far in the future because much work remains to be done. This New Year's Day reminds us that God is giving us another chance for a new beginning. Many people on this day make resolutions. A good one for us is to become more fully Catholic, to be a really active person of the Church.

The Church is the sacrament of the kingdom. That means

it is both a sign of what the kingdom is to be and a means for bringing it about. There is a blueprint, a plan, for this kingdom. It has been drafted for us in the Preface for the Solemnity of Christ the King which proclaims "a kingdom of truth and life, a kingdom of holiness and grace, a kingdom of justice, love and peace."

Our work as Catholics is to rise above the secular, materialistic, and narcissistic society in which we live to be disciples who embrace the truth of the Scriptures and the other teachings of the Church in order to be a people who protect, foster, and cherish human life in all its stages from conception through natural death. We follow Christ the King in order to be a people of holiness, rather than self-centered individuals, a people who worship the Father in spirit and in truth and who rely on his grace to serve him in holiness rather than depend on the scant satisfaction which comes from greed and consumerism.

As people of the kingdom we work toward the goals of justice, love and peace. We act in accord with the admonition of Pope Paul VI: "If you want peace, work for justice." And we see that love calls us even beyond what justice demands of us.

Anyone who opens the window and sees the people of the Church should be able to say, "Maybe a whole lot has not changed since last year, but I do see some progress because there are followers of Christ the King who believe in and work for a kingdom of justice, love, and peace."

Solemnity of the Epiphany, B

Children Show the Meaning of Christmas
Is 60:1-6; Eph 3:2-3, 5-6; Mt 2:1-12

Christmas is not over. It continues in the celebration of the Epiphany this Sunday. When adults reflect on the meaning of Christmas, they often think of children. Even though all through our lives Christmas continues to have meaning for us, it is never more exciting than in our years of growing up.

Of course children are thrilled by the idea of presents, but they are also impressed by the meaning of the birth of Christ. It is very touching to watch parents, holding little children by the hand, and leading them to the crib in church. They kneel down with them and point to the baby Jesus and whisper words of simple explanation for the profound mystery.

And yet Christmas really is for everyone. That is the essential meaning of the Epiphany. The Magi were not Jewish as were Mary and Joseph and their baby. Even Gentiles were welcomed at Bethlehem because this child was sent by God to be the savior of the world.

The Gospel story of the Epiphany by St. Matthew helps us to broaden our vision of the mission of Jesus. St. Matthew emphasized the Magi because he was writing for Gentiles, but we see other meanings for the Magi. In tradition they are called kings. We also speak of them as the Wise Men. Apparently they were wealthy since they presented to Jesus three gifts which were among the most precious items of the time: gold, frankincense, and myrrh.

St. Luke adds another dimension to the story by St. Matthew. St. Luke loved the poor and used every opportunity to proclaim God's love for them. He emphasized the shepherds who were simple men of little means who worked for others, but to them the angel proclaimed the good news of the birth of the Savior. At the crib they found a couple who were poor like themselves since Joseph was in the same economic and social class as the shepherds.

Old people are not excluded. In fact, in their wisdom they have a deep understanding of the meaning of Christmas. They are represented by Simeon, the old man in the temple who was waiting to die until he could hold in his arms his Messiah and Lord. There too was Anna, the eighty-four-year-old widow. When she saw Jesus, she "gave thanks to God and talked about the child to all who looked forward to the deliverance of Jerusalem."

No one need fear to approach Jesus as Savior; all are welcome. In fact a constant refrain in the Christmas story is that fear is out of place. To Joseph the angel said, "Have no fear about taking Mary as your wife." To Mary also the angel said, "Do not fear. You have found favor with God." And to the shepherds the angel said, "You have nothing to fear."

Angelic children, kneeling at the crib, help us to understand the angelic message. They are not afraid of the baby Jesus. They are fascinated by the truth that God can be smaller than they are. We ourselves find the Lord smaller than we are when he comes to us under the appearances of a little piece of bread and a swallow of wine in the Holy Eucharist. There is nothing to fear about God. Although Christmas is for everyone, we overcome fear and capture its joyful experience when we follow the command of Jesus and become like little children.

Feast of the Baptism of the Lord, B

Finding God on Earth
Is 42:1-4, 6-7; Ac 10:34-38; Mk 1:7-11

Some people picture God as being "up in heaven." We do it, too, at times when we raise our eyes to heaven in prayer. But when you think about it we do not look *up* so much as we look *out* from the world toward space. I suppose that only someone living at the top of the north pole would actually look up, and someone living at the south pole would look down.

The great feast of Christmas which we have just celebrated brings us the good news that God is not merely out there in space, whether we look up or down. Through the person of his beloved Son he has come close to us, he has become part of our human family, and he has entered our world.

Our Catholic doctrine tells us that what Jesus did during his time on this earth, he continues to do among us through the sacraments until the end of time. Pope Pius XII expressed it beautifully back in 1947 when he wrote in his encyclical on the Sacred Liturgy, *Mediator Dei*: "(In the Church) Christ continues that journey of immense mercy which he lovingly began in his mortal life, going about doing good with the design of bringing people to know his mysteries and to live by them" (165).

Pope Leo the Great (who was Pope from 440 to 461) insisted that we are more blessed than the people with whom Jesus lived. He pointed out that "Christ is more present to us now through the sacraments than he was to the people of his day through his humanity."

Jesus graced the wedding of the unnamed husband and wife at Cana, but he is the bond uniting every couple who are joined in the sacrament of marriage. He reached out and touched the sick of his day to cure them, but only a few persons so benefitted. Today he comes with his healing grace in the sacrament of anointing to all who are ill and who respond in faith to this sacrament of compassion. Jesus forgave the sins of the paralytic when his friends placed the young man on his pallet before him, but now in the sacrament of penance we are all invited to lay our sins before him so that he may lift their burden from us. Jesus fed more than five thousand people with the five barley loaves, but in the Eucharist for twenty centuries he has nourished untold numbers with his body and his blood.

Some people think they do not need the Church. Others reject the doctrine of the sacraments. This feast of the Lord's own baptism says something else. It declares that God's way has been to take the human way, to act among us in the Church through visible signs and audible words as he acted through the humanity of Jesus in Jerusalem and throughout Judea and Galilee.

For us the human nature of the Son of God has been extended through the human elements of the sacraments. Christmas teaches us to look down into a crib to see God, and the Catholic doctrine of the sacraments makes us realize that there is no need to look out from our world into space in a search for God; rather, we are to look right here within our world at the Church and the sacraments Christ has given us.

The Season of Lent and Easter
Cycle B

"By means of the yearly cycle the Church celebrates the whole mystery of Christ from his Incarnation until the day of Pentecost and the expectation of his coming again."
(*General Norms for the Liturgical Year*, 17)

First Sunday of Lent, B

Lent Is a Journey with Christ
Gn 9:8-15; 1 P 3:18-22; Mk 1:12-15

When you are going to go on an automobile trip, you have to make certain preparations. You pack your bags, lock up the house, and then get in the car with the conviction that you have forgotten something, but for the life of you, you cannot think of what it is.

The public ministry of Jesus was like a journey. Throughout the time after his baptism in the Jordan when he began to preach the kingdom of God and to gather disciples around himself, Jesus had "his face turned toward Jerusalem." Jesus was gradually and deliberately moving along a road mapped out by his Father which led inevitably up to the Holy City. There he would fulfill the purpose of his coming among us through his death and resurrection. Some scholars look upon the Gospel of St. Mark, which is featured this year, as a narrative of the passion with a long introduction. The point is that everything in the life of Jesus led to the cross. Jesus was getting ready for his journey to the cross even from the moment of his conception in Mary's womb, but he concluded his immediate preparation during forty days in the desert, as St. Mark tells us in the Gospel today.

The great event of the death and resurrection of Jesus is called his "Paschal Mystery." We know the meaning of this event from our Eucharistic acclamations at Mass when we proclaim to the Lord Jesus: "Dying you destroyed our death, rising you restored our life," and "By your cross and resurrection you have set us free; you are the Savior of the world."

The first great sacrament of Lent is baptism which is our initial sharing in the Paschal Mystery. This Sunday in the reading from the First Letter of Peter we are told that we are saved by a baptismal bath which is like the flood in Noah's time. The land, so to speak, died in the flood and was buried beneath its waters, but when the waters receded a new life blossomed, and God established a covenant of love with his people. In the waters of baptism we die as sinful people; then we rise to a new life in Christ, and we enter into the new and eternal covenant with God. Baptism is a living out of the acclamation, "Dying you destroyed our death, rising you restored our life."

Because in our weakness we fail to keep a perfect covenant with God after our baptism, we have another way of coming into contact with the saving death and resurrection of Jesus, and that is the sacrament of penance, the second great sacrament of Lent.

Penance is a living out of the eucharistic acclamation, "Lord, by your cross and resurrection, you have set us free; you are the Savior of the world."

The First Letter of Peter reminds us today that "Christ died for sins once and for all, a just man for the sake of the unjust, so that he might lead us to God." Lent is a time to get our bags packed for the journey toward the fulfillment of our existence on this earth. For the life of us we must not forget the map. We must keep our eyes fixed on Jesus as the Church presents him to us in the Lenten Scriptures. Jesus is a living map for us, leading us through the sacramental experiences of his Paschal Mystery to physical death and ultimate resurrection.

Second Sunday of Lent, B

All's Well That Ends Well
Gn 22:1-2, 9, 10-13, 15-18; Rm 8:31-34; Mk 9:2-10

In the midst of his public ministry, Jesus explained to his apostles that he had to go up to Jerusalem to suffer and die and then be raised up. Six days later he led Peter, James, and John up on a high mountain where he was transfigured before them. The transfiguration was a visualization of the meaning of the Paschal Mystery. Jesus wanted to teach his apostles that "he had first to suffer and so come to the glory of his resurrection" (Preface 13). The Paschal Mystery, which should fill our minds and hearts especially during Lent, gives light to our darkest days and eases the burden of our greatest suffering. Borrowing from the title of Shakespeare's play, "All's well that ends well."

Participation in the sacred liturgy, which is the indispensable source of the true Christian life, focuses our attention on the Paschal Mystery, the death and resurrection of Christ. The liturgy urges us to embrace a constant meditation and reflection on the Paschal Mystery because it is the fulfillment of Christ's coming into our world, it is the center of all liturgical celebration, and it must become the preoccupation of our prayerful thoughts.

The Paschal Mystery is God the Father's plan, and liturgical spirituality sees the Paschal Mystery everywhere. When night turns into day, that is the Paschal Mystery. When a seed dies in the earth and rises to become a fruitful vine, that is the Paschal Mystery. When a woman's birth pangs turn into the joy of giving birth to a child, that is the Paschal Mystery. When an alcoholic is recovering from the slavery of addiction to a new life of freedom, that is the Paschal Mystery. When food satisfies hunger and drink quenches thirst, that is the Paschal Mystery. When health overcomes sickness, when love drives out loneliness, when reconciliation is the fruit of repentance — all that is the Paschal Mystery. When one man, Abraham, becomes a great people, transcending even his physical descendants to include all who believe in Christ, that too is the Paschal Mystery. It is important to get the sequence right. Life is not ups and downs; life is downs and ups.

Our first sacramental experience of the Paschal Mystery is in baptism. We are a people who have been plunged into the death of Christ and we have been raised with him to newness of life. Baptism is a one time experience, but this initial sacramental sharing in the Paschal Mystery leads us to the eucharistic celebration of the Paschal Mystery. When bread "dies" to become the body of Christ, that is the Paschal Mystery. And when wine "perishes" to become the blood of Christ, that is the Paschal Mystery.

Our ultimate sharing in the Paschal Mystery is our physical death which brings us to enjoy the fruit of the resurrection, everlasting life. Liturgical spirituality never forgets the Paschal Mystery. It enlightens us with a faith that "Christ had first to suffer and so come to the glory of the resurrection," and it fills us with trust that God the Father includes us in his plan of the Paschal Mystery. The Paschal Mystery assures us that all's well that ends well.

Third Sunday of Lent, B

A Church Rises from a Temple Destroyed
Ex 20:1-17; 1 Cor 1:22-25; Jn 2:13-25

Imagine you are standing before the awesome grandeur of St. Peter's basilica in Rome when you hear someone declare: "Destroy this basilica and in three days I will build it up again." You, as well as the Pope, would be as shocked and incredulous as were the Jews who heard Jesus standing before their temple in Jerusalem declare: "Destroy this temple and in three days I will raise it up."

Scholars estimate that it was in the year 29 A.D. that Jesus made his declaration. At that time the temple to which Jesus referred had been in the process of being built over a period of forty-six years. It was not actually completed until shortly before it was destroyed by the Romans in 70 A.D. The people to whom Jesus spoke were thinking of this temple with a small "t." Through the teaching of St. John in the Gospel, we know that Jesus was speaking of a Temple with a capital "T," his body. That includes us.

The Jerusalem temple was sacred, a holy place wherein devout Jews came to worship the one true God. Infinitely more sacred was Jesus himself. He was a Temple in the sense that he was the perfect priest, the worshipper of his Father. He would fulfill his priesthood when the Temple of his body hung in death upon the cross.

Jesus' prophecy was fulfilled in his resurrection. That is why he did not say, "I will *rebuild* the temple," but "I will *raise* it up." From the death of Jesus flowed a fullness of life which not only raised him from the dead but also lifted us out of the grave of sin. This life which flows from the cross comes upon us in the waters of baptism and gives us new life in Christ, so that we become his body, his mystical body, the Church. From the destruction of the Temple of his body, Christ rose in glory as Head of the Church, his mystical body. All that Jesus said of his body as the Temple applies to us now since we have became part of him, many though we are, just as many elements went into the building of the Jerusalem temple.

Every Sunday we come together in a building which we call a church. As we enter the church (little "c") we should realize that through baptism we have been transformed into the Church (capital "C"), the new spiritual temple. The church becomes a place of worship when Christ gathers together his people, the Church, to join him in the worship of God the Father. More precious than the temple of Jerusalem is this new temple, the body of Christ. More magnificent than St. Peter's in Rome are we who gather in the name of Christ, for we are united with him as the Head of his body, which is the Church.

Statues and paintings in church serve to remind us of the many great men and women who have gone before us in faith. Today look around at the living statues and paintings, the people who are members of the body of Christ. See beyond their exterior. Be perceptive. Jesus stood in front of the temple, a mere building, but through his words he invited people to respond through faith to a reality deeper than the building before them. Equally he invites us to look beyond externals and to see that we, the people in church, are the Church, the body of Christ.

Fourth Sunday of Lent, B

Tragedy Turns into Triumph
2 Ch 36:14-17, 19-23; Eph 2:4-10; Jn 3:14-21

Some philosophers view life as essentially tragic. They come to this pessimistic conclusion because they observe that all life inevitably ends in death. The rose which blooms early this spring will have died long before summer arrives. New-born infants who brighten the life of loving parents will themselves follow their father and mother one day into the darkness of the grave.

In the far distant future the sun, which is our furnace, will exhaust its energy and the earth will endure a frozen death. Actually the entire universe is finite, limited in the resources which are needed for continued existence. Even at this moment the universe is slowing passing away.

If like some philosophers we relied only on our human intellects, we too would be pessimistic. But we have been given the gift of faith which is like a bright light shining on an awesome truth within God's plan. We call this truth the Paschal Mystery.

According to God's plan death leads to life. This plan applies to our world. In accord with the Sacred Scripture (see 2 Peter 3:13), the Second Vatican Council stated that "as deformed by sin, the shape of this world will pass away. But we are taught that God is preparing a new dwelling place and a new earth where justice will abide and whose blessedness will answer and surpass all the longings for peace which spring up in the human heart" (*Constitution on the Church in the Modern World*, 39).

This same plan applies to us. Some people manage to escape taxes but no one will escape death. The liturgy instructs us in our faith: "In Christ who rose from the dead, our hope of resurrection has dawned. The sadness of death gives way to the bright promise of immortality. (For the Lord's) faithful people life is changed, not ended. When the body of our earthly dwelling lies in death, we gain an everlasting dwelling place in heaven" (Preface for Masses for the Dead). In our eucharistic acclamation we cry out to the Lord, "Dying you destroyed our death, rising you restored our life."

In this Sunday's Mass St. John reminds us that "God did not send his Son into the world to condemn the world, but that the world might be saved through him." Theologically speaking, the "world" in this passage is to be understood as referring not only to the inhabitants of this planet but to the planet itself, and indeed to the whole universe.

Jesus declared that he must be lifted up. It was his way of referring to his crucifixion. The manner of his death was the kind meted out to criminals whose lives end in tragedy. The cross seemed to herald, not a victory, but a defeat. Faith tells us something different. The only "crime" Jesus committed was to rob death of its power. The cross was neither a tragedy nor a defeat but a glorious triumph. In that triumph we already share since God in his great love has brought us to life in Christ when we were dead in sin. He also has reserved for us a place in the heavens that in the ages to come he might display the great wealth of his favor toward us. (See the second reading for this Sunday.) Our life is not tragic because in Christ death leads to eternal life.

Fifth Sunday of Lent, B

God's Spiritual Big Bang
Jr 31:31-34; Heb 5:7-9; Jn 12:20-33

Many scientist subscribe to the "big bang" theory to explain the origin of the universe. Some fifteen or twenty billion years ago, they theorize, all matter and energy of the universe were concentrated into a space smaller than the head of a pin. When the density became intolerably intense, there was an enormous explosion which propelled matter into a constantly expanding space.

Leaving aside any judgment about the correctness of this theory within the providence of God, the truth is that there was a spiritual big bang less than two thousand years ago. All of God's love was concentrated in a single action. His love was so intense that it exploded with such force that it was propelled outward in a great sphere, moving not only forward but even backward in time. That action was the death and resurrection of God's Son. God's big bang is not a theory. It is a profound reality which we call the Paschal Mystery.

In the death and resurrection of Jesus we see the providence of God the Father. The Father's plan is that death unfolds into life. The death of God's Son led to his resurrection, and his death will lead to our resurrection as well.

Actually God's plan is a pervasive part of all reality, not only of our spiritual lives. That is why Jesus had no trouble finding analogies to illustrate the Paschal Mystery. He declared: "Unless the grain of wheat falls to the earth and dies, it remains just a grain of wheat. But if it dies, it produces much fruit."

We came into contact with the Paschal Mystery for the first time in our baptism. St. Paul wrote to the Romans: "We who were baptized into Christ Jesus were baptized into his death. We were indeed buried with him through baptism into death so that, just as Christ was raised from the dead by the glory of the Father, we too might live in newness of life" (6:3-4). When we come into church, we make the sign of the cross with holy water. That should remind us of our baptism and make us aware that we gather in church primarily to celebrate the Paschal Mystery.

Every time we participate in the Mass we do so in memory of Christ's death and resurrection, his Paschal Mystery. Once a year we celebrate the Paschal Mystery in a special manner during the three days which are called the sacred triduum. This solemn memorial begins with the Mass of the Lord's Supper on Holy Thursday night and concludes with evening prayer on Easter Sunday. Although the celebration encompasses three days in a reflection of the historical unfolding of these events of our salvation, the death and resurrection of Christ are one reality, his Paschal Mystery, always present before God the Father. Our liturgical celebration is more than a mere recalling of events of the past. It is a living memorial of the Paschal Mystery. Through the liturgy we enter into the memory of God.

Our final sharing in the Paschal Mystery comes through our physical death. Death for us means life. Then the eucharistic words of Jesus will be fulfilled: "Those who eat my flesh and drink my blood have life everlasting and I will raise them up on the last day." On that last day the echo of God's big bang will sound in our ears as the joyful announcement of everlasting life.

Passion or Palm Sunday, B

The Eucharist Is the Sacrament of Our Salvation
Is 50:4-7; Ph 2:6-11; Mk 14:1—15:47

This Sunday the liturgy begins to unfold a series of events which God the Father planned and which he guided by means of the Holy Spirit in order to accomplish our salvation. In the center of this divine drama stands, not an actor, but the eternal Son of God. He is Jesus, the Savior. He is the Christ, the one anointed by God to be the Lamb who takes away the sins of the world.

The week which is unfolding was once called the "Great Week," but now usually "Holy Week." It begins with the entry of Jesus into Jerusalem, and reaches a climax in the three days which we call the Triduum: Good Friday, Holy Saturday, and Easter Sunday. These days are truly the great, holy days of our faith.

On Thursday evening, already Friday in the Jewish liturgical reckoning, "Jesus realized that the hour had come for him to pass from this world to the Father. He had loved his own in this world, and would show his love for them to the end" (John 13:1). The Greek word used by St. John for "end" means not only "until the termination of his life" but also "to the fullest extent." Actually Jesus would show the fullest love by sacrificing his life for us.

On that awesome night of the Last Supper, Jesus was thinking of his final act of love while on this earth, his death on the cross. So that his followers might be able to share in his sacrifice throughout all ages, he instituted the sacrament of his Paschal Mystery, his death and resurrection. At this supper "under the appearances of bread and wine, Jesus offered his body and blood, gave them to his apostles to eat and drink, and then commanded them to carry on this mystery" (Roman Missal, 55).

The Church rightly understands that "the sacrifice of the

cross and its sacramental renewal in the Mass, which Jesus instituted at the Last Supper and commanded his apostles to do in his memory, are one and the same, differing only in the manner of offering, and that consequently the Mass is at once a sacrifice of praise and thanksgiving, of reconciliation and expiation" (*ibid.*, 2).

On Friday afternoon Jesus offered the sacrifice of himself which he had instituted as a sacrament on the previous night. On Saturday, the second day of the Triduum, Jesus was in the tomb. His burial indicated that his death was real, not a fiction or pretense. It is the day of supreme quiet, the great silence of the liturgy. The liturgy invites us to remain at the tomb of Jesus, in peaceful expectation of the bright morrow.

On Easter Sunday Jesus broke the bond of death. By dying he destroyed our death, and by rising he restored our life. Now in the eucharistic celebration his resurrection cannot be separated from his death. We proclaim, "Lord, by your cross and resurrection you have set us free; you are the Savior of the World."

Today we begin the great, Holy Week of our faith. It will culminate in the Sacred Triduum. The meaning of the three great, holy days of our faith is not lost in the past. It is a reality for us in every celebration of the Holy Eucharist.

Solemnity of Easter, B

Easter: Past, Future, and Present
Ac 10:34, 37-43; Col 3:1-4 or 1 Cor 5:6-8; Jn 20:1-9

Easter Sunday is a day of unparalleled significance. Its celebration is so great that it touches the past, the future, and the present. We remember the past in faith; we look to the future in hope; and we are called to live a life of love in the present.

We remember the past, the resurrection of Jesus from the dead. Because we were not eyewitnesses of the resurrection, we embrace this truth on the authority of God's revelation which he has communicated to his Church. The Church's faith is proclaimed to us within the liturgical celebration of Easter Sunday.

St. Paul put the event of the resurrection in perspective: "If Christ has not been raised, our preaching is void of content and your faith is empty too" (1 Corinthians 15:14). Easter Sunday is the first of all our feast days. Without the resurrection our faith about the past collapses, our joyful anticipation of the future gives way to sadness, and our celebration in the present is hollow. Thanks be to God, we have received the grace of faith which we proclaim in our eucharistic acclamation: "Christ has died, Christ is risen, Christ will come again."

Now comes the second step: we look to the future in hope. This hope is a conviction that we, like Christ, will be raised from death to the fullness of life. Perhaps we find it easier to accept the resurrection of Christ than our own. After all Christ is the divine Son of the Father, who came on this earth only for a time to work out our salvation. It seems natural that his death should lead to resurrection. We mere mortals are another case. And yet faith in Christ's resurrection leads us to faith in our own resurrection. An Easter celebration of the resurrection of Christ is devoid of significance unless we have a firm hope about our own resurrection.

The hope to which God invites us is based on the truth contained in another of our eucharistic acclamations which is addressed to the Risen Lord: "Dying you destroyed our death, rising you restored our life. Lord Jesus, come in glory." Death is the ultimate, inevitable act of this life. We cannot escape it, but only sin makes of death a tragedy. Jesus has destroyed death by overcoming sin. Death will not be a final step into oblivion. It will be a transition to a higher form of existence as it was for Jesus. Our well-founded hope is that death will lead to resurrection.

Then the third step: a confident hope in the future leads to a life of love in the present. If we want to live with Christ in the happiness of eternity, we must live with him now the way he lived on this earth. We understand clearly what that means. We know what the example of Christ is for us: to be unselfish, generous, caring, devoted to prayer which we offer to God and dedicated to service which we offer to our sisters and brothers.

Easter is past, present, and future. As we receive the Risen Christ in Holy Communion, we are strengthened in our faith in Christ's resurrection in the past, we are fortified to live the life of Christ in the present, and we are given a pledge of our own resurrection in the future. Easter is indeed the great celebration of our Catholic faith.

Second Sunday of Easter, B

What Do You Hear the Risen Christ Say?
Ac 4:32-35; 1 Jn 5:1-6; Jn 20:19-31

Place yourself in the upper room with the disciples on Easter Sunday evening. The Risen Lord stands before you. He greets you warmly, "Peace be with you." What do you expect him to say next?

I can imagine Jesus with arms raised above his head proclaiming, "I am the resurrection and the life." This was the proclamation he made to Martha to bolster her faith that he could raise her brother, Lazarus, from the dead. But on the evening of his own resurrection Jesus says, "Receive the Holy Spirit. Whose sins you shall forgive they are forgiven, whose sins you shall retain they are retained." That is somewhat surprising.

I can also imagine Jesus declaring, "I am the great healer." After all, in his ministry he cured the sick, cleansed the lepers, gave sight to the blind, and cared for every human ailment. But Jesus says, "Whose sins you shall forgive they are forgiven, whose sins you shall retain they are retained." Somewhat surprising.

I can imagine Jesus urging us, "Love one another as I have loved you." This was his command on the night before he died. He could now say, "In my death on the cross you have seen how deep is my love. That is the kind of love you are to have for one another." Instead he says, "Whose sins you shall forgive, they are forgiven." Surprising.

It seems that Jesus was intent on granting to the Church the power to forgive sins because forgiveness must come first in our relationship with God. Jesus is our resurrection and our life, but sin is an obstacle to that life. In fact, mortal sin is not life but everlasting death.

Jesus is indeed the great healer, but the most serious illness we face is not cancer or AIDS or anything else. It is sin. The disease of sin must be overcome before all else. Jesus wants us to love one another, but the great obstacle to this love is sin, especially pride, selfishness, and individualism. Sin must be wiped out so that we may become loving people.

Jesus forgives our sins through the ministry of the Church, and he does so in three specific ways. The first is the sacrament of baptism. The waters of baptism wash us clean of all sins, whether we are infants or adults. Through baptism we are born again to begin a new life as children of God. The second means of forgiveness is full, conscious, active participation in the liturgy of the Mass. Part of the initial rites of the Mass is our acknowledgment of our sinfulness and a plea for mercy. In Holy Communion we receive the body and blood of the Risen Lord who has triumphed over sin and death. Our devout participation in Mass grants forgiveness of venial sins. The third means is the sacrament of penance. When we confess our sins in sorrow, we hear the comforting voice of Christ, "I absolve you from your sins." This sacrament is necessary for the forgiveness of mortal sins.

On the night of his resurrection, having triumphed over sin and death, Jesus granted to his Church the ministry of forgiveness so that the power of his life, his healing, and his love might penetrate our lives and transform us into a new people. In faith we hear the Risen Lord proclaim first of all the forgiveness of sins.

Third Sunday of Easter, B

Toward a Glorious Future
Ac 3:13-15, 17-19; 1 Jn 2:1-5; Lk 24:35-48

Time is an elusive reality. The intriguing concept of "Back to the Future" was fascinating enough to produce three movies of that name. Even more fascinating is the truth of our faith about the future. It will be glorious.

The Easter season is a time for looking back to the past but always with an eye on the future. During this season we celebrate the great events of our salvation through the Paschal Mystery of the death and resurrection of Christ. That is the past. But our salvation will not be complete until we rise with Christ through the power of the Holy Spirit to everlasting glory in the home of our heavenly Father. That is our glorious future. When the disciples saw the risen Lord, "they were incredulous for sheer joy and wonder." Later Peter was able to proclaim to the people: "You put to death the Author of life, but God raised him from the dead and we are his witnesses."

We are favored by God to have received in faith this witness to the resurrection, and so it is proper for us during the Easter season to concentrate on the communion rite of the Mass which emphasizes our future sharing in his resurrection.

When Martha and Mary were in distress over the death of their brother, Lazarus, Jesus declared, "I am the resurrection and the life." He had already promised that he would give the gift of his body and blood, as St. John recounts in the sixth chapter of his Gospel. There St. John quotes Jesus as saying, "Whoever eats my flesh and drinks my blood has life everlasting and I will raise him up on the last day" (6:54). In Holy Communion we receive the glorified body and blood of the Lord, a pledge and promise of our own resurrection.

Just before we receive communion, the priest declares,

"This is the Lamb of God who takes away the sins of the world. Happy are those who are called to his supper." This is not a return to the past, to the Last Supper. The quotation is from the Book of Revelation (19:9). The context is that within a vision of heaven St. John was told by an angel, "Write this down: Happy are those who have been called to the wedding feast of the Lamb." This is the great feast of heaven. The eucharistic banquet prepares us for and leads us to this everlasting feast which God wishes us to enjoy in the fullness of our humanity, body as well as soul.

Throughout the communion rite the proper posture is standing since it is a sign of our faith in the resurrection of Christ and our own as well. It is especially inappropriate to fail to stand while the priest says, "This is the Lamb of God who takes away the sins of the world. Happy are those who are called to his supper."

The communion procession is a liturgical sign that we are a pilgrim people. In this life we are on a journey, not to a place, but to a destiny, the joy of everlasting life in union with our Father in heaven. As we walk toward the altar to receive Holy Communion, we ought to do so with the faith that we are moving onward toward a glorious future when we will share fully in the resurrection of Christ.

Fourth Sunday of Easter, B

Where Is the Good Shepherd Today?
Ac 4:8-12; 1 Jn 3:1-2; Jn 10:11-18

In ancient Christian art the most beloved image of Christ was that of the Good Shepherd. Even today, though most of us live in a society in which shepherding is mostly a thing of the past, we find solace and comfort in thinking of Christ as our Good Shepherd.

It is pleasant on a spring day to picture an idyllic scene of Christ with his sheep, resting in a pleasant pasture with a bubbling brook nearby. Perhaps we yearn to turn aside from all the hectic activities of modern life to enjoy the serenity and peace which such a picture suggests.

But the peace of this scene is soon to be disturbed. An intruder silently approaches the sheep. He is a wolf. On many occasions he has succeeded in snatching a lamb in his teeth, while the rest of the flock scatters. Now he awaits his opportunity. He has learned to be wary of the shepherd, and so his eyes scan the scene to see where the shepherd is. He hopes the shepherd is absent or asleep, or that he is actually a hireling, someone who works only for pay, and who has no concern for the sheep.

Will the vicious wolf succeed in our own times? Will he snatch away young people from the Church? Will he devour Catholics who are discouraged because no one seems to care about them? Will he scatter the people of a parish because contentious bickering, harmful gossip, and disruptive recalcitrance make them open to the fatal attacks of evil? The answer is ours.

It should be unnecessary to observe that bishops and priests are not our only shepherds. Today in the Church we are all called to be good shepherds to one another. We have responsibilities toward each other because it has pleased God to save us and make us holy, not merely as individuals without any mutual bonds, but by forming us into a single people. That is the solemn teaching of the Second Vatican Council (See *Lumen Gentium*, 9).

The first shepherds are parents. It is their privilege and duty to teach and guide their children, to care for them, to love them. Parents need to realize that Christ the Good Shepherd wants to live and act within them for the sake of their children. Next are teachers and all who care for the young.

Bishops and priests, of course, are shepherds, but in the Vatican II Church we have come to recognize that baptism is a sharing in the priesthood of Christ and a call to ministry. It is a beautiful thing in a parish when the sick and the elderly are not neglected because the parish has ministers who bring Holy Communion regularly to shut-ins. Those who drive people to church on Sunday, who do shopping for them, or take them to the doctor are shepherds.

Those who cannot provide active help to others but who dedicate themselves to prayer, even within their own homes, for those in need, are shepherds. The newspaper and TV news can provide them with many topics for prayer.

But perhaps most importantly of all we are shepherds when we give good example to one another, especially by our fidelity to Sunday Mass, by our active involvement in the parish, and by our charitable speech. The wolf need not succeed. We can help and defend each other against evil and hatred by allowing Christ the Good Shepherd to live and act within us.

Fifth Sunday of Easter, B

A Vine Is Fruitful in Its Branches
Ac 9:26-31; 1 Jn 3:18-24; Jn 15:1-8

Over the centuries a favorite image of Jesus has been that of the Good Shepherd, followed closely in more recent times by that of the Sacred Heart. At a distant third, or even worse, is that of Jesus as the Vine of which we are the branches. And yet Jesus presented this image to his disciples at the Last Supper on the night before he died, at a time when he wanted to impress upon them the most fundamental aspects of his teachings. The image of the vine and the branches presented an important truth.

After Jesus declared: "I am the vine, you are the branches," he applied the image to life: "Just as a branch cannot bear fruit on its own unless it remains on the vine, so neither can you unless you remain in me. Without me you can do nothing."

Every Sunday we come to Mass to intensify our union with Christ. We pray for God's mercy and ask that our sins be forgiven. We undergo a kind of pruning process. Then we partake of the body and the blood of the Lord, the nourishment which is necessary to keep vibrant and growing within us the life which comes from Christ, the Vine.

Christ extends himself in space and time through the members of his Church as a vine reaches outward by means of its branches. The purpose of the vine is to produce fruit, but grapes come forth from the vine through its branches. What is the fruit which Jesus wishes to produce through us?

The answer is multiple, but we know the specifics by reading the signs of the times. Catholics, according to the polls, rank very low among denominations for enthusiasm in spreading their message. We have the Good News; we should be eager to share it. Pope Paul VI and Pope John Paul II have called Catholics to evangelization. That does not mean standing on a street corner and preaching, but it does mean crossing the street from the church and carrying Christ into all the corners of our lives.

The first step is to appreciate the enormity of God's grace which has given us our Catholic faith. There is nothing more beneficial for God's glory and our salvation than being part of Christ in his one, holy, catholic, and apostolic Church. We should then encourage and support one another as Catholics and never fall into that spirit of carping criticism which makes us blind to the blessings we enjoy. Above all we must make Sunday Mass an absolute priority in our lives.

Everyone of us has a family member or friend who no longer goes to Sunday Mass. We ought never to stop praying for them, but we also need gently but persistently to invite them to return to their true spiritual home. Equally we should not be afraid to speak of our faith to those who are not Catholics and to urge them to look into the truth of the Church.

In every instance we must challenge ourselves with the question, "Am I thinking and acting as Christ would?" Have I allowed myself to be taken in by the values and slogans of a secular, materialistic society so that my thinking and way of acting are little or no different from that of those who have no religion? Christ wants to produce the fruit of truth and goodness through us who are his branches.

Sixth Sunday of Easter, B

The Solution for Our Planet
Ac 10:25-26, 34-35, 44-48; 1 Jn 4:7-10; Jn 15:9-17

IBM has adopted a new motto which concludes most of its advertising on TV and in magazines. That motto is: "Solutions for a Small Planet." The meaning seems to be that modern communications have in a sense shrunk the globe so that our planet has become smaller. People on one side of the earth can easily and quickly be in communication with people on the opposite side.

Long before IBM came into being, God the Father had a plan to bring people together, no matter what part of the planet they happened to inhabit. He sent his Son to be the link, the binding force of all the human race.

Before the coming of Christ almost all peoples had some kind of religion. Whether they believed in one god or many gods, they thought of their deity as belonging to them, limited to their nation or even their tribe. They not did not want to share their god with other people; they could not even conceive of the idea of a god who would be the Lord of two or several groups of people. The thought that there was actually only one, personal God for the entire world and for the universe was unimaginable.

It took the first disciples of Jesus, all of whom were Jewish, no little time and quite some anguish, to come to realize and to accept the truth that the God of Israel is the God of all people. St. Peter in particular as the head of the Church had to accept and implement the truth that Jesus had done something new, that Christianity was not a national religion, that it was meant for everyone.

The incident with Cornelius, a Roman army officer, was an object lesson for St. Peter. God had granted Peter a symbolic vision which represented the universal call to the Church. He was pondering that vision when the Holy Spirit informed him that two men were waiting to take him to Cornelius. After meeting Cornelius and seeing his faith, Peter exclaimed: "I begin to see how true it is that God shows no partiality. Rather, the person of any nation who fears God and acts uprightly is acceptable to him." St. John in his letter today adds: "Everyone who loves is begotten of God."

We say in our profession of faith during Mass: "We believe in one God." Because there is only one God, we are all actually one people. As our one true God excludes no one from his love, so we too must never exclude anyone on the basis of race, color, nationality, religion, or any other element which tends to separate people. In particular as Catholics, we profess that our Church is universal, such being the literal meaning of catholic.

All sins are serious, but racism, bigotry, and prejudice of any kind are a contradiction of what it means to be a Catholic. St. Peter was granted a vision to transform his outlook. We have something even greater. Every Sunday we celebrate together the Holy Eucharist, which is the sacrament of the body of the Lord given up not only for us but for everyone; the Holy Eucharist is the reality of the blood of Christ which was shed, not only for us but for everyone.

There is only one God and Father of us all. We must be most conscientious about overcoming the hatred and division which is part of secular society. The solution for our planet, large or small, is to share the love of Christ with everyone.

Solemnity of the Ascension, B

Praying for the Holy Spirit
Ac 1:1-11; Eph 1:17-23; Mk 16:15-20

After Jesus had ascended into heaven, his disciples returned to Jerusalem and went to the upstairs room where they were staying. They devoted themselves to constant prayer together with Mary, the mother of Jesus. Their time of prayer culminated in the sending of the Holy Spirit on Pentecost. To understand the work of the Holy Spirit, we turn to the liturgy, and in particular to the Second Eucharistic Prayer, since it is such a great expression of our faith. This brief prayer is based on a eucharistic prayer which goes back to about the year 215 and is the earliest written form of such a prayer that we possess. It singles out three activities of the Holy Spirit.

In the Preface of this prayer, we give thanks and praise to God the Father because "by the power of the Holy Spirit (Christ) took flesh and was born of the Virgin Mary." The moment of the Incarnation was the beginning of our salvation in Christ. It was the work of the Holy Spirit.

Next as the priest holds his hands over the bread and wine, he prays to the Father: "Let your Spirit come upon these gifts to make them holy, so that they may become for us the body and blood of our Lord, Jesus Christ." The sacrament of the Holy Eucharist, which renews for us the sacrifice of our redemption, is the work of the Holy Spirit.

After the memorial offering the priest says to the Father, "May all of us who share in the body and blood of Christ be brought together in unity by the Holy Spirit." The unity of the Church through the Holy Eucharist is the work of the Holy Spirit. These two invocations of the Holy Spirit are called the "*epiclesis*," a Greek word meaning "calling upon" someone to do something.

What the Holy Spirit does is to exercise his power over the body of Christ in its threefold reality: the physical body of Christ born of the Virgin Mary, the eucharistic body of Christ upon the altar, and the mystical body of Christ, the Church. These three actions of the Holy Spirit are closely related. Christ became human by the power of the Holy Spirit so that he could offer himself in sacrifice to the Father. This offering becomes a reality for us on the altar in the body and blood of Christ, a reality brought about by the Holy Spirit so that through our sharing in this sacrament we may be brought together in unity in the Church, the mystical body of Christ.

Sometimes in political history authors talk about the power behind the throne, an unseen and unheard person, often a woman, who has influence, sometimes even power, over the monarch. Without any of the suggestions of political intrigue, we can rightly say that the Holy Spirit is the power behind Christ. This power behind Christ is not that of military weapons or economic sanctions. It is the power of love. During these days between the Ascension and Pentecost we are invited to pray for a renewed coming of the Holy Spirit. These are special days devoted to "*epiclesis*," a calling upon the Holy Spirit to continue and fulfill the work he began in the womb of Mary so that through the Eucharist we may all become one body, one spirit in Christ.

Seventh Sunday of Easter, B

We Are Like Matthias
Ac 1:15-17, 20-26; 1 Jn 4:11-16; Jn 17:11-19

One of our marks as Catholics is our devotion to the saints. Some of us honor the saint of our baptismal name, and many of us have some other favorite whom we may consider to be our patron. The first reading tells the brief story of St. Matthias. He could well be a patron for all of us.

After the Ascension of Jesus into heaven, Peter determined that it was necessary to replace Judas among the apostles to bring the number to twelve. The disciples prayed, drew lots, and chose Matthias. Matthias, unlike the twelve apostles, was not chosen directly by Jesus but by the Church.

We are like Matthias in that we did not hear the voice of Christ calling us or feel his hand upon our shoulder in a gesture of welcome. Rather in the sacrament of baptism we were chosen by the Church.

St. Peter declared that the choice for a new apostle should fall upon someone who was a witness to the resurrection of Jesus. Apparently Matthias fit that criterion. Do we? Yes, we do, not as ones who have actually laid eyes upon the Risen Lord but as people who live by belief in the resurrection of Christ from the dead.

We have no record of what St. Matthias did after his choice. It is left to us to carry on the mission he was given as a witness of the resurrection. We express what we believe in the profession of faith during every Sunday Mass. We say, "He suffered, died, and was buried. On the third day he rose again." In our Eucharistic acclamation we say, "Christ has died; Christ is risen; Christ will come again."

These words of faith influence our actions in such a way that our lives would not make sense if we did not believe in the resurrection. We believe that Christ's resurrection is the pattern which will lead to our resurrection, that he will come again to raise us from the dead. If there is no future for us through our resurrection from the dead, then surely we should "eat, drink, and be merry for tomorrow we die." And yet we know that death is not the end, that a life lived faithfully with Christ will lead to the fullness of life in our resurrection from the dead on the last day.

During our time on this earth we give a further witness to the resurrection. The reason Jesus was raised from the dead is that the Father loved him in his humanity. The reason there will be a resurrection for us is that God sees the person of his Son within us. He values every human being as precious, body as well as soul, created as we are in the image and likeness of his Son. That is why the Church is pro-life, that is why we are called to honor and respect every human person, regardless of their status, from the moment of conception through natural death. Our Catholic respect for every human person is a powerful witness to our faith in the resurrection, both that of Christ and our own.

In our Blessed Sacrament, the Holy Eucharist, Christ is present as he has been raised from the dead in his glorified body. When we profess our faith in the real presence, we acknowledge that, to put it bluntly, we do not receive a dead body. The Mass is not a wake service or a funeral. It is a celebration of the great truth of which we are to be witnesses: "Christ has died; Christ is risen; Christ will come again."

Solemnity of Pentecost, B

Pentecost Is a Conclusion and a Beginning
Ac 2:1-11; 1 Cor 12:3-7, 12-13; Jn 20:19-23

Pentecost is not a name. In Greek it is a number, fifty. It is the conclusion of the fifty days of the Easter season. This great solemnity completes the mission of Jesus on this earth and inaugurates the life of the Church in his name.

The two great solemnities of our liturgy are Easter with Pentecost, and Christmas with Epiphany. Our Christian story began when the eternal Son of God became human in the womb of Mary, a Jewish maiden, and was born as an offspring of King David in Bethlehem. The Epiphany — and we remember that the Magi were Gentiles, not Jews — manifested that Jesus was born as the Savior, not only of the Jewish people from whom he had come, but of all people for whom he had come. His mission was universal.

The Son of God could have entered our world in any manner of his choosing, but the plan of his Father was that his Son was to be born human like us in all things but sin, not only so that he might live a human life but so that he might be able to die. In his divinity the Son could not die, but die he did in his humanity. His birth led to his death. Christmas was the prelude of Good Friday.

The day Jesus was born is bright and cheerful, filled with lights and good cheer. The day Jesus died seems to be bleak and sorrowful, but we call it "Good" because his death meant life for us. Jesus on the cross was like a woman who dies in childbirth. He gave up his life so that we could be born to new life. Our great tradition from the ancient Fathers and teachers of our faith is that from the side of Christ the Church, symbolized by the blood and water, was born from his death and received a share in his divine life through his resurrection.

As the Epiphany illuminates the meaning of Christmas, so Pentecost illuminates the meaning of Easter, the Paschal Mystery, the death and resurrection of Jesus. Pentecost celebrates that great event "when the Holy Spirit made known to all peoples the one true God, and created from the many languages of the human race one voice to profess one faith" (from the Preface). Pentecost shows that, as the mission of Jesus was universal, so the membership of the Church is universal. That is why we call ourselves Catholics. Christ is much more than "my personal Savior" because his mission transcends a merely individual relationship. We receive our life in Christ through the ministry of the Church and we live out that life within the family of the Church. We are one people who profess one Lord, one faith, one baptism, one God and Father of us all.

Pentecost concludes the mission of the Son of God upon this earth in his humanity, but it marks the beginning of the life and mission of Christ in his Church. The Church is now his body, his mystical body, filled with the life of his Holy Spirit, which is the soul of the Church. Through his Spirit, who fills the whole Church with life and love, Christ is faithful to his promise, "Know that I am with you always until the end of the world."

Christ has ascended to heaven, and yet he is truly with us in and through his Church.

Solemnity of the Trinity, B

Liturgical Prayer Is Trinitarian
Dt 4:32-32, 39-40; Rm 8:14-17; Mt 28:16-20

Before Christ ascended into heaven, he gave a final command to his disciples: "Baptize them in the name of the Father and of the Son and of the Holy Spirit." We began our lives as Catholics when that command of Christ was fulfilled in our regard. This blessing of God, our baptism, we renew every time we make the sign of the cross in the name of the Trinity.

Although we began our lives of faith in the light of the truth that God is three persons in one nature, it was not so for God's people of the Old Testament. Only through a long, tortuous history did God lead his people to the momentous truth which we celebrate every year on the Sunday after Pentecost, the truth of the Trinity.

Abraham, our father in faith, lived among people who worshipped many gods: a god of war, a god of fertility, a god of the tribe or the nation. Some worshipped the moon, or the sun, or the stars. To Abraham the Lord revealed himself as the one true God, the only God, the God who created the earth, the moon, the sun, and the stars.

Moses, living centuries after Abraham, preached to the people a holy God, a transcendent and powerful God who had brought them out of Egypt and formed them into his own special people. To Moses God revealed his personal name, a name so sacred that Jewish tradition forbids its being pronounced aloud, a name we translate as "LORD."

But how hard it was for the people to worship only one God. Incredible to us perhaps is the fact that again and again the people fell into idolatry, worshipping multiple false gods. The prophets repeatedly had to call the people back to the truth that there is but one God, the God of Israel.

Jesus gave us a new revelation. He proclaimed that God is his Father. He spoke of himself as equal to God. He promised to send the Holy Spirit. This revelation within the pages of the New Testament was not sufficiently precise to formulate a doctrinal statement about the Trinity. The Church pondered the revelation for some three centuries before it was ready to formulate our faith by means of the first two ecumenical councils, Nicea in 325 and Constantinople in 381 (Vatican II was the twenty-first council).

Despite the clear teaching of these two councils, heresies about the nature of God plagued the Church, and even now some forms of piety neglect the divine relationships which constitute the persons of the Trinity. Attention to the liturgical way of praying will both form us in sound doctrine and keep us faithful to it since the way we pray liturgically is the expression of our faith.

The liturgy proclaims to the Father: "All life, all holiness comes from you through your Son, Jesus Christ our Lord, by the working of the Holy Spirit." Liturgical prayer, in response to this doctrine, is addressed to the Father through the Son in the unity of the Holy Spirit. God the Son is our one Mediator and the Holy Spirit is our bond of unity. Our faith is reflected in the conclusion of the eucharistic prayer when the priest, elevating the body and blood of Christ, says, "Through him, with him, in him, in the unity of the Holy Spirit all glory and honor is yours, almighty Father, forever and ever." Liturgical prayer is the right way to pray because it flows from our faith in the Blessed Trinity.

Solemnity of the Lord's Body and Blood, B (*Corpus Christi*)

"Do This in Memory of Me"
Ex 24:3-8; Heb 9:11-15; Mk 14:12-16, 22-26

In 1944 the Allied troops under the command of General Dwight David Eisenhower invaded Normandy. It marked the inevitable defeat of Nazi Germany. One commentator observed that we must never forget the men and women who died in that terrible conflict for the survival of freedom, even though 1944 is a long time ago.

It is a beautiful thing to remember. Jesus wanted us to remember and never forget all that he would accomplish through his death and resurrection, the offering of himself in worship of his Father. He instituted the sacrament of his body and blood and he was so earnest about our remembering him that he gave us, not a polite request, but a command: "Do this in memory of me."

Do what? Do what he had just done in offering his body and his blood to the Father, the sacrament of his death and resurrection. The Eucharist instituted by Jesus at the Last Supper looked to the future, to the days of the Paschal Mystery of his death and resurrection. When we fulfill the command of Jesus by celebrating the Eucharist, we look to the past, to those same days of the Paschal Mystery of Jesus' death and resurrection. The Eucharist is the reality of the mystery we proclaim, that Christ by dying destroyed our death and by rising restored our life.

When two people are in love, they enjoy each other's presence. They may sit for hours without speaking or even looking at each other. But if a husband and a wife want a child, they must act. They must embrace each other in an act of love which is fruitful. They must give themselves to each other to bring about new life.

The Eucharist is a sacrament of life. It is, to be sure, the real presence of Christ. Bread and wine are really transformed into his body and blood. One cannot be a Catholic without believing that. But the Eucharist is immensely more profound than the presence of Christ, sacred and precious though that presence is. The Eucharist is dynamic. It is the offering of Christ to the Father for the sake of our new life in grace. It is the sacrament of the death and the resurrection of Christ. Our understanding of the Eucharist should move us to want more than to be in the presence of the Blessed Sacrament; it should motivate us to act in union with Christ.

When Jesus spoke of remembering, he was speaking within the context of the biblical meaning of liturgical remembrance. We have a Greek word for that kind of remembering: *anamnēsis*. To remember liturgically is to make an action present spiritually. We can see the invasion of Normandy as it was preserved in newsreels and depicted in movies, but in no way would we want that horrible conflict to become a reality among us again. But because by dying Christ restored our life and by rising he restored our life, it is a joy to remember and make present his sacrificial death and glorious resurrection. The Eucharist is celebrated, not primarily in honor of Jesus, but above all in his memory. It is the worship we offer through, with, and in Christ to the Father. As the Paschal Mystery was the most significant act of the life of Jesus on this earth, so our participating in the Eucharist, the sacrament of the Paschal Mystery, is the most significant act of our lives as Catholics. Although the death and resurrection of Jesus occurred a long time ago, we must never forget but always remember.

The Season of the Year
Cycle B

"By means of the yearly cycle the Church celebrates the whole mystery of Christ from his Incarnation until the day of Pentecost and the expectation of his coming again."
(*General Norms for the Liturgical Year*, 17)

Second Sunday of the Year, B

Jesus Says, "Come and See"
1 S 3:3-10, 19; 1 Cor 6:13-15, 17-20; Jn 1:35-42

When a child is born, good parents have hopes. They look down at the infant in his crib and say, "One day this kid could be President." Zechariah, the father of John the Baptist, looked down at his infant son and said, "You, my child, shall be called prophet of the Most High; for you shall go before the Lord to prepare straight paths for him."

John the Baptist did not fail to live up to this high expectation. Like the great prophet Samuel before him, he responded to God's call. His only desire was to find and identify the Messiah, and then to point him out to others. When he was convinced of the identity of Jesus, he quickly forgot all about himself and eagerly declared, "Look! There is the Lamb of God."

On the occasion of this Sunday's Gospel, John spoke to two men in particular who made a decision to follow Jesus. When they asked Jesus where he was staying, Jesus answered in a few words which were full of warmth and welcome. "Come and see," he said.

The evangelist does not tell us what transpired when they went with Jesus to his home. Did he speak to them at length about the kingdom of God? Did they dine with Jesus? Whatever happened, they left full of excitement and a sense of commitment. Andrew was one of the two. He was so thrilled that he rushed off to tell his brother, Simon Peter, that they had found the Messiah.

At the center of all four Gospels is the person of Jesus. In today's passage John the Baptist is like a light shining on Jesus so that others could see him and begin to grasp who he is. Andrew was not content to keep Jesus to himself. He felt compelled to invite his brother to share the good news with him.

The Church in her many centuries of tradition has continued the role of John the Baptist. To us today that tradition has pointed out Jesus as our Savior, as the Lamb of God who takes away the sins of the world. We have heard the invitation of Jesus, "Come and see where I stay." That invitation has led us within the walls of our spiritual home, the Church. We know what happens here. Jesus through the Scriptures speaks to us and proclaims the kingdom of God. Jesus dines with us, sharing with us the spiritual supper of his body and blood.

What then is the next step? Are we eager to go out to find someone with whom to share the good news? Perhaps some member of our family or a friend no longer comes to Mass. Maybe there was a misunderstanding, feelings were hurt, and the result was a rupture with the Church. With the eagerness of Andrew we should go to our spiritual brother or sister and gently invite them to return to the practice of their faith.

Do people we work with know that we are Catholic? Without being "preachy," do we let it be obvious that we have the conviction that we have found Jesus and that we center our lives on him by means of our Catholic faith? When our parish asks for volunteers to help in our religious education program for our children, do we volunteer to do whatever we can to be of help?

The vocation of John the Baptist can and should continue in us. The eagerness of Andrew should be part of our lives as Catholics. To others we should always be ready with the invitation: "Come and see where Jesus stays."

Third Sunday of the Year, B

God Is Big

Jon 3:1-5, 10; 1 Cor 7:29-31; Mk 1:14-20

Almost everyone has heard the story about Jonah's being swallowed by a whale. The point of the story is lost, however, if we do not know or remember how he got into that predicament. God called Jonah to be his prophet and to preach repentance to the Ninevites. Jonah was not merely a reluctant prophet, as were Isaiah, Jeremiah, and Amos. He revolted against God's wishes. His reason was that the Ninevites were not Jews. They were the enemies of the Jews. Jonah was afraid that the Ninevites would actually listen to his preaching, repent, and thereby find favor with God. That was the last thing he wanted to happen. Asking Jonah to preach to the Ninevites was like asking a Dallas Cowboy fan to pray that the San Francisco Forty-Niners would win the Super Bowl.

So Jonah tried to run away from God. He boarded a ship only to be tossed about in a life-threatening storm. When the sailors concluded that Jonah was the problem, they threw him overboard. He was swallowed by a huge fish. God commanded the fish to spew Jonah upon the shore. It was God's way of saying to Jonah, "Now will you please go and preach to the Ninevites whom I happen to love."

The book of Jonah is like the parables of Jesus, and like the parables of Jesus it has a very important lesson to teach. Jonah represents those people who are petty, selfish, and who do not want to share anything, not even God, with others. Jonah is symbolic of those who hate other people, hold grudges, and refuse to be reconciled with their enemies, even though they expect God to forgive their sins. Jonah represents those people who do not understand God.

God is big but we tend to be petty. God is forgiving but

we tend to refuse reconciliation with those who hurt us. God is generous but we tend to be selfish. The sign of how God is different from Jonah and those who are like him is the cross. In the second eucharistic prayer we say of Jesus that "he opened his arms on the cross." He did so in order to embrace men and women of every time and place. The Spanish translation makes the meaning clearer and more emphatic: "*Extendió sus brazos en la cruz.*" He extended his arms, that is, he reached out as far as he could so that no one would be excluded from his reconciling love.

Before he sacrificed himself on the cross for our salvation, Jesus set about to insure the continuance of his mission on this earth after his death and resurrection. At the beginning of his public ministry, he selected his apostles, those chosen disciples who would be the nucleus around which he would form his Church. They would become fishers of souls with a net so big that it was enormously larger than the fish which swallowed Jonah, a net so large that it would be big enough for everyone.

We call the Church Catholic because it is universal. It extends back through all the ages to the time of Christ and will remain until he returns in glory. It is catholic also in the sense that all people are included. Although the Church was founded in Jerusalem, it is not Jewish. Although the Church found its center in Rome, it is not Italian. Although the Church was spread mainly by European missionaries, the Church is not European. The Church is catholic, universal. All authentic Catholics do not close their hearts to others as did Jonah. Rather like Christ they open their arms — they extend their arms — to embrace everyone.

Fourth Sunday of the Year, B

The Holy One of God

Dt 18:15-20; 1 Cor 7:32-35; Mk 1:21-28

Sometimes beauty and truth come from unexpected sources. You would not expect a youngster to compose beautiful music, but as a child prodigy Mozart astounded his contemporaries. And when Jesus appeared in the synagogue of Capernaum, no one expected a man with an unclean spirit, a demon, to proclaim the truth about him. And yet his words addressed to Jesus are profoundly true: "You are the Holy One of God!"

The synagogue was a place for beauty and truth. It was there that the beautiful truth of God's inspired Word in the Hebrew Scriptures was proclaimed and reflected upon. A rabbi taught the meaning of the Scriptures and led prayers. From the beginning of his public ministry Jesus was acknowledged as a rabbi, a teacher. Later the people came to recognize him as a prophet, not merely a teacher but one who actually spoke in the voice of God.

Jesus was in the habit of going to the synagogue on the Sabbath. When he accepted the role of rabbi on those occasions, he fulfilled the promise of Moses who declared to the people: "A prophet like me will the Lord, your God, raise up for you from among your own kinsmen; to him you shall listen."

When Jesus began to teach in the synagogue of Capernaum, the unclean spirit shrieked, "You are the Holy One of God." By a supreme irony, the unclean spirit gave a "sermon" on the identity of Jesus. What he cried out was true. Then Jesus confirmed the testimony of the unclean spirit by his action: he drove the demon out of the possessed man. St. Mark who gave us this remarkable story wanted us to understand that the primary purpose of this incident was not to attract us to Jesus as a miracle worker but to move us to embrace him in his identity as the Holy One of God. St. Paul had much the same commitment in mind when he observed that celibate people can and should be concerned with things of the Lord. But married or unmarried, we all are called to dedicate ourselves to Jesus, the Holy One of God.

Still later in his public ministry Jesus would give a sermon in this same synagogue of Capernaum in which he would promise to give his body and his blood as food and drink for everlasting life.

Our earliest ancestors in the faith continued to go to the synagogue on the Sabbath; then on Sunday they met for the Eucharist in someone's home. When Gentiles began to enter the Church, the synagogue service of Scripture, sermon, and prayers was combined with the Eucharist on Sunday. The Word and the Sacrament, the Scriptures and the Eucharist, became so intimately connected that they formed but a single act of worship.

Every Sunday we are privileged to share in this act of worship which we call simply the Mass. Jesus is still with us in Word and Sacrament. The Church reminds us that "it is Christ himself who speaks to us when the Holy Scriptures are proclaimed in the liturgy." It is really Christ who speaks to us in the sound of human words. The Church insists that it is Christ himself who comes to us in his body and blood under the appearances of bread and wine. Holy Communion fulfills the promise of Jesus in the synagogue of Capernaum that he would give us his flesh to eat and his blood to drink. In the celebration of every Mass we are given the opportunity to embrace Jesus as the Holy One of God.

Fifth Sunday of the Year, B

No Rest for the Good

Jb 7:1-4, 6-7; 1 Cor 9:16-19, 22-23; Mk 1:29-39

Mothers-in-law have been the object of jokes, some humorous and some cynical, for a long time. One pundit observed, "Behind every successful man stands a surprised mother-in-law." Whether Peter's mother-in-law was surprised at Jesus' selection of him to be the head of the apostles, we do not know. In fact, she is mentioned only once in all the Gospels, but that one mention is important to us.

Peter, who at the time was still known as Simon, was worried about his mother-in-law. She lay ill with a fever. When Simon told Jesus about her, he took her by the hand and the fever left her. The action of Jesus is not surprising. But then, quite surprisingly, she immediately began to wait on Jesus and his disciples. You would think that she would take at least a few moments to rest, but that was not this woman's way.

Some cynics might picture her as a caricature of women who are destined, in their "inferior position in society," to wait on men. The truth is that she was a mirror of Jesus himself. She reflected the generous, outgoing spirit of Jesus in his ministry.

After dinner in Peter's house, Jesus, no doubt exhausted from the day's labors, was expected to cure the townspeople who were ill or possessed by demons. He responded in his characteristic way. The next morning despite his fatigue he rose early, as Peter's mother-in-law rose from her bed of illness. Jesus was in search of a quiet place for prayer, but there is no rest for the good. When Simon and the others found him, he knew that his few moments of peace were at an end for that day. His mission beckoned him. He recognized that his Father was calling him to lift people out of the kind of misery which Job felt when he protested, "I shall not see happiness again." So off Jesus went to the neighboring villages to proclaim the good news.

St. Paul was filled with a similar sense of service. To underscore his dedication to preaching the Gospel to which he had been called, he wrote: "I am under compulsion and have no choice." It was an emphatic way of expressing his profound sense of duty. He did not hesitate to highlight his generosity by reminding the Corinthians, "I offer the Gospel free of charge." In comparison with the exalted vocation of St. Paul, the simple service offered by Peter's mother-in-law may seem rather insignificant. The point, however, is that both of them reflected the generous and unselfish spirit of service of Jesus himself, Paul in his way and the mother-in-law in her way.

And what is our way? We can be like Jesus in the duties of our calling in life, whatever they may be. Peter's mother-in-law and Paul the Apostle show us that there is a wide range in the service to which disciples of Jesus are called. We need to reflect on how generous and unselfish we are in our lives as a parent, a spouse, a teacher, a worker, a volunteer, a student, a priest, a religious — whatever our calling may be.

There is rest for the wicked because they think only of themselves and their own comfort. There is no rest for the good, the people who follow the example of Jesus. They know that happiness and fulfillment in this life come from imitating the generous, unselfish spirit of Jesus.

Sixth Sunday of the Year, B

Who Are the Contemporary Lepers?
Lv 13:1-2, 44-46; 1 Cor 10:31-11:1; Mk 1:40-45

The disease of leprosy has pretty much been eradicated from contemporary society, but in Jesus' day it was the most dreaded of all illnesses. It gravely disfigured its victims, forced them to live in the desert apart from family and friends, and rendered them unfit for public worship.

When the leper approached Jesus to seek a cure, he was really out of line. He had no business leaving his place of exile to go where people gathered. He was an ostracized degenerate. Rather than asking for help from Jesus, he should have been crying out, "Unclean, unclean!" so that no one would have to come near him.

The episode in today's Gospel is altogether extraordinary. Jesus not only welcomed the man; he actually reached out and touched him. He was not repulsed by this poor disfigured person. More than that, Jesus invoked an authority higher than that of the levitical law. Anyone who touched a leper was rendered levitically unclean, which meant that he was unfit for worship. Jesus implicitly rejected such legislation, and by his action he declared that charity is higher than any law. He told the man to show himself to the priest of the temple so that the priest could declare him cleansed of his leprosy and admit him once more to public worship.

Jesus wanted to change the attitude toward lepers. He wants to change our attitude too toward the outcasts of our society. We need to accept a challenge from Jesus, not regarding lepers whom we never see, but regarding those people who are held in contempt by our contemporaries.

The most dreaded disease in our times is AIDS. It is, in a way, the leprosy in our society. Some people are quick to condemn every person who is afflicted with AIDS as a moral degenerate, and to go so far as to say that God has punished them, that they have gotten only what they deserve. But Jesus did not question the leper about his morality. He did not make judgments about him even though he could have read his heart. Jesus knew that his Father is a merciful and forgiving God, and so Jesus came to this leper's assistance. That tells us what our attitude should be.

Some of our fellow citizens want to drive aliens from our land. They have a self-righteous attitude toward undocumented immigrants as criminals because, as they protest, they are breaking the law. The Church does not advocate violating any just law, but the Church does teach, as Jesus exemplified, that charity is higher than any law.

Some people look down on those who are on welfare, they castigate unwed mothers, and they are quick to vilify members of races or nationalities other than their own. Can anyone who hears the Gospel be so ready to despise others? Can anyone who follows Jesus in his journey of mercy and compassion treat others with such disdain? Can anyone who prays the Lord's Prayer, "Forgive us our trespasses as we forgive those who trespass against us," be so bold as to condemn others?

Relatively few people have leprosy today, but rampant among us is the disease of hatred, self-righteousness, and rejection of fellow human beings. Conscientious people must have no part of a spirit which is so foreign to that of Jesus.

Seventh Sunday of the Year, B

The Divine Way Takes the Human Way
Is 43:18-19, 21-22, 24-25; 2 Cor 1:18-22; Mk 2:1-12

There are some things you cannot do. You cannot drive a car with only water in the gas tank. You cannot keep food cold and fresh in a refrigerator if you do not plug it in. And no one can forgive sins on human authority alone.

The scribes who observed Jesus as he declared that sins were forgiven were quite right in their objection, "Who can forgive sins except God alone?" But they missed the point since they did not know the identity of Jesus. Because Jesus is divine, equal to his heavenly Father in all things, he could and did forgive sins on his own authority. He did so, however, in a human way. Jesus could very easily have forgiven the sins of the paralyzed man by a simple act of his will. Instead he looked with compassion on the paralytic and spoke powerful, but human words: "My son, your sins are forgiven." In Jesus we see that the divine way was to take the human way.

Jesus confirmed the power of his words by a miracle. Because the remission of sin is invisible, there was no test to the power of his words, but when he said to the paralytic: "Stand up, pick up your mat, and walk again," everyone turned to the paralytic to see whether Jesus' words had actually had an effect. When the man stood up, it was a sign for everyone that Jesus had not only cured the man with his words, but he had equally forgiven his sins with his words.

In Jesus God was doing something new. Never before had anyone heard words of forgiveness like those of Jesus. His words and his power continue in the Church, because God's divine way is still to take the human way.

A priest does not forgive sins on his own. He needs "to be plugged" into the Church since according to the will of Christ forgiveness comes in and by means of the Church. That is why the words of absolution in the sacrament of penance include this important prayer: "Through the ministry of the Church may God give you pardon and peace."

But who is the Church to forgive sins? As with Jesus, it is a question of identity. The Church is much more than a society or an assembly of people. The Church is a mystery. The Church is actually Christ himself, continued in space and time and communicated to his people (Bishop Bossuet's definition). Through the Church Jesus has freely chosen to carry on in a human way his divine mission of reconciliation.

The paralytic must have been almost giddy with delight to have regained his ability to walk. He was more profoundly blessed to have had his sins forgiven, and to have experienced a miracle which confirmed his freedom from sin. Like the crowd he must have been awestruck. With them he must have given praise to God.

As Catholics one of our greatest gifts from God is the sacrament of penance. We are blessed to be able to hear a human voice express our forgiveness and to feel the reconciling touch of a human hand. When we couple this human experience with faith we too should be awestruck and give thanks and praise to God for such a generous and wonderful favor from our great, good, and merciful God.

Eighth Sunday of the Year, B

God Is Catholic and So Is His Church
Ho 2:16-17, 21-22; 2 Cor 3:1-6; Mk 2:18-22

Most Catholics today feel that there is a lot of controversy in the Church. It is hard for them to imagine a more turbulent era in our religion, and yet almost immediately after the death and resurrection of Jesus, the Church was faced with disputes so grave that they threatened the meaning of all that Jesus had come to accomplish.

The disputes centered on the nature of the Church and the identity of Jesus. Was all that Jesus taught and done nothing more than a reformation of Judaism? Had he established a movement which was similar to others of the day, a kind of sect or religious expression within Judaism? Did he mean only to patch the torn fabric of the ancient religion? Was he content with the old, seasoned wine of his ancestors? More fundamentally, just who is Jesus? What does the New Testament mean by naming him God's Son?

The question about the Church was answered by the Council of Jerusalem around the year 50 A.D., as recorded in the Acts of the Apostles (chapter 15) but the answer was rooted in controversies during the public ministry of Jesus. In the Gospel of this Sunday, for instance, Jesus was faced with the objection that his disciples did not follow the prescriptions about fasting which were practiced by the Pharisees and the disciples of John the Baptist.

Jesus made it clear that he was not trying to repair defects in the old religion. He insisted that he offered a new wine which could not be put into the old wineskins. What then was so different about the new wine? Remember the marriage feast of Cana? The wine was not only better than the old; it was generously abundant. That first of Jesus' miracles demonstrated that because of God's abundant grace the Church is open to everyone, not just those who were physical descendants of Abraham. The Church of Jesus Christ is Jewish in origin but universal in its membership. It is open to every human being who responds to the grace of faith. The Church is catholic.

Jesus could do all that he intended and claimed because of the answer to the second great question about the identity of Jesus. The earliest ecumenical councils, of which Vatican II was the twenty-first, determined and confirmed that Jesus is the divine Son of God, equal to the Father in all things. He is more than a prophet, greater than a king, and holier than any priest. He is the unimaginable fulfillment of messianic expectation because he transcends any particular race or nation. He is the bridegroom, the spouse not only of Israel but of all God's people. The Church of Jesus Christ is catholic, universal, and not limited to a few because Christ with the Father and the Holy Spirit is not a national or ethnic deity but the one God of all humanity. As Catholics we believe that there is one Lord, one faith, one baptism, one God and Father of us all. We express this by the way in which we pray at Mass as one people, united by the ministry of the presiding priest who bears the person of Christ who offers the Mass in the name of all his members. Whatever controversies may swell within the Church today, there must never be any question about who Jesus is or what the nature of the Church is. There can be no stance which denies Jesus' role as the universal Savior or a snobbery which excludes any fellow human being from his Church.

Ninth Sunday of the Year, B

Keep Holy the Lord's Day
Dt 5:12-15; 2 Cor 4:6-11; Mk 2:23-3:6

The observance of the Sabbath among the Jews was already an ancient practice by the time Jesus was born. Following the return of the people from exile in Babylon long after the era of Moses, detailed regulations developed with a demand for exact observance. To some extent this rigidity seemed more of a burden than a favor. It lost sight of the purpose of the Sabbath as a day of rest in recognition of the Lord's rest after the six days of creation.

Jesus insisted on a reasonable interpretation of the Sabbath which took account of human need. He taught that the law was not an end in itself. After his death and resurrection, the disciples in Judea continued to observe the Sabbath. They went to the synagogue on Saturday and celebrated the Eucharist in their homes on Sunday. Since Sunday was a work day, the Eucharist took place in the evening, which accounts for some of our liturgical observances, such as the use of candles despite the availability of electric lights. When large numbers of Gentiles began to be baptized, the Church was justified in changing the Sabbath observance to Sunday. The synagogue service of Scripture and prayer became joined to the liturgy of the Eucharist to form the Mass.

St. Justin, who composed an informative document on Church practices in Rome around the year 150 A.D., gives us important testimony. He wrote: "We hold our common assembly on Sunday because it is the first day of the week, the day on which God put darkness and chaos to flight and created the world, and because on that same day our Savior Jesus Christ rose from the dead." This practice of observing Sunday as a special day of prayer and rest has endured to our own times. Like the

Catholics who lived at the time of St. Justin, we too hold our common assembly, the Mass, on Sunday.

The Second Vatican Council in its *Constitution on the Liturgy* (106) insisted on the importance of Sunday. The Council taught that "Sunday, the Lord's day, is the original feast day, and it should be proposed to the piety of the faithful and taught to them in such a way that it may become in fact a day of joy and freedom from work." The Council also made clear that on Sunday "the faithful should come together into one place so that, by hearing the Word of God and taking part in the Eucharist, they may call to mind the death, the resurrection, and the glorification of the Lord Jesus and may offer thanks and praise to God."

Mass on Sunday unites us back through the centuries with all the faithful who have gone before us in Christ, as well as all faithful Catholics in the whole world today. It is the Mass that matters. It is what we do as Catholics. Celebrating Mass on Sunday is our distinguishing characteristic. Failing to celebrate Mass on Sunday is acting like a husband and wife who refuse to live with each other. A Catholic without the Mass is like a musician without his instrument, or an astronaut without his space ship.

The Mass is our loving union with God, a union which is like the covenant between husband and wife. The Mass is our opportunity to join together in a beautiful symphony of praise and thanksgiving which transports us high above the earth to our ultimate home in heaven. The Mass marks us out as Catholics. Always and everywhere our priority is to come together for our common celebration of Mass on Sunday, the Lord's Day.

Tenth Sunday of the Year, B

Reconciliation Is the Gift of God
Gn 3:9-15; 2 Cor 4:13-5:1; Mk 3:20-35

The story of Adam and Eve in the Book of Genesis is not only the way it was with our first parents; it is pretty much the way it often is with us today. The sin of Adam and Eve was one of disobedience by giving in to the temptation that they could be independent of God. After their fall they were like little children looking for someone to blame after they have been caught at something. Adam complained to God: "The woman whom you put here with me — she gave me fruit from the tree and so I ate it." Eve was not to be outdone in looking for someone to blame. She looked at the serpent, who represented the devil, and said to God, "The serpent tricked me into it." The serpent squirmed off into the grass and said nothing because he knew he did not have a leg to stand on.

Suppose things had been different. Imagine that when Adam was confronted by God, he had said, "I confess to almighty God and to you, my wife, that I have sinned through my own fault." Do you believe that God would have said, "You had your one chance and you failed. Do not look for mercy from me"? Suppose Eve had taken her husband's hand and said, "May almighty God have mercy on us, forgive us our sins, and bring us to everlasting life." Do you think God would have said, "Forget it. I am too angry for this"?

From what we know about God, I believe that he would have been understanding and merciful. But the fact is that Adam and Eve made excuses for themselves and manifested no signs of repentance, only the effects of sin. Sin separates; it divides. Sin separated Adam and Eve from God. Sin separated Adam and Eve from each other. Sin separated their inner longings from their natural inclination for God. Sin is like the example given by Jesus in the Gospel: "If a household is divided according to loyalties, that household will not survive."

Even though we may at times be like Adam and Eve in that we commit sin and look for excuses, God has been and continues to be most merciful toward us. He sent his Son into the world as our Savior who overcomes sin by bringing about its opposite, its antidote. As sin separates and divides, so Jesus' saving action brings about reconciliation and harmony. He unites us again with his Father, he brings us into the one household of the Church, and he repairs the internal, spiritual injuries we suffer through sin. Reconciliation is the gift of God through his beloved Son.

Our first, fundamental reconciliation is through baptism. Our harmony with God, with each other, and within ourselves is strengthened by confirmation. When we commit sin after baptism, the sacrament of penance is always available for a new reconciliation.

Jesus does all this for us through the ministry of the Church, the household of God. He does so because he refuses to remain separated from us even in our sins, provided we make the effort to do the right thing, to do the will of God. Jesus looks at us with great compassion and says, "These are my mother and my brothers and my sisters. Whoever does the will of God is mother and brother and sister to me." Even though Adam and Eve are our first human parents, Jesus assures us that he is our brother and that God in heaven is truly our loving Father.

Eleventh Sunday of the Year, B

The Mystery Which Is the Church
Ezk 17:22-24; 2 Cor 5:6-10; Mk 4:26-34

Jesus today expresses a truth which we all recognize, at least upon reflection. After seed is planted in the ground, it develops into a full grown crop. With only some water, warm sunshine, and a little patience the marvelous growth takes place. How that can happen we do not know. Even more mysterious is the fact that when a shrub is pruned, when some of its branches are cut away, it actually becomes more vigorous and productive.

There are mysteries in nature which can be described but not explained. We glibly state that what goes up must come down, but we don't know why gravity works, only that it does. Why should all bodies be drawn to the center of the earth and not moved away from it? No one completely understands this.

Jesus' intention was not to teach a lesson about agriculture or physics, but to move us to ponder a deeper mystery, the mystery of the reign of God in the Church. Jesus said that the reign of God is like a mustard seed which can grow into the largest of shrubs. We can readily perceive the truth of his comparison. The Church began as a small group of disciples in Jerusalem. From there it spread north to Antioch in Syria, and then across the Mediterranean to Rome, throughout Europe, and eventually to the whole world.

How all this happened is even more of a mystery than the growth of a seed into the largest of shrubs. A mystery should not, however, put us off. A mystery is not a truth about which we can know nothing. A mystery is a truth about which we cannot know everything. Something we can know about the mystery which is the Church is that the Holy Spirit is at work. Vegetable life needs light and water to grow. The Church needs the Holy Spirit. After the day of Pentecost when the Holy Spirit was sent upon the Church, it began to grow and to spread.

This work of the Holy Spirit in the Church should not surprise us. Jesus himself was conceived in Mary's womb by the power of the Holy Spirit. During the eucharistic prayer we ask God the Father: "Let your Spirit come upon these gifts to make them holy so that they may become for us the body and blood of our Lord Jesus Christ." Then we ask, "May all of us who share in the body and the blood of Christ be brought together in unity by the Holy Spirit." That unity is the Church, the mystical body of Christ.

The Holy Spirit formed Christ in the womb of Mary. He continues to form Christ in the Eucharist as well as in the Church, this Church which is universal and which we call catholic because it reaches out to embrace every human person. The Holy Spirit is like the force of gravity, drawing all people to the center which is Christ.

To be a Catholic is to think big, to realize that we are part of a Church which reaches back through the centuries to Christ himself and which now circles the globe and is found in every place. The Church, though universal, is not perfect, we must admit. Weaknesses and mistakes, whether our own or those of others in the Church, should never discourage us. Just as a shrub occasionally needs pruning for health and growth, so the Church needs repentance and renewal which are also the work of the Holy Spirit. We are privileged indeed to be part of this great Catholic Church.

Twelfth Sunday of the Year, B

Who Can This Be?
Jb 38:1, 8-11; 2 Cor 5:14-17; Mk 4:35-41

The *Titanic* was touted as the ship which would never sink. And yet after hitting an iceberg in its first voyage, the *Titanic* sank to the bottom of the North Atlantic in what seemed to the passengers to be a few minutes. The ocean, mightier than any ship, had swallowed the *Titanic* as if it had been a can of sardines.

There is a profound mystery about the sea, and it is no wonder that power over the mighty waters is considered to be a divine attribute. In the Book of Job God himself gave witness to his divine authority by citing his power over the deep waters. The apostles who were fishermen needed no one to tell them of the awesome and at times frightening aspect of the Sea of Galilee. Sudden squalls were by no means unusual. The Sea is 685 feet below sea level, and is surrounded by mountains. As the warm air rises in the evening, cool air rushes down from the mountains and in almost an instant transforms the calm water into dangerous waves of seven or eight feet.

That is precisely what happened on that eventful evening when Jesus got into a boat with his disciples on the Sea of Galilee. It was as if from the day of creation, the elements of nature were waiting for that moment when their Lord and Master would assert his power and manifest his divinity. After Jesus calmed the sea by his word, the disciples were stunned and kept asking one another, "Who can this be that the wind and the sea obey him?"

The wind and the sea knew who Jesus is, and so do we. We can answer the apostles' question. If we were without faith, we would have to regard him in terms of mere human judgment, but because of our faith we can acknowledge that Jesus is Lord and Savior. As our Lord and Savior he wishes to free us from the terrors in the ocean of life: the fear of diseases such as cancer or AIDS, anxiety about an uncertain financial future, the concern about children in a society given to drugs and promiscuity, the instability of a marriage, the pangs of loneliness and isolation, the terror which the prospect of death can engender.

In our eucharistic acclamation we cry out, "Lord, by your cross and resurrection you have set us free." After the Our Father, we pray, "Deliver us, Lord, from every evil and grant us peace in our day. In your mercy keep us free from sin and protect us from all anxiety." These prayers are meant to be an expression of our faith, but the degree of our peace and serenity depends not on the expression of our faith, but on its depth. Our faith must be as deep as the sea.

When the *Titanic* sank, the number of fatalities was multiplied because the ship had not been equipped with enough lifeboats. We have more than a lifeboat to save us when we are sinking in the tempests of life. We have the person of Jesus Christ, always present to us in the Church, and to whom we can turn with confident prayer. In the storm on the lake, the disciples complained, "Teacher, doesn't it matter to you that we are going to drown?" With faith we know that it does matter to Jesus. It matters so much that our salvation comes not from words, however powerful, such as "Quiet! Be still!" Our salvation comes from the sacrifice of the cross. Our faith is: "Lord, by your cross and resurrection, you have set us free. You are the Savior of the world."

Thirteenth Sunday of the Year, B

Jesus Has Time and Concern for Us
Ws 1:13-15; 2:23-24; 2 Cor 8:7, 9, 13-15; Mk 5:21-43

Each of the four evangelists has his own distinctive emphasis in his Gospel. St. Mark, whose Gospel we are following during most of this year, highlighted the humanity of Jesus. He emphasized those truths which reveal that the Son of God really is the Son of Mary, that the divine person comes to us in the simplicity of our human nature. St. Mark delighted in showing Jesus as a person who understands us and sympathizes with our needs.

In today's Gospel while Jesus was preparing to preach to the crowd, Jairus, an official of the synagogue, asked him to go with him to his home to cure his little daughter who was critically ill. St. Mark leaves it to us to imagine the frustration of Jesus in being called away from his ministry of preaching, but he shows that Jesus responded with compassion to the man's plea. Then a woman from the crowd interrupted Jesus by touching his cloak. Jesus insisted on knowing who had touched him, not to admonish the woman, but to be able to look directly at her and tell her tenderly, "Daughter, your faith has cured you."

Then Jesus continued his journey to look after the little girl, only to be told that she was already dead. Undaunted Jesus entered the room where the child was lying. Taking her hand he spoke the words of life, "Little girl, get up." The little girl arose. Imagine the scene. The parents, crying and laughing at the same time, hugged their little girl and danced around the room with her. Jesus, always attentive and aware of human needs, became very practical. He said to the parents, "Give her something to eat."

This Gospel narrative tells us that Jesus had time for people, both important people like Jairus, one of the leaders of the synagogue, and this poor woman who was insignificant in the view of most and whose name even St. Mark did not know. St. Mark shows us that Jesus was concerned about the profound sorrow of the father and mother whose little girl had died, but he wanted us to know that Jesus did not neglect the woman whose illness obviously was not fatal. He felt the anguish of the helpless parents, but he also recognized that the woman had her share of misery too.

St. Mark shows us that Jesus loved with a human heart. His emphasis on the humanity of Jesus should make us realize another important truth, that as Jesus acted through his humanity during his public ministry, so he acts now through the ministry of the Church, and in particular by means of the sacraments. God's way had been to take the human way. The human way for us now is through the sacraments of the Church.

In the sacrament of baptism Jesus took us by the hand, called us by name, and raised us from the death of sin, and restored us to God our Father as his children. Then Jesus told the Church to give us something to eat. That something is the wonderful sacrament of his body and blood.

We should remember that Jesus through the ministry of the Church has time for all of us, whether we happen to have some important position in society, as Jairus did in the synagogue, or whether hardly anybody knows our name, as was the case with the woman with the hemorrhage. All of us are important to Jesus, and all of our needs are his concern. We have a God who has time for all of us.

Fourteenth Sunday of the Year, B

Is Jesus in the Church Too Much for Us?
Ezk 2:2-5; 2 Cor 12:7-10; Mk 6:1-6

In most instances people will back a hometown boy or girl who does well in sports, or entertainment, or politics. They are proud of their product and feel part of this successful person. Why then did the people of Jesus' own hometown reject him? The Gospel says that they found him too much for them. Too much what? The meaning seems to be that he was making too much of himself in their opinion, that in their view he was just an ordinary person, a carpenter, Mary's son. Who was he to have turned prophet?

Preaching like a prophet aroused the animosity of Jesus' townsfolk. If Jesus had been a sports figure, an entertainer, or even a politician, he would have been no threat to the people. They would have been proud of him. But a prophet? A prophet can upset people. A prophet can present a challenge or a rebuke. A prophet proclaims the truth. Jesus' neighbors were afraid of him. Fear leads to rejection. The people of Nazareth became like their ancestors to whom God had sent the prophet Ezekiel. They were hard of face and obstinate of heart. What a shame it was! There was Jesus, actually more than a prophet, the Son of God himself right in their midst. Would we have turned against Jesus?

The truth is that Jesus is still with us. He speaks to us when the Scriptures are read during the liturgy, and he instructs us by means of the other teachings of the Church. At times are we afraid to listen? Do we fear that we may have to change our manner of thinking and our way of acting? Do we tend to excuse ourselves from difficult teaching because, as we protest, the matter is controversial or complicated? Do we find that we favor secular views rather than the teachings of the Pope and the Bishops?

The Second Vatican Council warned that abortion is an unspeakable crime, and yet many in our country say that the right to choose is more important than the right to life. The Pope has warned us against the culture of death, and yet the way is being cleared for assisted suicide and euthanasia. Together with the Bishops the Pope has urged that the death penalty is permissible only in the most extreme circumstances when society cannot defend itself except by execution, and yet some politicians gain votes by advocating capital punishment. Many of these same politicians want to blame immigrants, documented or undocumented, for our economic problems, but the Catholic view is that these people must be respected as children of God and it is God to whom belongs this country in which it is our privilege to have a home.

Some people are so self-righteous that they hold in contempt anyone on welfare, they despise those who are afflicted with AIDS, they condemn those who are enslaved by drugs, and they look with disdain on minorities and those who are of an ethnicity different from their own. Even some Catholics protest that the Church should stay out of politics and stick to the business of saving souls. They make the mistake of thinking that we live in two worlds, one religious and one secular. They conclude that the religious should not intrude upon the secular. The truth is that we live in one world, God's world. Is the Church too much for us? It will not be if we remember that Jesus is not dead, that he is alive, and that he continues to speak to us through the Scriptures and the other teachings of the Church.

Fifteenth Sunday of the Year, B

The Father's Plan for Us
Am 7:12-15; Eph 1:3-14; Mk 6:7-13

Before a building is constructed, an architect must complete a blueprint. Before a professional football team takes the field, the coaches have to devise a game plan. And before we can make sense of our lives we need to see a blueprint; we need to know what the game plan is.

Jesus presented that plan while he was here on this earth. He sent the Twelve on journeys to extend his teaching, and he continues that teaching today through the Church. The truth is, however, that God's plan is not an abstract truth or an ethereal ideal. God's plan is a person, the person of his Son, Jesus Christ. Jesus is like a blueprint which has taken on flesh and blood. Jesus is the plan for our lives.

St. Paul in our remarkable reading from his Letter to the Ephesians explains the plan which God the Father was pleased to decree in Christ, namely to bring all things in the heavens and on earth into one under Christ's headship. Christ is the Head, we are the members of his body, his mystical body which is the Church. The body is to be like the Head.

Because we are one with Christ in the Church, we share in his relationship with the Father. As he is the eternal Son of the Father in the Trinity, so we have become sons and daughters of God in the Church. God is a family of Father and Son united by the love of the Holy Spirit. The Church is our spiritual family here on earth. We are born into this family by baptism and confirmed as sons and daughters by the anointing of the Holy Spirit.

St. Paul wrote that we were sealed with the Holy Spirit. This expression refers to the practice whereby a king or other such person pressed his identifying ring in hot wax and sealed a letter or other important document to give it authenticity. When the recipient saw the king's seal, he knew the document was valid. The Holy Spirit through the sacrament of confirmation has imprinted a seal on our souls to identify us as really the children of God. We are authentic.

Our relationship with God in the Church calls us to respond in two ways. The first is liturgical. St. Paul emphasizes that "we must praise the divine favor God has bestowed on us in his beloved," that "we are predestined to praise his glory." We fulfill this response chiefly by means of the sacred liturgy, our prayer together as the Church. The second response is to strive "to be holy and blameless in God's sight, to be full of love." This second response indicates the way in which we are to live. It means that we are to be like Christ himself, not only in our being, but in our thoughts, our words, and our deeds.

Because Christ is the blueprint, the plan for our lives, the liturgy never tires of presenting the Gospel to us in every Mass. Over the course of three years on Sundays we cover virtually every word of the four Gospels. In the Gospels we witness Jesus in action. We see our blueprint come alive in the person of God's Son. We are presented with the ideal for correct living. In receiving the body and the blood of the Lord in Holy Communion, we are strengthened to follow God's plan for us. "Praised be the God and Father of our Lord Jesus Christ who has bestowed on us in Christ every spiritual blessing in the heavens!"

Sixteenth Sunday of the Year, B

We Need a Balance
Jr 23:1-6; Eph 2:13-18; Mk 6:30-34

Almost everyone recognizes a need for balance in life. An extrovert who loves being in the public eye does at times yearn for solitude and silence. An introvert who values moments alone occasionally is uplifted by being part of a jubilant crowd.

Jesus gave us the example of the balance we need in our spiritual life. Jesus had the custom of going to the synagogue for communal worship every Sabbath and he participated in the temple liturgies in Jerusalem at the appointed times. He also went off by himself and spent whole nights in prayer to his heavenly Father.

As today's Gospel unfolds, the apostles were returning to Jesus after a missionary journey for which he had sent them out two by two. It had been for them a time of preaching to the people and of praying with them. Jesus said to them, "Come by yourselves to an out-of-the way place and rest a little." They went off with Jesus in a boat to a deserted place. Jesus understood the necessity of balance in their lives as his disciples.

Jesus wants us, too, to maintain a balance. Foremost in our spiritual lives is the celebration of the liturgy together. Full, active, and conscious participation in the sacred liturgy, especially that of Sunday Mass, is the indispensable source from which we are to derive the true Christian spirit. And yet we too must at times go to a deserted place to pray alone with Jesus in quiet and recollection. We need the opportunity to pray in our own way and for our own intentions. Both public and private prayer are to be part of our Catholic lives. We should never want the liturgy to be what it is not: a form of private, individual prayer. Equally we should never neglect individual prayer in our private lives.

Sometimes people who experienced the former liturgy complain that they cannot pray at Mass anymore. What they mean is that formerly during Mass, which then was in Latin and almost entirely in silence, they could pray in their own way for their own needs. Now they are called to worship as a family, a community. They, and all of us, must recognize that taking our religion seriously involves much more than Sunday worship, even in the area of prayer. Outside the liturgy we must make time to pray in our own way in order to fulfill our personal religious needs so that we may come to the liturgy ready and eager to join with our spiritual sisters and brothers in the family worship of God our Father.

Those who are enthusiastic about the liturgical renewal and who find in public worship an uplifting and satisfying experience must recognize that they too need to make time for personal, private devotion. Keeping the balance is important. Private devotion should not ordinarily take on the character of public worship through the recitation of many vocal and communal prayers. The need is for quiet, contemplative prayer, a reflection on the meaning of life and our place within it, a meditation on the teachings and example of Jesus, and the expression of our personal relationship with God. We should not want the Mass to be like quiet, personal devotion, nor should we turn private religious expressions into community type prayer. Jesus has taught us the importance of balance in prayer and he has given us an example. The effort and time we put into both liturgical and private prayer are our way of responding to his teaching and his example.

Seventeenth Sunday of the Year, B

The Gospel Reflects the Mass
2 K 4:42-44; Eph 4:1-6; Jn 6:1-15

By the time St. John wrote his Gospel some sixty years after the death and resurrection of Jesus, the celebration of the Eucharist on Sunday had been firmly established as an expression of what it means to be a disciple of Christ. St. John constructed his sixth chapter in such a way that his readers would be drawn to see their Sunday observance reflected in his Gospel. Almost twenty centuries later we do well to see the reality.

The sixth chapter opens with the marvelous narrative of how Jesus fed five thousand people with five barley loaves and a couple of fish. It was, in St. John's words, a vast crowd. The Mass is not a private devotion or the privilege of a few. It is the celebration of the "vast crowd" throughout the world who are God's people.

St. John remarks that the Jewish feast of Passover was near. That was not so much a designation of the time of the year as it was an indication of the meaning of the Eucharist. The Eucharist is our Christian Passover, the celebration of the sacrifice which has given us the gift of freedom from sin and established us as God's people. In the fourth eucharistic acclamation we cry out: "Lord, by your cross and resurrection you have set us free; you are the Savior of the world."

St. John goes on to observe that when it was time to feed the people, a lad came forward with five loaves of bread and a couple of fish and gave them to Jesus. It seemed like almost nothing compared to the need of so many people. In the same way at Mass some of the people bring forward bread and wine to begin the preparation of the gifts. They are that lad of the Gospel and the gifts they present to the priest seem insignificant in comparison with what they will become.

In the story about the loaves Jesus performed eucharistic actions. Jesus took the loaves of bread and gave thanks (the word "Eucharist" means just that: to give thanks). At this point St. Matthew in his narrative helps us with an important detail. He says that after Jesus had looked up to heaven and given thanks, he broke the bread and gave the loaves to his disciples who distributed the bread among the people. That looks exactly like what happens at Mass when the priest is assisted by the special ministers of the Eucharist.

What about the fish? They are not part of our eucharistic meal but a fish is an ancient, and still current, Christian symbol. The initial letters in Greek for "Jesus Christ, God's Son, Savior" form an acronym which spells out the Greek word for fish: "ICHTHUS." For people alert to the meaning of symbols, any mention of a fish makes them remember that God loved us so much that he sent his only Son who became our Savior through the sacrificial offering of himself on the cross. The Eucharist is the living memorial of that sacrifice. During the celebration we exclaim to Christ: "Dying you destroyed our death; rising you restored our life."

For the next four Sundays we will be hearing parts of this sixth chapter of St. John's Gospel, and with each Sunday we will see more deeply into the meaning of the Holy Eucharist.

Eighteenth Sunday of the Year, B

Faith in Christ Demands Faith in the Eucharist
Ex 16:2-4, 12-15; Eph 4:17, 20-24; Jn 6:24-35

Last Sunday at Mass we began reading from the sixth chapter of the Gospel according to John. It is a chapter of seventy-one verses, second in length in the New Testament only to St. Luke's first chapter of eighty verses.

 St. Luke's first chapter tells of those events which led up to the coming of Jesus, born of the Virgin Mary. St. John's sixth chapter unfolds the teaching of Jesus which proclaimed the purpose of his coming as manifested in the gift of himself in the Holy Eucharist.

 This chapter of St. John is so lengthy that the liturgy has divided it into five parts over five Sundays. In order to perceive the beautiful meaning of the picture which John painted, it is helpful to step back and to view the chapter as a whole.

 The story began last Sunday with the familiar episode of the miracle of the loaves. Jesus fed five thousand people with five barley loaves and a couple of fish. The importance of this event can be seen in the fact that it is the only miracle of Jesus which is recorded in all four Gospels. The manner in which it is related by each evangelist makes people of faith think of the Eucharist. St. John, for example, in his version says that Jesus gave thanks before he distributed the bread. The word in his original Greek for "giving thanks" is "Eucharist." The point of the story is that Jesus had in mind something more than ordinary food.

 This Sunday the scene shifts from the shore of the Sea of Galilee where Jesus worked the miracle to the synagogue at Capernaum where Jesus preached a sermon on the Eucharist. Jesus began the sermon by calling for faith in himself, the one whom God had sent into the world. Such faith is necessary since accepting the Eucharist depends entirely on the word of Jesus.

On the third Sunday the sermon continues. In this part of the sermon Jesus makes a transition from faith in himself to faith in his gift of the Eucharist. The one faith must lead to the other.

On the fourth Sunday Jesus clearly and without equivocation proclaims his doctrine. He declares in no uncertain terms: "The bread that I will give is my flesh for the life of the world." After a negative reaction from the crowd, he speaks even more emphatically: "My flesh is real food and my blood is real drink."

The final Sunday presents a challenge. People may not remain indifferent to the promise of Jesus. Once they have heard his teaching, they must either accept it or reject it. St. John tells us that "many of his disciples broke away and would not remain in his company any longer." Even the apostles had to make up their minds. Jesus asked them, "Do you want to leave me too?" Peter answered, "Lord, to whom shall we go? You have the words of eternal life."

Try reading the entire sixth chapter in one sitting. That will help you to appreciate the doctrine of the Eucharist which the liturgy will unfold for us over the next three Sundays.

Nineteenth Sunday of the Year, B

Straight Talk About a Vital Truth
1 K 19:4-8; Eph 4:30-5:2; Jn 6:41-51

Sometimes we need to hear straight talk about important truths, such as God is good; sin is bad. Simple, direct statements about what is really important in life can make us stop and take notice.

In the synagogue at Capernaum Jesus decided that straight talk was necessary about an essential truth. He wanted his hearers to take notice. And he wants us to stop and ponder the truth of his words.

The day before his simple, direct statement Jesus had fed a vast crowd of people with five loaves of bread. He expected them to see in this miracle a sign that he had something more to give, something greater than all the bread in the whole world. He would give himself as spiritual nourishment

The leaders of the people objected to what Jesus promised. They saw him as altogether too ordinary, despite the sign he had just given them in the multiplication of the loaves. They kept saying, "Is this not Jesus, the son of Joseph? Do we not know his father and mother?"

Jesus heard their murmuring but did not tolerate it. He refused to back down, despite their objections. He insisted: "I am the living bread come down from heaven. If anyone eats this bread he shall live forever." Then came the simple direct statement, a declaration which contains a truth which is essential to our Catholic faith, a pronouncement which was prompted by the loving concern of our all good God, a proclamation of a doctrine which men and women throughout the centuries have given their lives in martyrdom to uphold, a promise which reveals the beautiful love of the heart of Christ. Jesus said, "The bread that I will give is my flesh for the life of the world."

Nothing could have been more direct. No other expression could have been clearer. There was no equivocation. Jesus did not say that the bread would be like his flesh, or that it would be a reminder of his flesh. Quite plainly he said, "The bread I will give *is* my flesh for the life of the world."

Jesus fulfilled his promise on the night before he died. For his apostles and for all the generations that have followed them and will follow them until the end of the world, he instituted the Holy Eucharist.

Rich and poor, saints and sinners, people of every race and culture, have been called to the table of the Lord. How happy are those who have been so invited, how blessed have been those who have responded in faith. The bread and the wine which are the outward appearances of the Eucharist may seem too ordinary, too simple in the eyes of many, but people of faith see that we have been given a great gift from God through his Son.

When we pray for our daily bread, we ask not only for the food that will sustain us on this earth but for the heavenly nourishment which will lead us to everlasting life. Make no mistake. Keep to your Catholic faith. The bread that Christ gives is his flesh for the life of the world.

Twentieth Sunday of the Year, B

The Eucharist Is All About Life
Pr 9:1-6; Eph 5:15-20; Jn 6:51-58

More books have been written about the Holy Eucharist than about the other six sacraments combined, so rich is this wonderful gift from God. The word "Eucharist" means "thanksgiving" and refers to the action of the Mass. And yet if there is to be one word which must be associated with the Eucharist that one word could well be "life."

In promising us the Eucharist Jesus declared, "The bread that I will give is my flesh for the life of the world." In the Eucharist Jesus gives us himself under the appearances of bread and wine, food and drink, because he is the spiritual nourishment of our spiritual life.

St. Thomas Aquinas reasoned that we can begin to understand some of the effects of the Eucharist by reflecting on the relationship between ordinary nourishment and human life. His process is clear and simple.

He first observes that food and drink are necessary to sustain life. Without food and drink we die. Next he comments on how food and drink help us to grow. Thirdly he points out that food and drink are necessary for health and for healing the effects of wounds and illness. His fourth point is a truth which we all appreciate: food and drink give delight. It is proper to apply these truths to the Eucharist.

In baptism we are born of water and the Holy Spirit as the children of God. God is our Father and we share in his divine life. To sustain this life within us we need divine nourishment, and God the Father gives us the most precious nourishment possible, the body and the blood of his own Son. Jesus declared, "Just as the Father who has life sent me and I have life because of the Father, so the one who feeds on me will have life because of me."

The life we receive in Christ at baptism is not static. We are called to grow more and more into the likeness of Christ, but we cannot do so on our own efforts. The Eucharist is the means to become more and more like Christ himself. The Eucharist is a sacrament of transformation and of growth.

In our passage through life we make mistakes. We injure ourselves through sin. Even after sin has been forgiven, sometimes we feel the effects of sin. We are weak, like a person recovering from a high fever. The Eucharist is our strength to overcome the effects of sin and to repair its injuries.

And if we could only appreciate with profound faith the marvelous abundance of God's love for us in the Eucharist, we would be the happiest people on earth. We would come to the Eucharist as to a delightful celebration of the wonders of God's grace.

The Eucharist, simply put, is the sacrament of divine life. This sacrament sustains that life, helps us to grow in that life, repairs injuries done to that life, and celebrates in joy the gift of that life.

The Eucharist means life. Eucharistic life, however, is not mortal. It will not end in death. It is a sharing in the everlasting life of God. Jesus' own summary of the Eucharist is emphatic: "Those who eat my flesh and drink my blood have life eternal and I will raise them up on the last day."

Twenty-first Sunday of the Year, B

A Determined Decision for a Lifetime
Jos 24:1-2, 15-17, 18; Eph 5:21-32; Jn 6:60-69

Daily decisions are a part of life: how to dress, what to eat, when to go to bed. In these matters our decisions are constantly changing, but there are some decisions which by their nature should be permanent. These are fundamental choices which we make by our own free will, an excellent example of which is the decision to marry. Marriage is a covenant, a permanent, loving relationship of fidelity in which a man and a woman become one.

God invited his people of the Old Testament to become his partner in a covenant which was a spiritual form of marriage. Joshua, the leader of God's people after the death of Moses, understood the importance of this covenant. He challenged the people: "If it does not please you to serve the Lord, decide today whom you will serve.... As for me and my household, we will serve the Lord." Joshua had made his decision.

Centuries later Jesus confronted those who had heard him preach. He challenged them to make a decision about himself. He had proclaimed a doctrine which they clearly understood: "The bread that I will give is my flesh for the life of the world. Those who eat my flesh and drink my blood have life everlasting and I will raise them up on the last day." They understood Jesus so clearly that they objected, "This sort of talk is hard to endure! How can anyone take it seriously."

But that they take it seriously is exactly what Jesus demanded. When his objectors turned their backs on him to walk away, he let them go. It was the day of decision. It was not possible to profess faith in Jesus and at the same time to reject his promise of the Holy Eucharist. Jesus then challenged those closest to him, the Twelve: "Do you want to leave me too?" Peter, in a protestation of loyalty which has been repeated down through the ages by men and women of faith, declared, "Lord, to whom shall we go? You have the words of eternal life. We have come to believe; we are convinced that you are God's holy one."

Peter's profession of faith was not forced upon him. He had received a grace which was not unlike a proposal of marriage. To this grace he freely responded. He had made a decision to bind himself so closely to Christ that, despite his later momentary lapse, he would be of one mind in faith with Christ. In effect he said that he wanted to enter into a permanent, loving relationship of fidelity with Christ.

We have the same grace which means we have the same challenge, the same decision to make. Christ made faith in the Eucharist the ultimate test of faith in himself. Appropriately the Eucharist is the sacrament of the new and everlasting covenant. To embrace the Eucharist and to make the celebration of this sacrament the center and heart of our lives is to live out the permanent, loving relationship which makes Christ and ourselves two in one flesh.

Why do we believe in the Eucharist? Why do we value this wonderful sacrament? Why is the Mass the highest expression of Catholic devotion? Because Christ has the words of everlasting life and we believe that he is God's holy one.

Twenty-second Sunday of the Year, B

Inside Is What Counts

Dt 4:1-2, 6-8; Jm 1:17-18, 21-22, 27; Mk 7:1-8, 14-15, 21-23

One evening at a baseball game when the crowd stood for the "Star Spangled Banner," a young boy failed to remove his cap. A burly man behind him leaned forward and said, "Hey kid, take off your hat." The child's father bristled but he waited until the end of the singing, and trying to control his quivering voice, he said quietly to the man, "My son has been undergoing radiation treatment for cancer and he has lost all his hair!"

The boy was not disrespectful during the singing of the national anthem; he was simply too embarrassed to remove his cap. The burly man learned a lesson: externals do not always indicate what is in the heart. That is also the lesson the Pharisees had to learn in the Gospel episode for this Sunday's Mass. They were upset with Jesus' disciples because they failed to follow the regulations for a ritual washing of hands before eating. Their concern was not hygiene but adherence to the letter of the law.

When the Pharisees demanded of Jesus why his disciples acted as they did, he refused to answer. Instead he warned them, in the words of the prophet Isaiah, "This people pays me lip service but their heart is far from me." He went on to explain that internal dispositions are more important than external observance.

As a liturgical people we need to reflect on Jesus' teaching. The liturgy as a matter of fact is concerned with lots of externals, such as gestures, standing, sitting, kneeling, processing, singing and reciting prayers, as well as the use of vestments, candles, and decorations. In fact, the Church teaches in the *Constitution on the Liturgy* that full, active, conscious participation in the sacred liturgy is the indispensable source of the true

Christian spirit, and the same Constitution makes it clear that participation is accomplished "by means of acclamations, responses, psalms, antiphons, and songs, as well as by actions, gestures, and bodily attitudes" (14 and 30).

And yet the chief element of worship, Pope Pius XII taught, is internal. That means that what we do externally is intended to express and to intensify sincere interior dispositions, such as faith, hope, and love. Sometimes the best measure of our devotion is not what we do during Mass but how we act outside of Mass.

Is the faith we express liturgically the guiding norm of our conduct so that we live in such a way that if God did not exist our lives would not make sense? Does our faith make us different from others whose values are secular and materialistic? Does the virtue of hope brighten our outlook and make us basically optimistic people? Does our hope give us a trust in God which moves us to embrace his will? Does the love we express for God during our worship guide and direct the way in which we live? Do our lives reflect the truth we are taught that we are all brothers and sisters of one another in Christ?

Externals are important but of themselves they do not make us holy any more than a patriotic bumper sticker makes a driver a good citizen. St. James today tells us, "Welcome the word with its power to save you. Act on this word. If all you do is listen to it, you are deceiving yourselves." That is his way of saying that worship must lead to life, that externals must express sincere and honest internal dispositions. It is what is inside us that counts.

Twenty-third Sunday of the Year, B

Faith by Hearing, Worship by Speech
Is 35:4-7; Jm 2:1-5; Mk 7:31-37

Our senses are our contact with the world outside ourselves. It is difficult to determine which is more precious, our sight or our hearing, but the man in the Gospel had no hesitation. He was deaf. He knew exactly what was important to him.

Being deaf prevented him from speaking plainly; he could not hear how words were pronounced. He could not even ask Jesus for the favor he needed. Fortunately some concerned people brought him to Jesus and explained his situation. Jesus cured him, and by giving him the ability to hear he made it possible for the man also to speak plainly. We are not surprised that Jesus was so compassionate. What may surprise us is that all of us at one time were in somewhat the same predicament as the deaf man, not physically but spiritually. Before baptism we were spiritually deaf. We were without the gift of faith. As a consequence we could not hear God speaking to us, and we could not speak to God as we should.

Faith comes by hearing, not through our physical auditory apparatus, but by means of the gift of faith which we receive in baptism. Especially during the celebration of the liturgy of the Mass we have the opportunity to listen in faith. We should in the first place think of hearing the Scriptures as the source of our faith, but there are other opportunities during Mass. The creed after the homily expresses our faith, as do the hymns we sing and the prayers we say, especially the eucharistic prayer. An ancient axiom states that the way we pray expresses what we believe (*lex orandi, lex credendi*).

Faith is incomplete, however, until we speak to God the way we should, until we respond in worship. Liturgical prayer serves a twofold purpose: it teaches us our faith and it gives us the proper words to express our worship. What this comes down to is that we worship God by telling him what he has revealed to us. To put it another way, we offer thanks and praise to God by telling him what he has done and continues to do. In the Gospel episode the people honored Jesus by simply recounting what he was doing. They said, "He makes the deaf hear and the mute speak."

For example, in the third eucharistic prayer we say, "Father, you are holy indeed and all creation rightly gives you praise. All life, all holiness comes from you...." God has revealed that he is the source of all life and holiness; we praise him by proclaiming to him that very truth. The psalms too are fruitful in helping us to pray by revealing God to us. In today's responsorial psalm (Psalm 146) we say, "The God of Jacob keeps faith forever, secures justice for the oppressed, gives food to the hungry. The Lord sets captives free." These words are both a revelation and a prayer.

God does not need us to remind him of how great he is and how wonderful are the things he has done. And yet even in human relationships we praise people by telling them what they have done. To a friend who has invited you to a home cooked meal you might say, "You fix the best lasagna I have ever tasted." God does the best in every way for us. That is what we learn as we listen to all the forms of revelation. We are wise when the worship we offer God is in accord with what he has told us of himself, when we speak to him in prayer the way we should.

Twenty-fourth Sunday of the Year, B

Eternal Life Is Certain
Is 50:4-9; Jm 2:14-18; Mk 8:27-35

A little girl of seven takes off in an airplane to fly across the country, accompanied by her father and a flight instructor. The flight ends in disaster. Several young people are determined to climb the highest mountain to which they can travel, despite their inexperience. A rock gives way, the person in the lead slips, and all fall to their death.

What motivates people to take on risk, to overcome fear, and to go ahead with a dangerous adventure? For the little girl, Jessica Dubroff, and her father, it was the possibility of setting a record. For the mountain climbers it was the excitement of conquest. Sometimes thrill seekers are fatalistic. They say that there is a risk whenever you drive a car, and so we should not worry about the hazards of living life to the full.

Jesus was not a fatalist, but he knew how his life would end. It was his Father's plan that he should die on the cross, not so he could set a record as was the ardent wish of Jessica's father, but so that he could bring to us the gift of eternal life. He knew that his ministry, like that of the prophets before him, would bring on the wrath of enemies strong enough to condemn him to death, but he willingly climbed the mountain of Calvary to open his arms on the cross to embrace all of us in his divine love. His death was not a disaster but the accomplishment of his mission on this earth. It was a great conquest over sin and eternal death.

There was no risk for Jesus. Risk means a chance of injury or death. For Jesus death was a certainty. When Peter, with the best of intentions, tried to dissuade him from following the way to the cross, Jesus responded harshly: he told Peter that he was not judging according to God's standards. In the deep mystery of God, the death of his Son was necessary for our salvation.

We may feel that there is a risk in following Jesus, but not so. There is a certainty. If we follow him faithfully we must, as he teaches us, "deny our very selves, take up our cross, and follow in his steps." Our cross does not mean a literal crucifixion. In Catholic terminology we say of people who have particularly difficult burdens to bear in life that they have a heavy cross. We understand that the cross for us may mean the loss of a job, or grave illness, or the necessity of making significant sacrifices to take care of a family member who has suffered a debilitating stroke. The cross for parents may be seeing their children leave the Church and take on the worship of drugs and sex. The cross for children may be the grief of living with alcoholic parents or the sorrow which divorce inflicts upon them. The cross for all of us is the death of a loved one.

The cross in our lives may not be dramatic. It will not win national attention, as did the flight of Jessica Dubroff. It will not involve the thrill of mountain climbing. More importantly the cross will not bring on tragedy. It will not mean disaster. Instead enduring our cross in accord with the will of God will lead to everlasting life. The cross means living in union with Jesus. It means sharing his suffering and his death which will grant us the Father's gift of eternal happiness with his Son and the Spirit in our heavenly home. We should not fear the cross. When the cross is God's will for us, it is the real way to live life to the full.

Twenty-fifth Sunday of the Year, B

Recognizing the Source of Our Worth
Ws 2:17-20; Jm 3:16-4:3; Mk 9:30-37

I suspect we have all had one of those embarrassing moments when someone has overhead us saying something which was intended only for special ears. That happened to the disciples one day in the presence of Jesus. It was not Judas saying to one of his companions about Jesus, "I'm getting sick and tired of his holier than thou attitude." No, it was a debate among the apostles. They were arguing about who was the most important. Instinctively they realized their debate was so distasteful to Jesus that when he asked them about it they simply fell silent.

The amazing thing about their argument is that Jesus had just taught them that he was going to be delivered into the hands of men who would put him to death. As the humble servant of his Father he was willing to undergo death in contrast to those whose only thought was to rise to prominence and power. He said to the apostles, "If anyone wishes to rank first, he must remain the last one of all and the servant of all."

The disciples failed to understand Jesus' words. No wonder. God's values are upside down as far as secular standards are concerned. And so Jesus resorted to an example which was a favorite with him. In a very touching scene he took a child and put his arms around that fortunate youth and said, "Whoever welcomes a child such as this for my sake welcomes me." Children are the living example of the humility and simplicity we are called to practice.

There is an age when humility and simplicity lead most children to take it for granted in the best sense that they are loveable. Usually this age is before they go to school and enter into the world of competition. The sad truth is that in school some children begin to lose confidence in themselves. They are expected to produce, to get good grades, and perhaps a little girl hears, "Why can't you be like your big sister who gets all A's?" The competition makes her doubt herself. A young boy playing Little League strikes out with the bases loaded in the ninth inning. The ride home in the car is silent except for the sound of his sobbing. He has failed. His mind is filled with doubts. These little kids think their worth depends on success, but good parents love their children for who they are and not for what they accomplish.

One of the apostles, St. James, eventually learned the lesson of the importance of humility. He wrote in his epistle: "Where there are jealousy and strife, there also are inconstancy and all kinds of vile behavior." He went on to say that conflicts and disputes come from inner craving. That craving is the desire to be tops, to be first, to be better than anyone else.

Maybe many adults have this craving because they think their worth depends on accomplishments. Perhaps that is why they want to look and feel important. The fact is, of course, that if you want to get ahead, if you want a better job and bigger pay, you are going to have to accept the competitive system. You are going to have to prove yourself and you will have to do better than others.

Whatever the situation in the competitive, dare we say "cut throat," world, we need to recognize God's system of values. We have to remember that we are children of the perfect Father who indeed loves us for who we are. We must never doubt that his love for us is the source of our worth and our value.

Twenty-sixth Sunday of the Year, B

The Mother of Discovery
Nb 11:25-29; Jm 5:1-6; Mk 9:38-43, 45, 47-48

It has been said that necessity is the mother of invention. When an industrialized era made it necessary to have better lighting than candles and oil lamps could provide, Thomas Edison invented the electric light bulb. Necessity was the mother of invention. In the Church necessity is the mother of discovery. There is a difference. We have an example in the first reading.

When Moses recognized that the Israelites in the desert were becoming too numerous for him to take care of, he complained to God about his burden. God told him to assemble seventy elders of good reputation. Upon them God sent some of the spirit of Moses, which meant that God shared some of Moses' authority and power with them. By necessity Moses discovered that he did not have to do everything by himself, that God wanted others to share in his mission of guiding and directing the people.

Unfortunately Joshua failed to understand God's plan and at the time he was not big enough to be willing to share the spirit of Moses with Eldad and Medad who were not present when the spirit came on the others. Something similar happened with Jesus and his apostles. Jesus shared his mission with his apostles, but when John saw a man, not one of the apostles, using the name of Jesus to expel demons he became resentful, just as Joshua had. Jesus, however, was not controlled by jealousy. He was eager only that his mission be extended.

In the Church today the principle that necessity is the mother of discovery continues. Because of movements within the Vatican Council the Pope and the Bishops remembered that God in an earlier era had given the Church an ordained ministry known as the diaconate. It was a form of discovery occasioned by a need in the community. Before Vatican II a priest alone gave communion (even a seminary deacon needed special permission). After the Council as the number of Catholics going to communion greatly increased, the Church discovered that lay people may become special ministers of Holy Communion, that such a ministry was permitted by God and pleasing to him. Before Vatican II the priest did everything at Mass, including the reading of the Scriptures, but after a return to the vernacular, the Church discovered an ancient lay ministry known as lector or reader.

Unfortunately some of us are like Joshua or John. We resist discovery. We may resent that married men may be ordained deacons. We may reject the idea of special ministers of communion and insist that they should be tolerated under only the most extraordinary circumstances. Other of us cannot abide the fact that lay people, especially women, proclaim the Scriptures during Mass.

Because of necessity a light has gone on in the Church today, a light much brighter than that invented by Thomas Edison. It is the light of the Holy Spirit shining upon the truth for the Church to see in greater clarity. In the responsorial psalm we uttered the refrain that the precepts of the Lord give joy to the heart. That is true provided our hearts are open to the movement of the Spirit in the Church today. Rather than being resentful of ministries in the liturgy, we should be thankful to God and pray that the generous outpouring of his Spirit will continue in the Church.

Twenty-seventh Sunday of the Year, B

A Love Like That of Jesus

Gn 2:18-24; Heb 2:9-11; Mk 10:2-16

On their wedding day a bride and her groom declare before God, each other, and all present that they take each other for better or for worse, for richer or for poorer, in sickness and health, until death. A marriage is supposed to last a lifetime. But it does not always work out that way. A generation or so ago when Catholic married couples had a problem, they recognized that they had to try to work things out. The last thought to occur to them was to get a divorce. Now it seems that divorce is the first solution that some couples think of when they have a problem.

The Church has struggled to be compassionate rather than rigid regarding marriage. When it can be shown that there was an obstacle to a valid marriage from the beginning, the Church grants an annulment. This is not a divorce. It is a recognition that a valid, sacramental marriage did not exist. The process for securing an annulment is long and often tedious only because the Church is commissioned by Christ to safeguard and promote the nature of marriage as a lifelong commitment, a commitment which cannot be taken on lightly and which cannot be dismissed except for a grave cause. It must be observed that some marriages become impossible even when they cannot be annulled. Divorced Catholics who have not remarried may and should receive Holy Communion.

We must, however, keep marriage in perspective. Marriage did not evolve in society nor was it instituted by secular practices. Marriage is God's creation. That is the teaching of the Book of Genesis. God wanted marriage to reflect his own love for his people, a love which never fails and which grants the gift of life. Therein lies the difficulty with marriage. Marriage is a challenge to be like God. No wonder that marriage is not easy.

God is faithful. He does not love us only when we love him. He does not abandon his affection for us because he has fallen in love with someone else. God does not find it too troublesome to put up with our faults. He does not become irritable when we do things to get on his nerves. God does not fear that it will be too demanding to care for us when we have contracted a long, debilitating illness. God's love is patient, generous, and thoughtful. Above all, God's love never fails. God's love is the challenging ideal for every married couple.

Being parents is part of most marriages. Having children can bring many blessings but it can also be very demanding. No wonder. Having children is being like God. God's love is fruitful. Flowing from him is the gift of life. Jesus loved little children. In them he saw not only the fruit of love between husband and wife; he also saw the outpouring of life from his heavenly Father.

Jesus is the model of love for spouses and parents, especially in his sacrifice on the cross. Sacrifice is necessary for marriage. Only love can make sacrifice possible. That love can be derived from Jesus, especially in the Holy Eucharist. Catholic couples ought to receive Holy Communion together with a prayer in their hearts: "Lord Jesus, help us to love each other and our children with the love you show to us, especially through your suffering and your death on the cross. May our love never die but grow deeper and stronger as the years go on. May our love be like yours." It won't be easy, but it will be possible, and it will be worthwhile.

Twenty-eighth Sunday of the Year, B

Overcoming the Obstacle
Ws 7:7-11; Heb 4:12-13; Mk 10:17-30

Several years ago the state of California was faced with a major decision. In the work of expanding Highway 101 into a freeway from Los Angeles through Ventura County, the planners faced a mountain directly in their path. A decision had to be made. It was possible to continue the freeway by directing the roadway to the north in what was in effect a detour around the mountain's summit. The alternative was to go straight ahead, dynamite a path over the Conejo grade and so continue the freeway on a direct path. The alternative was chosen. It was the right choice.

Jesus invited the rich man in the Gospel to make a choice. He urged him to sell what he had and give the proceeds to the poor so that he could follow him. The rich man made the wrong decision. He was too attached to his wealth to give it up. His possessions were like a mountain, separating him from Jesus. He saw that obstacle as too great to overcome. We do not know what happened to him. Maybe eventually he found a round-about way of following Jesus and did become a disciple, but he missed his first opportunity.

Some men and women throughout the history of the Church have responded to the invitation of Jesus in a literal way. They have actually given up all their material possessions in order to lead the life of hermits or monks or nuns. Most of us are not very eager to follow their example, and the truth is that the Church and society could not exist if we all did. Not everyone in the Church has the same vocation or calling, and yet we cannot simply dismiss the invitation of Jesus as irrelevant or impossible.

It is reasonable to conclude that Jesus is not concerned with wealth as such but with obstacles. Jesus spoke to the rich young man about giving up wealth because wealth was his problem, his preoccupation, his attachment. Jesus through this Gospel speaks to us about whatever it is in our life that prevents us from becoming better disciples and more committed members of the Church. When we take the word of Jesus seriously, we will find that it is sharper than any two-edged sword. It will cut out of our lives our attachments, our sins, our failures, and our obstacles to accepting the grace of discipleship.

What must we do? That is a question each of us must answer. Perhaps the obstacle is being selfish or sullen in a marriage, always wanting our way and being disruptive when we don't get it. Maybe it is being prone to gossip, taking delight in putting other people down or spreading terrible stories about them. We may be the type of person who looks down on the homeless, holds in contempt those who are on welfare, and feels hateful toward immigrants. We must search our consciences. Would it not be wonderful to have Jesus stand in front of us and give us the answer? Maybe. Perhaps his words would hurt, like that two-edged sword. Perhaps we would turn away as did the rich young man. But in this Mass God's grace is with us, challenging us with the Gospel but strengthening us through Holy Communion to accept the challenge. These days Highway 101, thanks to the right decision, crosses the Conejo grade into what is known as Pleasant Valley. When we make the right decision about eliminating obstacles to discipleship we will find that our lives, though not always easy, will be lived in the Pleasant Valley of Christ's love for us.

Twenty-ninth Sunday of the Year, B

Upside Down Is Right Side Up
Is 53:10-11; Heb 4:14-16; Mk 10:35-45

Pineapple upside down cake is a favorite of some people. While it is baking, it looks very plain and ordinary. When it is served, the sweet, juicy part is on top. We can safely presume that Mary never baked a pineapple upside down cake for Jesus (no imports to Judea from Hawaii at the time), but if she had, it probably would have been a favorite of Jesus. The reason is that an upside down cake represents Jesus' values which themselves appear to be upside down.

Secular society says, "Get ahead. Be competitive. Don't let anyone take advantage of you. Show who is boss. Make people think you are important. Take care of number one. Just do it." Even though the apostles did not live in our era (no upside down cake for them), they were tainted with the kind of ambition which our society advocates and which Jesus rejected.

Ambition in the hearts of James and John was so strong that it emboldened them to demand of Jesus that they be seated in the place of honor, at his right and his left, when he came into his glory. They were insistent; they said, "See to it." We are not sure how long the apostles had been with Jesus at this point, but James and John had obviously failed to understand both the teaching and the example of Jesus.

Jesus' constant teaching was that we must be humble and not proud, that we must be willing to serve others, not dominate them. Since James and John, and the other apostles as well, had failed to grasp his teaching, Jesus became as explicit as possible. He said, "Anyone of you who aspires to greatness must serve the rest; whoever wants to rank first among you must serve the needs of all." That summarized his teaching.

Jesus' example was even more powerful than his teaching.

Jesus, the eternal Son of God, left his throne in heaven to become one of us. He abandoned all that secular society lusts for. Jesus was so humble because he was thinking, not of himself, but of us. He became human so that he could become our priest, our Savior, the one to whom we can confidently turn for mercy and help in time of need. That was his example which he explained by declaring, "The Son of Man has not come to be served but to serve — to give his life in ransom for the many."

When we come to Mass, we have still another testimony to the humility of Jesus. Jesus comes to us in Holy Communion, not in the trappings of royalty or amidst the trumpet blasts of the angels of heaven. No, he comes in humility. He willingly transforms ordinary, simple bread into his body, and he changes plain, inexpensive wine into his blood. He does so in order to be at our service, not merely to give us food and drink, but to be himself our spiritual nourishment. Could even God have thought of a more compelling example of humility and service? Let those who wish try to lord it over others. For us we have the example and teaching of Jesus. Some people put on airs to appear important. Jesus says, "Just don't do it!"

It's too bad that the apostles never ate an upside down cake. It could have been for them, as it should be for us, a sign that with Jesus upside down is right side up.

Thirtieth Sunday of the Year, B

Even the Blind May See
Jr 31:7-9; Heb 5:1-6; Mk 10:46-52

To be able to see is a wonderful ability. An infant, released from the darkness of his tiny world in the womb, gazes upon a magnificent earth. He sees faces which he will one day recognize as those of his father and mother, the two people who gave him life, who nourish him, and who love him.

Through sight we become aware of the world around us. We can see reality outside ourselves. We use the verb, "to see," not only to indicate the power of sight, but also to express perception, the work of our minds. When someone asks us whether we understand a point they are making, we respond by saying, "I see what you mean." The blind beggar in today's Gospel represents us before baptism. We were poor like him, lacking as we were in God's grace, and like him we could not see spiritually, deprived as we were of the gift of faith. Through baptism we received a share in God's riches and through faith we enjoyed the gift of sight.

Now we can look out at the world around us and see it for its true meaning. We have all heard that a pessimist looks at a glass and sees it as half empty and an optimist looks at the same glass and sees it as half full. The person of faith looks at the glass of water and says, "Thanks be to God." That person understands water to be the great gift of God, which is not only necessary to sustain our human lives, but which is the means by which God gives us a share in his life through baptism.

We can see our parents with a much deeper appreciation than can an infant who looks at the faces of his father and mother. Through faith we can realize that parenthood represents the truth that all life comes to us from God the Father. We can look at children and be charmed by their beauty and simplicity. Faith leads our perception of children to see the truth that God the Father loves us his precious children in Christ.

After Jesus cured the blind man he said to him, "Be on your way." The man stared at Jesus for a moment and thought to himself, "Where should I go except wherever Jesus leads me?" St. Mark then tells us, "He started to follow Jesus up the road." But we do not know whether he persevered. Did he follow Jesus up the road that led to Jerusalem where Jesus was crucified? Did he stand faithfully at the foot of the cross with Mary, the other women, and the beloved disciple? St. Mark does not tell us. Perhaps he wanted us to see ourselves in the person of that man who had been blind and to answer the questions by the way we live.

In every Mass we follow Christ, in a sense, up the hill of Calvary because in the Mass we stand at the foot of the cross, sharing in the one sacrifice of Christ. The Mass is an invitation for us to offer ourselves with Christ, our great High Priest, to the heavenly Father, to pledge that we will persevere in our Catholic faith, and that we will be loyal and faithful to Christ and his Church until death.

Today we can ask, "Where shall we go or to whom shall we turn?" How could we ever abandon Christ who has given us the gift of faith, who has made us children of God, and who promises us everlasting life? When we get to heaven we will enjoy the Beatific Vision of God. Faith will be transformed into sight, and we will say, "Now I see the meaning of all that Jesus has done for us."

Thirty-first Sunday of the Year, B

"I Didn't Know I Couldn't"

Dt 6:2-6; Heb 7:23-28; Mk 12:28-34

When President Harding died in the summer of 1923, his Vice President, Calvin Coolidge, was helping his father on his farm in Vermont. His father was a notary public. While still at the farm he administered the presidential oath of office to his son. Someone later asked him, "How did you know that you could administer the presidential oath to your own son?" He replied, "I didn't know I couldn't."

That laconic response, characteristic of the Coolidges, expresses a sentiment which many of us share. We want freedom. We want to believe that whatever is not forbidden is allowed. Perhaps to our surprise, Jesus felt the same way. He favored freedom.

The question which the scribe posed to Jesus was not an idle one: "Which is the first of all the commandments?" He was thinking, of course, of all the regulations found in the Old Testament. The rabbis had analyzed the Law and determined that it consisted of 613 distinct commandments, 248 positive and 365 negative. The scribe was sincere when he asked, "Which is the first?" by which he meant, "Which is the greatest?" Jesus did not hesitate. He immediately quoted from the Book of Deuteronomy, our first reading for this Sunday, "You shall love the Lord your God with your whole being."

Jesus didn't dismiss the 613 commandments enumerated by the rabbis. Rather in an instant he taught that they were all summed up in one great commandment, the love of God. But Jesus did not stop there. Although to the question, "Which is the first commandment?" there should be only one answer, Jesus insisted on adding a second: "You shall love your neighbor as yourself." This commandment he quoted not from the Book of Deuteronomy, but that of Leviticus.

So we might question Jesus, "Is there one great commandment, or are there two?" Jesus would respond, "There is actually only one because you cannot truly love God if you do not love your neighbor, and you cannot properly love your neighbor if you do not love God." Jesus reached out to the Book of Deuteronomy and then to the Book of Leviticus and joined their separate commandments into one.

Some Catholics have complained about all the post-Vatican II talk concerning love. They want us to go back to the old way of insisting on lots of laws and regulations. They have a point. We may not dismiss all of the laws in Scripture and the other regulations of the Church. But we must remember that Jesus did not dismiss all the laws of the Old Testament. He did not say that they were useless, but he did maintain that they were all summed up in the one commandment of love.

Actually it is easier to follow minute regulations than it is to love God completely and to love our neighbor as ourselves. Love sets us free from the self-centeredness which is the root of all sin. True freedom is not license to do whatever we want. It is the liberty to do whatever we must to love God and others.

According to legend when St. John was a very old man, he consistently preached only one message: "Love God; love your neighbor." When some of his disciples, somewhat in frustration, asked him why he persisted in the same message of love, he replied, "Because if we follow it, that will be sufficient."

Thirty-second Sunday of the Year, B

A Widow Shows Us the Way
1 K 17:10-16; Heb 9:24-28; Mk 12:38-44

You may have seen on TV one of those experiments in which someone places a penny on a busy sidewalk to see whether anyone will take the trouble to stoop and pick it up. Usually no one bothers because a penny these days is almost worthless.

Two small copper coins, worth about a penny, were all that the widow in today's Gospel had to contribute to the temple. In modern terms this woman surely is not the young, svelte widow in halter and shorts who runs through the neighborhood in Nike athletic shoes. She is more like the little old lady in tennis shoes from K-Mart, maybe even a homeless person or a bag lady, who enjoys little or no respect in our society.

Jesus did not neglect the little old lady in the Gospel. He was impressed by her. He did not fail to appreciate the gifts of the wealthy, the sizeable amounts which they chose to contribute, but he did take special notice of the widow. Her two small copper coins were far from worthless in the eyes of Jesus because they represented an extraordinary generosity: they were all that the woman had to live on.

I hope that this generous lady overheard what Jesus was saying about her. In a way one wonders why Jesus did not speak to her directly and praise her for her goodness. Maybe Jesus could see into her heart and recognize that by God's grace this woman had grasped the meaning of the example from the Book of Kings which forms the first reading for this Sunday. The widow in Zarephath was blessed by God for her generosity in feeding the prophet Elijah. In spite of the famine she and her son were able to eat for a year from the flour and the oil which she had shared with the prophet.

We are often called to be generous. A Catholic Mass seems

almost incomplete without some mention of a special collection that will be taken up to help those in need in various ways. Because some government officials want the open hand of welfare to change into a closed fist, the need for us to be charitable becomes even more imperative. Every city has homeless, hungry people, whom it is easy to dismiss as lazy or irresponsible, but a Catholic view sees them as Christ in need. Every Catholic must oppose abortion and stand for life, but we ought also to come to the aid of indigent women, whether wed or unwed, who have the courage to give their unborn children a chance to be born.

When we are generous, it is not wrong for us to want to overhear Jesus telling his Father how good we are, but more importantly we have to keep our eyes fixed on Jesus. The example of Jesus is that out of generous love for us he gave his life on the cross. Jesus reached down to pick up everyone from the depths of sin and to draw us to himself. No human person is so insignificant to him as to be like a penny which is not worth bothering with. We are all precious in his eyes.

When we come to Mass we experience the generosity of Jesus in the Holy Eucharist. He feeds us with his body and blood. The Eucharist is a gift even greater than that granted to the widow of Zarephath as Jesus himself is greater than his prophet Elijah.

With the gift of the Eucharist as our motive and our strength we can begin to match the generosity of the little old lady, the widow, who gave all that she had to live on.

Thirty-third Sunday of the Year, B

We Will Hear and See in Heaven
Dn 12:1-3; Heb 10:11-14, 18; Mk 13:24-32

Ludwig van Beethoven was one of the greatest composers of all time. While he was still creating masterpieces, he gradually lost his hearing. After he had become completely deaf he composed his great choral Ninth Symphony. He heard not a single note. Some people say that geniuses are immortal because of their works. They believe that Beethoven lives on in his music, Shakespeare in his plays, and Edison in his inventions. Beethoven knew better. When he was dying, he said, "I shall hear in heaven." He was right.

We believe that Beethoven is now hearing, not only his own masterpieces, but the music of the great master, God himself. Beethoven is privileged to join the angels and the saints in their endless song of joy. Shakespeare now knows that all of his picturesque words were but a faint echo of the eternal Word spoken by the Father in eternity, the Son of God himself. Edison was thrilled to invent the electric light bulb, but now he is bathed in the fulgent light of the Beatific Vision. He now knows the truth of the reading from the Book of Daniel. The background of that book is that Israel was occupied by the Syrians who tried to impose on the Jews a foreign language, culture, and religion. Many Jews chose death rather than capitulate. The author of the book offered a message of hope to the survivors by declaring that the "wise shall shine brightly... and those who lead the many to justice shall be like the stars forever." Edison's invention, and even its development, is but a dim reflection of the light of everlasting life, the great gift Christ will bestow when he comes again to raise the dead to life.

Shakespeare never imagined a scene like that of Christ, the Son of Man, coming in the clouds with great power and glory, nor could he have found words to describe it. Neither can we. And we are at a loss to understand fully the words we have in today's Gospel. What it will all be like, or even when it will happen, only the Father in heaven knows.

Meanwhile we are not unlike those Israelites who suffered in their own land from the occupation by the Syrians. We are surrounded by the army of the culture of death. This army wages war on the dignity and value of human life. It attacks its own fellow human beings when they are most vulnerable: when they are at the beginning of life in the womb and when they are near the end of life in old age. It rejects those who are in most need of our country's abundance for their survival: the homeless, the hungry, the welfare recipients, and the immigrants.

While remaining faithful to our Catholic faith and the values it teaches, we have not suffered death; at least not so far. But we are in danger of allowing ourselves to be influenced, however subtly, by secular values which are selfish, individualistic, chauvinistic, and xenophobic. To resist these influences, we should reflect on the promise of everlasting life to those who remain faithful. We should also remember that the Eucharist is a pledge and promise of the everlasting life which should be one of our motives for remaining faithful. Christ will fulfill the words of today's first reading: "Those who lead the many to justice shall be like the stars forever." Besides shining like the stars we will hear and we will see God himself.

Solemnity of Christ the King, B

Who Is Your King?
Dn 7:13-14; Rv 1:5-8; Jn 18:33-37

In 1925 Pope Pius XI instituted a feast in honor of Christ the King to be observed on the last Sunday of October. The Church for centuries had honored Christ as King in the procession on Palm Sunday, but the Pope saw the need for a special feast as an antidote to the secularism and materialism of the era. In our country that era was called the Roaring Twenties.

Pope Pius XI placed the feast on the last Sunday of October so that it would be followed by the observance of All Saints, the liturgical recognition of those disciples who had entered into the heavenly kingdom. The Vatican II renewal moved the Solemnity of Christ the King to the last Sunday of the liturgical year in order to symbolize that the kingdom, although present among us, is still to come: "We wait in joyful hope for the coming of our Savior, Jesus Christ," who will bring his kingdom to perfection when he returns in glory for the general resurrection.

The encyclical of Pope Pius XI in 1925 concerning Christ the King brought to the attention of the world the need to establish spiritual values as the guidelines for life. The Pope's words for the most part went unheeded. The United States in particular continued to follow the gospel of greed, to insist that everyone had a right to be rich, and that there could be wealth without work. People of every economic level, "even shoeshine boys" as one historian put it, were into the stock market. The crash of 1929 was as devastating as it was inevitable.

It is disturbing to realize that the encyclical written by the Pope in 1925 could have been composed by the Pope last week. The secularism and materialism which led to the failure of financial institutions in 1929 are almost the same as those which have led in our time to our enormous deficit and the scandalous Savings and Loans debacles of recent years.

Our liturgical celebration of Christ as our King challenges us to ask whether the fault lies in our financial policies or in our spiritual attitudes. What is ultimately important is not that greed leads to financial collapse but that it rejects the teachings and the example of Christ the King.

Secularism insists that the kingdom of wealth is here on this earth. It rejects every form of religious faith and worship. Materialism preaches the doctrine that comfort, pleasure, and wealth are the only or the highest goals of life. The god of secularism and materialism is not nailed to a sacrificial cross but lolls on luxurious, licentious bedding.

In contrast are the witnesses of the wisdom of the Christian Gospel; they are the citizens of the heavenly kingdom. They show us that unselfishness is the way to happiness as greed is not, that spiritual reality is true and real as the sham of secularism is not, and that religion is ultimately rewarding as materialism is not.

The Preface of this Sunday declares that Christ the King rules an eternal and universal kingdom, a kingdom of truth and life, a kingdom of holiness and grace, a kingdom of justice, love, and peace. That is the kingdom which is worth working for.

A PLEDGE OF ALLEGIANCE TO CHRIST THE KING

This Sunday is an appropriate time to pledge our allegiance to Christ the King. The following suggested form, which is based on the Preface of the Eucharistic Prayer for this Solemnity, may be used at Mass by having the people repeat the lines of the pledge after the priest or other minister.

> We pledge allegiance to Christ the King.
> We embrace his eternal and universal kingdom.
> We acknowledge his kingdom to be one of truth and life,
> of holiness and grace.
> We wish to do what we can through prayer and action
> to bring to the world his kingdom
> of justice, love, and peace.

The C Cycle of Readings

"As the time approached when he was to be taken from this world, Jesus firmly resolved to proceed toward Jerusalem."
(Lk 9:51)

The Season of Advent and Christmas
Cycle C

"Advent has a twofold character: as a season to prepare for Christmas when Christ's first coming to us is remembered; as a season when that remembrance directs the mind and heart to await Christ's Second Coming at the end of time. Advent is thus a period for devout and joyful expectation."
(*General Norms for the Liturgical Year*, 39)

First Sunday of Advent, C

Advent Reflects Life
Jr 33:14-16; 1 Th 3:12-3:2; Lk 21:25-28, 34-36

Some people come to church to get away from the hectic and disturbing aspects of life. They like that. Some people complain that church is unreal since it bears no resemblance to the life they lead. They do not like that. What is the truth? Is what we do during the celebration of the liturgy an escape from the realities of life?

In reflecting on the season of Advent, we have the means for seeing that the liturgy is real, that it reflects life as it is, but the liturgy is also an ideal since it gives a direction and purpose to life.

One of the aspects of life is that we are constantly looking to the future. It begins early when adults insist on asking a child, "What do you want to be when you grow up?" It continues during school years, especially as graduation approaches, when consideration has to be given to what we will do next. Most people look forward to marriage, to having children, to advancing at work, to retirement, and then to that which in youth seems uncertain and distant, old age and death.

Looking to the future is an inescapable part of life. Advent, therefore, reflects life in that it looks to the future. It does so in two ways, first by being attentive to an uncertain, and seemingly distant, future when Christ will come again to our world to bring his kingdom to perfection. You might say that is the graduation ceremony of the world. Secondly Advent looks to the future by preparing to celebrate on December 25th the birth of Christ.

The two are not unrelated. About Christ's second coming we have sure hope because we accept his first coming with firm faith. What God promised was fulfilled in the first coming of Christ and what God still promises will be fulfilled in the second coming of Christ. Because we believe that Christ came once, we believe he will come again. One promise fulfilled is a pledge of a promise yet to be fulfilled.

God taught his people through the prophets to hope for salvation despite their sinfulness. He so loved the world that in the fullness of time he sent his only Son, born of the Virgin Mary, to be our Savior. In fulfillment of God's will, the Son gave himself up to death, but by rising from the dead he destroyed death and restored life.

That wonderful story of our faith is meant to engender within us a great confidence about our ultimate future.

The First Preface for Advent Masses summarizes the meaning of this liturgical season. It states: "When Jesus humbled himself to come among us as a man, he fulfilled the plan you formed long ago and opened for us the way to salvation." That is the event we will celebrate every Christmas. Next the Preface states: "Now we watch for the day, hoping that the salvation promised us will be ours when Christ our Lord will come again in his glory." That is the future we await in hope.

Hoping for a bright future is a real part of life, and it is of the essence of the season of Advent.

Second Sunday of Advent, C

The Baptist Deserves Imitation
Ba 5:1-9; Ph 1:4-6, 8-11; Lk 3:1-6

On this Sunday and the next John the Baptist fills a prominent role in the Gospel. The liturgy emphasizes him, not because of any personal qualities he possessed, but because of his relationship with Jesus.

John was born by the special providence of God of parents who were far beyond the age for child bearing. When the time came to circumcise the infant and give him his name, Zechariah his father was filled with the Holy Spirit. Looking at his son, Zechariah declared: "You, my child, shall be called the prophet of the Most High, for you shall go before the Lord to prepare his way."

This declaration John the Baptist fulfilled precisely. In the Gospel of this Sunday, we hear of him that his message was: "Make ready the way of the Lord, clear him a straight path." Next Sunday we will hear him protest, "There is one to come who is mightier than I. I am not fit to loosen his sandal strap."

The purpose of John's entire life was to point to the Messiah. In fact, we do not think of John without thinking of Jesus. The two go together as the dawn precedes the day, as opening a book reveals its contents, as the work of the chef in the kitchen leads to a banquet in the dining room. Quite an honor for the Baptist and surely an appropriate model for us all.

The Church's prayer book during morning prayer repeats what is called the canticle of Zechariah (or in Latin the *Benedictus*) within which we hear the words he addressed to his son: "You, my child, shall be called the prophet of the Most High, for you will go before the Lord to prepare his way." These words we should hear as addressed equally to ourselves. In baptism we were given a name, not just our personal name, but our family name, "Christian." We fulfill our Christian identity when we direct our lives to Christ and manifest him to others.

To be a "prophet of the Most High" means that our words and actions proclaim our faith in Christ. Our way of living is such that Christ is the truth who guides us in everything. We have his values, we follow his teachings, we embrace his dedication to his Father.

As dawn reflects the rays of the sun which is about to rise, so the love we extend to others begins to warm their hearts and enlightens them to know that Christ is not dead but alive and active within us.

The devotion we show for the liturgy, especially the celebration of the Holy Eucharist, makes it clear that we know that Christ prepared a banquet for us through a special labor, his sacrificial death on the cross, and that in the Mass we delight in that "divine meal in which Christ is consumed, the memory of his passion is recalled, our souls are filled with grace, and we receive a pledge of future glory" (St. Thomas Aquinas).

The liturgy of these two Sundays affords us the grace to imitate John the Baptist. We become like him, not by wearing sackcloth and dining on grasshoppers, but by living in such a way that it is obvious that if our faith in Christ were not true, our lives would make no sense.

Third Sunday of Advent, C

Christmas Leads to Easter
Zp 3:14-18; Ph 4:4-7; Lk 3:10-18

During Advent we love looking forward to Christmas because it is such a happy event. St. Paul today before December 25th occurs invites us to "Rejoice in the Lord always!" Is Christmas our favorite day among all the Church's celebrations? Possibly it is, and yet there is a day which is even more important. That day is Easter.

While keeping, and even enhancing, all the wonderful feelings we have about Christmas, we should try to appreciate the connection between what we celebrate at Christmas and what we celebrate at Easter. There was a Christmas only so that there could be an Easter. John the Baptist proclaimed the coming of the Messiah. He helped people to see that the Messiah was present among them. But there was more. St. Luke throughout his Gospel shows Jesus, the Messiah, in a relentless journey to Jerusalem, the city where he would die and be raised from the dead. The birth of Jesus led to the Paschal Mystery of his death, burial, and resurrection.

The Paschal Mystery was considered so central to our faith, so essential to why we gather to give thanks and praise to God our Father, that the early Church for almost three hundred years celebrated no aspect of the life of Christ other than the Paschal Mystery. There was no celebration of Christmas until around the year 336, but even then Christmas was seen only in relationship to the Paschal Mystery.

Our Catholic faith is precise. The Son of God exists from all eternity, which is to say that he is without beginning and without end. The Son is divine, equal to the Father in all things. The Son is God. As God he cannot suffer, he cannot die. But when the Son was conceived by the power of the Holy Spirit in the womb of Mary, he took human nature to himself and was given the name of Jesus. Jesus is one Person, the Son of God, but in Jesus there are two natures, one divine and one human. That is what we mean by the technical term, "the hypostatic union."

Once the Son of God became human, he freely subjected himself to all things human except sin. Then he could and did suffer and die. Awesome though it is, the Son of God died on the cross in his human nature. That statement may seem outrageous to anyone who fails to understand or to accept Catholic doctrine, but it is perfectly correct. In fact, if the Son of God did not die for us, we are still in our sins and we are most pitiable indeed.

But the Son of God did die. The truth is that the value of all that Jesus said and did came from the fact that he is one divine Person, the Beloved Son of the Father, who took on our human nature so that he could fully enter into our human condition, even to the extent of suffering and dying for us.

For our salvation the Son came down from heaven. Born of the Virgin Mary, he became human. He suffered, died, and was buried. This he did for our sake. Christmas is incomplete without Easter. The crib leads to the cross. A child is born so that we may be reborn through his death and resurrection. Rejoice in the Lord always! I say it again. Rejoice, because Christmas leads to Easter.

Fourth Sunday of Advent, C

Mary Manifests the Christmas Spirit
Mi 5:1-4; Heb 10:5-10; Lk 1:39-45

I cannot define the Christmas spirit, but I know what it means. I think we all do. It is distinguished by cheerful kindness and unselfish generosity. It is just the opposite of the attitude of Dickens' fictional character, Scrooge, who greeted Christmas with "Bah! Humbug!"

A real person, and not a fictional character, exemplifies the Christmas spirit. That person is Mary. She does so in an eminent manner in the episode which forms the Gospel for this Fourth Sunday of Advent, an event which we call the Visitation. Mary had just conceived Jesus by the power of the Holy Spirit. It all seemed impossible, just too good to be true. To give Mary assurance, the angel informed her that Elizabeth, her elderly relative, had also conceived and that she was already in her sixth month. Impossible? The angel said, "Nothing is impossible with God."

It was as if, however, Mary needed no assurance. As soon as she learned about Elizabeth, her thoughts turned immediately from the magnificent reality of what had just occurred in her womb and focused on her relative in need. She forgot about herself. She spent not even a moment in reflecting on how blessed she had been by God. St. Luke in the Gospel tells us that Mary set out, proceeding in haste to Elizabeth's home. She went in haste, so eager was she to help the old woman who, Mary realized, at her age would find extra difficulties in her pregnancy. Mary would shower Elizabeth with cheerful kindness and unselfish generosity. Even before Christmas existed, Mary manifested the Christmas spirit.

I find a model of the Christmas spirit in what is expected of a priest at Mass. After receiving Holy Communion, a priest is required to minister the body and the blood of the Lord to his people. He is not allowed to pause for personal devotion, to retire to his chair to rest and reflect on the magnificent gift God has given him. Often he may want to meditate on how he has been blessed in a manner which is not entirely unlike what happened to Mary when the Son of God became flesh in her womb. Instead he is directed to be like Mary, to go, as it were, in haste to serve God's people. Personal piety comes later.

All Catholics must seek from the liturgy the models of their Christmas spirit. Reflect on what happens to you at Mass which suggests the spirit of cheerful kindness and unselfish generosity.

After the homily we find petitions in the Prayer of the Faithful which are basically unselfish, outgoing, for the sake of others who are in need. When you are invited to offer a sign of peace, see in that gesture a reminder that you are to have care and concern for others.

Notice the ministers at the altar. The girls and boys are called "servers." They suggest that we must serve one another. The lector, or reader, nourishes us with the truth, just as we must speak the truth in love to each other. The ministers of Holy Communion bring the Lord to you, as we must bring the Lord to each other through our eagerness to help anyone in need.

Mary did not say "Bah" to Elizabeth or to anyone in need. She had no "humbug" within her. She exemplifies for us the true Christmas spirit.

Solemnity of Christmas, C

God Gives All That He Has
Is 62:1-5; Ac 13:16-17, 22-25; Mt 1:1-25

When people are preparing a list of those to whom they wish to give Christmas presents, they may come across the name of a person about whom they ask themselves, "What do you give to someone who has everything?"

We can turn the question around and ask, "What does the person who has everything give to others?" The answer is that he gives everything, and the person is, of course, God.

The "everything" that God has given us is eternal life. He has wrapped his gift, so to speak, in the humanity of his divine Son. That is what St. John had in mind when he wrote in his First Epistle, "God has given us life, and this life is in his Son."

God chose to give us the gift of eternal life, not in some vague or nebulous fashion. Rather he chose a reality, the Incarnation of his Son, of which again St. John wrote in the introduction to his First Epistle: "This is what we proclaim to you... what we have heard, what we have seen with our eyes, what we have looked upon and our hands have touched — we speak of the word of life. This life became visible; we have seen and bear witness to it."

We give our Christmas gifts only once a year, but God continues to give us his gift every Sunday, even every day, whenever we participate in the Mass. He gives this gift as a continuation of the Incarnation. God gives us the gift of his life in his Son through the Word and the Sacrament of the Mass. When we listen to the Scriptures at Mass, we hear the Word of Life and the voice of Christ. When we receive Holy Communion, we receive the life-giving body and blood of Christ.

For many of us Christmas is a time of abundance. With all the food and drink, the cookies and the candies, we have to be practical at some point and warn ourselves that we can have too much of a good thing. God always offers us an abundance at Mass, but of his wonderful generosity we need never say, "Too much of a good thing." In fact, we can never have too much of the Eucharist. With each Holy Communion we are offered the grace of growing in such a way that we become more open to receive the fullness of God's life. God's gift is never limited, only our capacity, and that capacity can increase by cooperating with the gift of the Eucharist.

The Church in order to act in accord with God's generosity offers us the Mass not just once a year at Christmas, not just once a week on Sundays, but even every day.

The truth of Christmas is beautiful, that in the flesh of an infant the eternal Son of God, in whom dwells the fullness of divinity, came to live among us. The scene of the crib is touching. Christmas cards which depict that scene can be beautiful. But we must remember that the reality of God's gift, two thousand years after the event, is presented to us again and again in the celebration of the Holy Eucharist.

Solemnity of Christmas, C (alternate)

Come to Bethlehem
Is 62:11-12; Tt 3:4-7; Lk 2:15-20

We believe that the birth of Jesus is the birth of the Messiah. For centuries the Chosen People looked for him. When he appeared he did so in an unexpected way, not in the pomp of a mighty monarch, but in the humble littleness of an infant.

In accord with the manner of Jesus' coming among us, the first people to be called to the crib were humble, poor people. They were the shepherds living in the fields whose task was considered menial and whose status was thought to be lowly. After hearing the message of the angel, they said to one another, "Let us go over to Bethlehem and see this event which the Lord has made known to us."

There was some surprise in the message of the angels. Even though Bethlehem was David's city, no king had sat on his throne for centuries, most people had forgotten that a royal Savior was to come from that village, and no one thought he would be found in a cave that sheltered animals, in a manger from which the animals were fed.

And yet the shepherds, in response to the good news from the angel, did the right thing in going to look for Christ and they went to the correct place. They manifested a profound wisdom even before the arrival of those travelers from the East whom we now call the Wise Men.

Throughout life we must look for Christ and hope that we do not miss him wherever he may be found, since he will often show up in unexpected circumstances. He is with the homeless and the undocumented for whom there is no room in the inn of our society. He is with the hungry who would be happy to be as well fed as many animals and pets in our society. He is with those who accept the most humble and menial tasks, as did the shepherds who first went to Bethlehem. We must never miss Christ no matter where he may be found.

 Wherever we search for Christ, we must above all else return to our Bethlehem. The literal meaning of this word in Hebrew is "House of Bread." Jesus was made flesh in the womb of Mary and born in Bethlehem, the "House of Bread," so that he could give us his flesh as our spiritual bread. His birth was the turning point in history. How privileged was Mary to give birth to this child. How blessed was Joseph to share Mary's joy. How favored were the angels to announce this good news. How fortunate were the shepherds to witness the event. And yet we need not feel deprived. Every church where Mass is celebrated becomes a new Bethlehem, not only at Christmas but every day of the year.

 The church is not the only place to find Christ. We can never forget his presence in people, especially in the poor, and yet the church during the liturgy is the most important presence for us. In our response to the Gospel, the good news, we are not contemporary shepherds in our journey to Bethlehem since now it is Christ who is the Shepherd who searches us out and beckons us to the liturgy. Within the celebration of the Holy Eucharist, he feeds us with his own body and blood and the church becomes a new Bethlehem, a house of spiritual bread. We do the correct thing when we come to church, our Bethlehem, to find Christ.

Feast of the Holy Family, C

It's Tough to Be a Family
Si 3:2-6, 12-14; Col 3:12-21; Lk 2:41-52

This Sunday's feast of the Holy Family presents a model for all Christian families. Some people think the model is not really very practical. After all, what kind of a model is a family comprised of two saints and the Son of God? It seems too much to ask any of us today to follow the example of the Holy Family.

Actually the ideal is even more demanding than it seems at first glance, since the Holy Family in Nazareth was founded upon the Divine Family in heaven. Jesus could have come into our world as an adult of the rabbinic age of thirty, the age at which he began his public ministry, but such was not the Father's will. God the Father brought his Son into our world within a family because he wanted the earthly beginnings of his Son to reflect his eternal origin in the Trinity. God's life is a family life: from all eternity the Father gives life and being to his Son through the love of the Holy Spirit.

The Church in the liturgy of this Sunday proposes the Holy Family of Jesus, Mary, and Joseph as a model to be followed, but we must realize that the ultimate model is the life of God himself. St. Paul wrote to the Ephesians, "I kneel before God the Father from whom every family in heaven and on earth takes it name" (3:14).

We should not think of the Trinity as if it were some kind of mathematical puzzle. One word summarizes the inner life of the Triune God; that word is "relationships." God is relationships. The Father gives himself completely to the Son. The Son responds with complete absorption in his Father. The two are devoted to each other in the unifying love of the Holy Spirit.

The Holy Family reflects these relationships of God as

three persons who are devoted to each other in love. The realization that God's life is the ultimate model for human families should not discourage us from striving for the ideal. Rather it should help us to understand why we seem to fail in reaching the ideal. In trying to live a life of family love, we are reaching beyond the stars to become like God.

That kind of an ideal is worth working toward. God thinks so too. That is why he placed Jesus, not only within the family of Nazareth, but within the family of the Church, especially during the celebration of the liturgy of the Mass.

At Mass we constantly hear the guiding word of Jesus, his advice and teaching, on how to live a life of love. At Mass we receive the power to follow that teaching as we receive the body and the blood of the Lord in Holy Communion. In the liturgy God shows that he is earnest about our both knowing and following the ideal of family life.

The life of the Holy Family should not seem lost to us in the pages of the New Testament. Even the family life of the Trinity should not seem distant from us in some far-off heavenly country. God is close to us in the liturgy. He wants to make his family life come alive in our human families as he made it come alive in the Holy Family of Jesus, Mary, and Joseph.

New Year's Day, C

A New Year's Meditation on Time
Nb 6:22-27; Gal 4:4-7; Lk 2:16-21

During a football game on TV some announcers at intervals indicate, "Time out on the field." That leads me to wonder whether "time is out" somewhere other than on the playing field. Certainly not in the real world. Time we cannot stop.

Cardinal Henry Edward Manning in his book on the priesthood wrote, "Time is so precious that God gives it to us only moment by moment and he never gives us a single moment without taking the previous moment away."

Time is God's precious creation and priceless gift to us, even though God lives in eternity, without beginning, without interval, without end. The concept of eternity is completely befuddling to us, but time itself is by no means easy to comprehend. We measure a year by the journey of our planet around the sun, which consumes 365 days, 5 hours, 48 minutes, and 46 seconds. Having looked up that precise information in an astronomy book, we feel no closer to understanding time.

We experience time, but we are defeated in trying to define it satisfactorily. What is clear to us is that God is not only the creator of time but its master, and that God from the inscrutable point of eternity chooses to work in time, indeed to accomplish our salvation within time.

The liturgy, borrowing as is its wont from Scripture, acknowledges before God: "In the fullness of time you sent your only Son to be our Savior" (see Galatians 4:4 and the Fourth Eucharistic Prayer). That is a curious expression, "the fullness of time." It makes us wonder precisely how time can be full, or empty for that matter.

That expression suggests to me that God took all the moments of time from creation until the coming of his Son, and pressed them together, so to speak, into one supreme moment in which all the events which had transpired until that instant found their meaning and purpose. Or perhaps better, God placed all the previous moments, one on top of the other, until they reached a pinnacle, a summit which, if your imagination will allow it, reached high enough to touch heaven and summon into time the eternal Son of God.

As from that moment all previous moments derived their significance, so all moments which have followed flow from it and take their meaning. Where we are going in time depends on whether we have grasped in faith the meaning of the Incarnation, the coming of God's Son into the world and into time. Time has meaning for us because the Son of God gave it meaning.

You may be thinking, in the lyrics of William Gilbert, "poor wandering one." Yes, these thoughts are somewhat meandering but it is overwhelming to meditate on what deceptively seems to be such a simple thing, a reality which we usually take for granted, but which on this New Year's Day demands profound gratitude to an eternal God who has blessed us with the gift of time within which he has sent to us his divine Son.

Solemnity of the Epiphany, C

The Journey of the Magi
Is 60:1-6; Eph 3:2-3, 5-6; Mt 2:1-12

The feast of the Epiphany has a special character because of our image of the Magi. Today the elegantly robed Magi and their majestic camels become part of the crib. Soon the crib will be taken down and there will be nothing to do with the Magi except to put them back into their box until next year.

I wonder what became of the real Magi after they had offered their homage to the Divine Infant. T.S. Eliot composed a poem which he entitled, "The Journey of the Magi," in which he presents one of the Magi as telling their story. The poem begins:

> "A cold coming we had of it,
> Just the worst time of the year
> For a journey, and such a long journey:
> The ways deep and the weather sharp,
> The very dead of winter."

That introduction dispels any romantic notions we may have about how the Magi came from their homeland to a distant land to greet an unknown King. Eliot then reflects that the Magi after their arrival did more than admire or even honor Jesus. They somehow came to realize that Jesus wanted to become the King of their hearts, and that such an enthronement required a change in their lives. Jesus' birth meant that they would have to die to a life which did not include him. The poem continues:

> "… were we led all that way for
> Birth or Death? There was a Birth, certainly,

We had evidence and no doubt. I had seen birth and death,
But had thought they were different; this Birth was
Hard and bitter agony for us, like Death, our death."

Eliot does not tell us what he thought finally happened to the Magi (and neither does St. Matthew in his Gospel story), but he offers us an opportunity to speculate on the outcome as we read the final words of the narrator:

"We returned to our places, these Kingdoms,
But no longer at ease here, in the old dispensation,
With an alien people clutching their gods.
I should be glad of another death."

The Magi had to face something called death in the moment in which they were experiencing a birth. In the liturgical celebration of the Solemnity of the Epiphany, we do the same. The Gospel narrative of the manifestation of Jesus to the Magi leads us to the celebration of the Eucharist, the sacrament which is the living memorial of the sacrifice of Christ, his death and resurrection.

We make a leap in time, so to speak, from the simple, precious days of Jesus' infancy to the awesome moments of his maturity in which he offered himself on the cross for the world's salvation. Jesus, King though he was, did not deem majesty a greater reality than his Priesthood. The reason Jesus was born, the reason he came into the world, was to be a witness to the truth that God his Father wanted us and everyone to be saved through his sacrifice.

The human birth of Jesus meant he would die. Our birth through baptism requires that we must die with him by our sharing in the Eucharist. Celebrating the Eucharist means that we must not attempt to live like pagans clutching our gods of sinfulness.

Through our devout sharing in the Holy Eucharist we determine how our journey as present day Magi will end.

Solemnity of the Epiphany, C (Alternate)

Epiphany Leads to Pentecost
Is 60:1-6; Eph 3:2-3, 5-6; Mt 2:1-12

Christmas does not seem to be the time to think about Good Friday and Easter Sunday, and today's feast of the Epiphany does not seem to have anything in common with Pentecost. The truth is that all of these great events are related.

First, the purpose of the birth of Jesus is revealed through what happened on Good Friday. Jesus became human because in his divinity he could not suffer and die. Dying was the means for overcoming sin and death. When he took a nature like our own, when he became human like us in all things but sin, it became possible for him to fulfill his Father's plan for our salvation. When we celebrate Christmas we do not remove the crucifix from our churches. We know that the crib leads to the cross. The cross does not confuse or embarrass us since we also know that the tomb of Jesus was empty on Easter Sunday because Jesus had been raised from the dead.

Christmas celebrates the coming of God's Son into our world to be our Savior. The events of Good Friday and Easter Sunday reveal just how Jesus was to be our Savior, which was through his death and resurrection. Christmas is really incomplete without the death and the resurrection of Jesus.

Today's feast of the Epiphany shows that Jesus became human in order to be the Savior for everyone, that one day he would open his arms on the cross to embrace us all, that he was the Savior not only of the Jewish people but of all of God's people.

Pentecost confirms the meaning of Jesus' mission as a universal Savior. As Epiphany manifests the meaning of Christmas, so Pentecost manifests the meaning of Good Friday and Easter Sunday. Looking at these realities more profoundly, we can say that Christmas celebrates the birth of Jesus, and Good Friday and Easter celebrate the birth of Christ. The first part of this statement is obvious; the second may not be so. The writings of the New Testament, especially the Acts of the Apostles and the epistles of St. Paul, have given the term "Christ" a technical significance beyond its literal meaning of "the anointed one." It refers to Jesus who through his death and resurrection has been exalted as Lord and Christ, the Head of the mystical body, the Church.

Jesus was born as an individual so that he could gather the people of his Church into one body, his mystical body, the Church. Jesus Christ is now more than an individual. He is the Head of his body, the Church. He is inseparably united with his members.

Christmas is clear. We need to be clear about the meaning of the death of Jesus. The Church teaches us that "it was from the side of Christ as he slept the sleep of death upon the cross that there came forth the wondrous sacrament which is the whole Church." "The Church appeared before the whole world on the day of Pentecost." (See the *Constitution on the Liturgy*, 5 and 6.)

The Solemnity of the Epiphany should not be seen in isolation. It is an integral part of the central truths of our faith.

The word "epiphany" means "manifestation" or "revelation." What God revealed in the event we call the Epiphany was proclaimed on the day of Pentecost. What Jesus accomplished through his mission on this earth, he did for the whole world, for all people of all time.

Baptism of the Lord, C

With Christ Up to Jerusalem
Is 42:1-4, 6-7; Ac 10:34-38; Lk 3:15-16, 21-22

We have been commemorating the beautiful events of the infancy of Jesus since Christmas day. In the liturgy of this Sunday, however, we witness Jesus as an adult. We see him being baptized, and we hear the voice of God the Father saying to him: "You are my beloved Son. On you my favor rests."

The liturgical feast of the Baptism of the Lord concludes the Church's celebration of Christmas. It helps to remind us that Jesus was born to be our Savior. His baptism marks the beginning of his public ministry which culminates in his paschal sacrifice, his death and resurrection. Jesus was born to die. He came into the world to offer himself in a perfect sacrifice to his heavenly Father for the salvation of the whole world.

This year will feature the Gospel according to St. Luke. All through his Gospel St. Luke presents Jesus as on a relentless journey to the city of Jerusalem since it is there that he will fulfill his mission. Remember that forty days after his birth, Jesus was brought by Mary and Joseph from Bethlehem to the temple in Jerusalem. That event symbolized that the purpose of his birth would be accomplished in the Holy City.

When Jesus was twelve, Mary and Joseph feared that he had become lost during their pilgrimage to Jerusalem for the feast of the Passover. Jesus seemed surprised that they did not understand that he would be in his Father's house, the temple of Jerusalem. That temple he would replace in his own person through his sacrifice on the cross, and he would thereby fulfill the meaning of the Passover which his parents had come to Jerusalem to celebrate.

At a critical moment during his public ministry, Jesus said to the apostles, "We must now go up to Jerusalem so that all that was written concerning the Son of Man may be accomplished. They will scourge him and put him to death, and on the third day he will rise again" (Luke 18:31-32).

Although the baptism of Jesus was not the sacrament which we receive, our baptism is related to his. Our baptism marked the beginning of our Christian lives. God the Father looked upon us with pride and declared, "You are beloved children, my sons and daughters, upon whom my favor rests."

Because we are the sisters and brothers of Jesus as part of God's family, we share his destiny. Baptism begins our journey up to Jerusalem with Christ to share in his Paschal Mystery. The journey will culminate for us, as it did for Jesus, with death and resurrection. But the Christian life is a constant, relentless journey with Christ up to Jerusalem.

The church, our place of worship, is our Jerusalem. Our gathering every Sunday is the enduring characteristic of the sons and daughters of God. The Eucharist is our paschal sacrifice, our sacrament of sharing in the death and resurrection of Christ. Do you not know that on the Lord's day we must all be in our Father's house? As we enter our spiritual Jerusalem we find a font. We bless ourselves with its holy water. That action is meant to be a reminder of our baptism, that great event which brought us into God's family and formed us into such an intimate union with the Son of God that his destiny is our own.

The Season of Lent and Easter
Cycle C

"Lent is a preparation for Easter.
The fifty days from Easter Sunday to Pentecost
are celebrated in joyful exaltation as one
feast day, or better as one 'great Sunday.'"
(*General Norms for the Liturgical Year*, 22 and 27)

First Sunday of Lent, C

Keep Your Bags Packed
Dt 26:4-10; Rm 10:8-13; Lk 4:1-13

The genial Pope John XXIII was seventy-seven years of age when he was elected to the papacy in 1958. He realized that his time as Pope would probably be brief because of his age, but he faced that possibility without hesitation. He used to say, "I keep my bags packed." He was ready to begin his journey into eternal life whenever God chose to call him.

St. Luke the evangelist shows us that Jesus throughout his life was on a relentless journey up to Jerusalem where he would fulfill the Paschal Mystery of his death and resurrection. Before he began his public ministry, Jesus went into the desert to prepare himself for his spiritual journey.

In the desert Jesus, so to speak, emptied his bags of the temptations which became part of him when he entered our human condition. First, he threw out selfishness. The devil tempted him to use his power for himself, for his own convenience, by turning stone into bread. But Jesus patiently was awaiting the day when he would turn bread into his body and wine into his blood as the living memorial of his sacrifice on the cross for our sake.

Next Jesus threw out the false worship which is known as materialism. The devil promised him the power and the glory of the kingdoms of this world if only he would fall down and worship the devil. But Jesus was preparing to proclaim the coming of the kingdom of God, not that of Satan.

Finally Jesus emptied his bags of pride. The devil tempted Jesus to throw himself off the parapet of the temple in a spectacular show of his power before the crowds who had gathered for a Jewish feast. But Jesus was about to proclaim the doctrine of simplicity, humility, and meekness as the characteristics of those who would become like little children in the kingdom of God their Father.

Having emptied his bags of all the junk, Jesus who was himself already full of the Holy Spirit, filled his bags with gifts of the Holy Spirit for us, such as faith, hope, and love. Then he set out on the journey of his public ministry, a journey to be completed in the city of Jerusalem. There he would suffer, die, and be raised up on the third day.

We began our journey when we were baptized. We were given the grace to throw sin into the trash can and fill our bags with the gifts of faith, hope, and love, but throughout life we seem to keep making the mistake of putting the wrong stuff back into our bags. God is patient with us and our mistakes. Every year he gives us the season of Lent as our opportunity to reject the wrong values and to choose the right ones. Lent is the time for looking into the bags where we keep what is most important to us and to decide what we will throw out and what we will put in.

John XXIII who kept his bags packed had much in common with Jesus, even though when Jesus began his public ministry he was about forty-seven years younger than the Pope was when he began his papacy. Whatever our age, Lent means going on a journey toward Easter and the celebration of the Paschal Mystery. It is a journey we will take every year until we finally pass through the doors of death and enter eternal life.

Second Sunday of Lent, C

Lent Is a Time for Growth
Gn 15:5-12, 17-18; Ph 3:17-4:1; Lk 9:28-36

We can look at Lent in one of two ways. We can see it negatively as a time of deprivation, or we can see it positively as an opportunity for growth. The Church hopes that we can all have a positive spirit because Lent offers us the opportunity for the transformation of our lives. That is real growth.

Jesus in the Gospel of this second Sunday of Lent reveals the great Lenten theme of transformation. He begins to reveal the Paschal Mystery. He went up a mountain to pray. There he became transfigured. His face changed and his garments became dazzlingly white. This manifestation prefigured the glory that would come to him through his death and resurrection. It helps us to understand that it pleased God to lead his Son through suffering to joy, through humiliation to exaltation, and through death to life. That is the transformation which is at the heart of Lent.

To some people human existence appears to be a relentless journey in which we go full circle from nothing to nothing. In Shakespeare's play, *As You Like It*, one of the characters, Jaques, reflects on seven phases of life from birth to death. His soliloquy is famous because of its opening lines, "All the world's a stage, and all the men and women merely players." He concludes by saying, "The last scene of all that ends this strange eventful history is second childishness and mere oblivion." Shakespeare loved the stage but he disagreed with the character he had created, and so do we. The Paschal Mystery of the death and resurrection of Jesus tells us that life does not end in oblivion.

God's plan for us is to share in this mystery. We began our sharing through baptism. With Christ we died to sin so that we could begin a new life. It was a transformation for us. We were given a white garment to remind us that we had become like Jesus in his transfiguration. As the transfiguration for Jesus was but a prelude to his resurrection, so baptism directs us to a future event. That event is our sharing in the glory of Christ's resurrection.

The body and the blood of the Lord in the Eucharist nourish us on our way to our destiny. At Mass we go in procession to the communion station, a symbol of a people who are on a journey. Standing to receive communion is a sign of our faith in the promise of Jesus, "Those who eat my flesh and drink my blood have life eternal and I will raise them up on the last day" (John 6:54).

As baptism begins our sharing in the Paschal Mystery, so the Eucharist will perfect and complete it. We must never forget that the Mass is our means for participating in the Paschal Mystery since the Eucharist is the sacrament of the death and the resurrection of Christ. In the Mass we find the meaning and purpose of human existence.

The world is not a stage upon which a play is enacted. Rather the world is part of God's kingdom of truth and life. And the truth is that we are on a journey, but our journey is not a death march. We do not end as we began in a "second childishness." Instead we come to the fullness of our likeness to Christ as the mature children of God. Our inheritance from a loving Father is everlasting life.

Third Sunday of Lent, C

The Three Realities of Lent
Ex 3:1-8, 13-15; 1 Cor 10:1-6, 10-12; Lk 13:1-9

Most children, especially in the "old days," did not like the season of Lent. The reason was that at the insistence of their parents they had to give up things they liked, such as eating candy and going to the movies. Not eating candy was hard enough, but not going to movies was really a sacrifice because there was no television. Of course parents had in mind only the spiritual welfare of their children.

The Church, like a good parent, has our spiritual welfare in mind during this season of Lent, but we must rise above childish limitations to appreciate its value. To begin with, the Church sees Lent as related to three realities of our life of faith.

The first reality is the Paschal Mystery, the sacrificial death and resurrection of Jesus which brings about our salvation. The Church developed Lent precisely as a preparation for the celebration of this great event at Easter. The Paschal Mystery is at the very heart of our faith in Christ.

Through the Paschal Mystery the Church came into being. Pope Pius XII wrote in 1943: "The Church was born from the side of our Savior on the cross like a new Eve, mother of all the living" (*Mystici Corporis*, 29). From this truth flows the second reality, Christian initiation. Very early in our history it became clear that the most appropriate time to introduce new members into the Church through the spiritual birth of baptism was at that time when the Church was celebrating her own birth. Lent became a season of special preparation for baptism, and Easter was understood to be the ideal time for the celebration of this sacrament or for its renewal.

The third reality is repentance and renewal. The Church recognizes that Easter is the time for Catholics to become reconciled to God and his Church through repentance and the celebration of the sacrament of penance. Each year one reality takes on a prominence, and this year it is the turn of repentance to occupy the center of our attention. The Church gives this emphasis through her selection of the Gospels for the Sundays of Lent. (When candidates for baptism are present, the readings of the A cycle which are important to Christian initiation may be used.)

This Sunday you will hear Jesus refer to tragedies which had recently occurred. From these two mishaps he drew a lesson: to judge the victims as guilty of sin is not the correct response, but to think about one's own need for repentance is. Next Sunday you will hear Jesus tell a beautiful story which illustrates how eager God the Father is to offer forgiveness to all his children when they repent. This story has come to be known as the parable of the prodigal son. On the Fifth Sunday of Lent you will see Jesus forgiving the woman who was caught in adultery. He saw in her heart the spark of repentance which he turned into a flame of love. Jesus wants the same for us.

All three realities are present in every Lent, but this year we should turn our attention to our need for repentance, and we should begin to make plans to celebrate the sacrament of penance as an important part of our preparation for Easter.

Fourth Sunday of Lent, C

Penance Is a Goal of Lent
Jos 5:9, 10-12; 2 Cor 5:17-21; Lk 15:1-3, 11-32

Jesus' parables are so drawn from experiences in life that the fictional characters in them seem to be real people. Perhaps most realistic is the prodigal son. His story illustrates for us the meaning of the sacrament of penance. Lent is a particularly appropriate season to celebrate the sacrament of penance, especially during one of the penance services before Easter.

This Sunday we see in St. Luke's Gospel how happy the father was when his prodigal son returned home. The fact that the father insisted on an elaborate banquet to celebrate the return of his lost child should encourage us to prepare for the sacrament of penance with confidence in God's mercy. God our Father eagerly wishes to celebrate our repentance.

The young son's repentance is our model. After having squandered his inheritance, he came to his senses. He abandoned his dissolute way of living and resolved to return to his father. He prepared to confess his sins and to make an act of contrition. Before asking to be forgiven, he resolved to change his life.

In an earlier era of the Church people confessed their sins to the bishop on Ash Wednesday. Sackcloth was given them to wear, ashes were sprinkled on their heads, and their names were entered in the book of penitents. The bishop assigned a penance which was to be performed during the entire season of Lent. This penance was medicinal rather than punitive; it was a way of bringing about a cure for the disease of sin rather than a form of punishment for a crime. That is the spirit of the prodigal's father.

The penance was suited to the sin. If people had been selfish and greedy, they were required to distribute alms to the poor. If they had been guilty of self-indulgence, they were directed to fast and abstain from choice foods. If they had been negligent of God, they were given a regimen of prayer, The purpose of the penance was to effect a change of heart. In a special ceremony on Holy Thursday morning the penitents received absolution from the bishop and that evening they participated in the celebration of the Mass of the Lord's Supper. In our times we have inverted the order of the sacrament. We confess our sins, receive absolution, and then only later do we perform our penance. From the earlier practice of the Church, we can learn an important lesson, that we should not wait until we go to confession and receive an official penance from the priest. We ought to practice penance long before we approach the priest. In other words, we ought to be working during the entire season of Lent to change our lives.

The first step is to examine our conscience, to come to our senses about the way we are living. We need to have an honest talk with ourselves, as did the prodigal son, about what we have done and what we have failed to do in our relationship with God and his people. We need to ask ourselves where we are going in life. When we recognize what we must change, we should decide on a penance, a practice that will turn our lives around.

If we enter into the spirit of repentance and participate properly in the sacrament of penance, at the end of Lent we will hear God our Father say, "Let us eat and celebrate for my children have come back to me."

Fifth Sunday of Lent, C

Christ Casts No Stones
Is 43:16-21; Ph 3:8-14; Jn 8:1-11

Lent is drawing to a close and it is time for conscientious Catholics to plan to celebrate the sacrament of penance. The liturgical Scriptures of this Sunday, only two weeks before Easter, help us to understand the disposition we should bring to the sacrament.

The dramatic scene of this Sunday's Gospel is the familiar one in which the scribes and Pharisees led before Jesus a woman who had been caught in adultery. The situation has given an expression to our language: "Don't be the first to throw a stone." We might well conclude, then, that the message of the Gospel is that we should not be quick to judge others. And that is indeed a valid application, as well as often a necessary one.

On the other hand, this episode tells us something very important about Jesus, our Savior. The scribes and the Pharisees thought they could trap Jesus in a dilemma. If he agreed that the woman should be stoned, they could accuse him of cruelty. If he declared that the woman should go free, they could accuse him of violating the law of Moses. When they asked, "What do you have to say about the case?" Jesus as usual refused to answer the question. Instead he first dismissed their stance as completely inane, as insignificant as the scribbles he traced on the ground with his finger. When they persisted in their questioning, he uttered his challenge: "Let the man among you who has no sin be the first to cast a stone at her."

Of course they all walked away. Jesus, who could have met his own challenge, preferred to offer the opportunity for conversion. He did not condone the sin the woman had committed. He granted her pardon, but he did instruct her, "From now on, avoid this sin." Jesus did not throw a stone at the woman, and he does not throw stones at us. God does not will the death of sinners but only that they be converted and live.

The vivid imagery of Isaiah in this Sunday's first reading is readily applied to Jesus: "… the Lord opens a way in the sea and a path in the mighty waters." In his compassion for us, Jesus always opens a way amid the sea of sin and shapes a path through the mighty waters of doubt and confusion. He is always eager to offer us forgiveness, as long as we try to follow his exhortation: "From now on, avoid sin." We must do the best we can.

What could have turned the woman away from adultery? What can turn us away from our sins, whatever they may be? St. Paul gives us his answer: "I have forfeited everything for Christ. I have accounted all else as rubbish so that Christ may be my wealth and I may be in him." Christ is rich in mercy; that is the wealth which can be ours through repentance.

On the first Sunday of Lent we saw the devil tempting Jesus to turn stones into bread. Stones do not interest Jesus, but bread does. In every Mass he transforms bread into his body and wine into his blood. Stones Jesus does not offer us, but he does offer his body given up for us and his blood poured out for us so that sins may be forgiven. The Eucharist is the sign that we need never fear to stand before Christ and acknowledge our sinfulness in the sacrament of penance. Christ casts no stones.

Passion or Palm Sunday, C

The Passover Moon of Easter
Is 50:4-7; Ph 2:6-11; Lk 22:14-23:56

In one week we celebrate the great feast of Easter. It is the Sunday which follows the first full moon after the spring equinox. This full moon signifies the Passover of our ancestors in faith. It is a sign of the fullness of God's love which he manifested toward his people when he freed them from slavery in Egypt. That same moon now shows the fullness of God's love for us which he manifested through the death and resurrection of his Son. St. John in his Gospel wrote: "Before the feast of the passover, Jesus realized that the hour had come for him to pass from this world to the Father. He had loved his own in this world, and he would show his love for them to the end" (13:1).

The moon is full each month when it turns its face directly toward the sun. It then reflects as completely as it can the light of the sun. The sun represents God. We are the moon.

At times in our lives we reflect, like a full moon, the love and goodness of God. One of these times is the great celebration of Easter. Catholics who have been away from church for a year, or possibly longer, return home like prodigal children. Those who have stayed home all the time learn the lesson the father wanted to teach the prodigal's older brother: "You are with me always and everything I have is yours, but we have to celebrate and rejoice because those who were lost have been found." Faith now reflects God's love and goodness.

The people who prepared for Easter by means of the sacrament of penance are resolved to follow the urging of Jesus to the woman whom he had forgiven, "From now on, avoid sin." And especially at Easter the men and women who have been initiated into the Church through the sacraments of baptism, confirmation, and First Eucharist are filled with a joyful love which reflects in a beautiful luster the splendor of God's goodness. Their lives have become like the full moon.

In nature the full moon inevitably wanes. Little by little it reflects less and less of the sun's brilliance. It need not be that way with us. We do not have to see our fervor fade and allow our lives to become spiritually dull or dark. God's light and warmth are always before us. We must make sure we do not turn our face away from God, our Sun.

The first day of the week has been named for the sun. We also call it the Lord's Day. The Second Vatican Council has reminded us that, although Easter is our great memorial of the death and resurrection of Christ, we celebrate this Paschal Mystery every Sunday, the Lord's Day, and that "on this day Christ's faithful should come together into one place so that, by hearing the Word of God and taking part in the Eucharist, they may call to mind the death, resurrection, and the glorification of the Lord Jesus, and may thank God who has begotten us again through the resurrection of Jesus Christ from the dead unto a living hope" (*Constitution on the Liturgy*, 106).

Easter is our great day, and every Sunday is a little Easter. The celebration of Sunday Mass allows us to turn our faces toward God, the true Sun of our lives.

Solemnity of Easter, C (Saturday Evening)

Easter Means We Are Sure to Follow

Ex 14:15-15:1; Rm 6:3-11; Lk 24:1-12

Easter is meant to be a happy day. We should try to put aside, at least for today, our troubles and our worries and to open ourselves to a spirit of joy which is expressed in the one great word of Easter, "Alleluia." This Hebrew word need not and should not be translated. It is an expression of the heart more than of the mind. It suggests feelings which transcend the intellectual and represents a euphoria, a sense that all is right after all, that God is good and he is our God.

On the other hand, life is serious and Easter is concerned with the ultimate meaning and value of human existence. A reflection on its profundity lends a somewhat sober note to our otherwise jubilant celebration. This is what I mean. Easter is concerned with two realities about which no one alive has any direct experience. These two realities are death and resurrection. We have never personally gone through the awesome, dark doors of death. Nor have we heard from anyone who has passed to the "other side." Houdini, the famous magician, spent a fortune and endured an agony of effort in trying to contact his dead mother, all to no avail. No voice from the dead.

Since we have not experienced death, we have not experienced resurrection. And yet death is more real to us than resurrection. The reason is that we have observed death. We know its results. We have all lost loved ones, and we recognize that the loss cannot be recovered on this earth. Nothing seems more final than death. Resurrection is a hope which may seem weak in comparison with the obvious power of death.

Unlike Houdini, through faith we have heard a voice from beyond the grave. It is the voice of Jesus who says, "Peace. Do not be afraid." Our Savior has gone before us to lead the way and to show us that death will lead to the everlasting life of resurrection. Union with Christ is the motive for our hope.

I see an image of a train moving along its tracks at high speed. The passengers have never traveled this route before. Suddenly they enter a tunnel and the entire train is plunged into darkness. Surprised and shaken, the people wonder what has happened and worry whether there will be a disastrous crash.

What they do not see is that the engine has already emerged into brilliant daylight. The coaches in which they are riding are sure to follow. The only condition is that they remain coupled to one another and to the engine.

Christ has emerged from the dark tunnel of the tomb to the brilliant day of resurrection. We are sure to follow him — united as we are with each other and with him in the Church. Those who have been baptized have died and been buried with Christ, but they have also shared in his resurrection because they have received new life, the life of Christ. On this night all of us, newly baptized and veterans, receive the Holy Eucharist. The Holy Eucharist is the sacrament of unity. Through this great sacrament our bond with Christ is strongly forged. We receive the grace to be coupled with him by an unbreakable link. In our Easter celebration we hear the firm, uplifting words of Christ: "Peace. Do not be afraid." To Christ, our Savior, we respond with our jubilant Easter acclamation, "Alleluia."

Easter Sunday, Solemnity of the Resurrection, C

Too Good to Be True?
Ac 10:34, 37-43; Col 3:1-4; Jn 20:1-9

If you are like many people, every now and then you receive a large envelope in the mail. On the outside are imperatives such as "Urgent" and "Open Immediately." There is also a sentence which moves you to follow those imperatives. It says, "You may have already won five million dollars." Possibly you have spent a small fortune on first-class stamps in order to mail back the certificates for these sweepstakes. Maybe you have given up because you have concluded that to win five million dollars seems too good to be true.

Perhaps the disciples of Jesus thought his resurrection was too good to be true. Maybe that is why they were hesitant to accept the testimony of the women who came to tell them the news about an empty tomb. The apostle Thomas was so incredulous that he has given an expression to our language; we speak of someone as being "a doubting Thomas." He had learned of the death of Jesus. It was so horrible and it seemed so final that he just could not make himself believe that Jesus had really come back to life until he actually saw and touched him.

What made Judas betray Jesus? Speculation about that has gone on for centuries. He witnessed Jesus in the weakness of his humanity. He was with him when after a journey by foot Jesus was sweaty and tired, hungry and thirsty. He saw Jesus dismayed by those who misunderstood his message, frustrated by those who rejected his proclamation of the kingdom, and infuriated by those who profaned his Father's temple. And Judas saw Jesus with tears in his eyes when he wept over the city of Jerusalem because of the sins of her people. Could this man

Jesus, so obviously human, be the Messiah? It was too good to be true.

On Easter Sunday we come to church as people of faith. We Catholics believe very extraordinary things. We embrace the truth that Christ has died, Christ is risen, and Christ will come again. We believe that he will come to raise us from the dead because by dying he destroyed our death, and by rising restored our life. We praise him as the Lord who by his cross and resurrection has set us free.

We believe even more. We believe that the Holy Eucharist is the sacrament of his Paschal Mystery, the reality of his death and resurrection for us on the altar. It is his body given up for us and his blood poured out for us. We believe that when we eat his body and drink his blood, we are proclaiming his life-giving death until he comes again.

While receiving Christ in communion, we ought to hear the echo of his wonderful promise; "You who eat my flesh and drink my blood have life everlasting and I will raise you up on the last day."

If we were to win five million dollars, the government would take a big chunk. Then we might make the mistake of going to Las Vegas to try to double what we had left and blow everything. God does not tax his gifts. We won't lose what he has promised us provided we live according to our faith. With God life is not a gamble. God has given the great gift of faith. We believe most extraordinary things. We have come to know and to believe that with our God nothing is too good to be true.

Easter Sunday, Solemnity of the Resurrection, C (alternate)

Seeing the Whole Picture
Ac 10:34, 37-43; Col 3:1-4; Jn 20:1-9

Easter is the celebration of life, God's life, which God has shared with us. Celebrating Easter Sunday without Good Friday, however, is like coming in late toward the end of a Disney movie. We see the handsome prince awaken Sleeping Beauty with a kiss, they marry and live happily ever after. By coming in late we have failed to understand how an evil spell was cast upon Sleeping Beauty and why only the prince could awaken her to a new life.

So that we may see the whole story, the Church does not take down the cross or hide it on Easter Sunday. We are not ashamed of the cross, nor are we embarrassed that Jesus had to die on it. Jesus on the cross was like a woman who dies in childbirth. She gives her life so that her child may live. When Jesus died, his life flowed out from him into his disciples of all times. When Jesus' physical life on this earth ended, his mystical life began. He gave the gift of life to his mystical body, the people of his Church of all times and places.

It is very sad when a woman dies in childbirth because she becomes separated from her infant and cannot nourish the child of her womb. But Jesus has been raised. He is alive. And so he can and does nourish us after our birth. A woman nourishes her child with milk which she makes within her body. Jesus goes even further. He nourishes us with his body and his blood in the Holy Eucharist.

When Jesus was dying on the cross, the soldier pierced his side with a lance. Water and blood flowed from the wound. The Church sees in this a sacramental symbol. The water symbolizes baptism, which gives us birth, and the blood symbolizes the Eucharist, which nourishes our life. The great sacraments of

Easter are baptism, which is completed in confirmation, and the Holy Eucharist.

Within the Easter celebration the elect are baptized and others are received into full communion with the Church. Those who have already been baptized are invited to renew their baptismal commitment. Easter is the springtime of the Church, the time for the great sacraments of baptism and Eucharist.

Easter is incomplete without Good Friday, and our view of the resurrection is also incomplete unless we include the Church. We can be so dazzled by the resurrection that we fail to look with the eyes of faith to see that Jesus opened his arms on the cross to embrace us all, and that he has united us so intimately to himself that we form one body, one spirit in Christ. This union is what the Church is.

Easter is the celebration of both the death and the resurrection of Jesus. Even though these two events transpired over a period of three days, they are now one reality which the Church calls the Paschal Mystery.

Jesus is the Savior who awakens us from the sleep of sin. He has overcome death and given us life. In faith we cry out: "Dying you destroyed our death; rising you restored our life. Lord Jesus, come in glory." And Jesus does come in the celebration of Easter to renew and to nourish within us his great gift of divine life.

Second Sunday of Easter, C

God's Abundant Forgiveness
Ac 5:12-16; Rv 1:9-11, 12-13, 17-19; Jn 20:19-31

It seems at times that God is more eager to grant us forgiveness than we are to receive it. On the very night of the resurrection, Jesus appeared to the apostles. He offered them a sign of peace, and immediately added: "As the Father has sent me, so I send you. Receive the Holy Spirit. Whose sins you shall forgive, they are forgiven them." The power to forgive sins was a beautiful Easter gift to the Church, a sign of God's special love which we call his mercy.

Elizabeth Barrett Browning began what is perhaps the most eloquent love poem in the English language by asking, "How do I love thee? Let me count the ways." On this Second Sunday of Easter we can do well to count the ways in which God shows his love for us, especially through his mercy and forgiveness.

Baptism is first. Through the waters of baptism we are washed clean and with all sins forgiven we are born anew as daughters and sons of God. We enter the family of God on this earth, his Church. Throughout our lives as God's children, like other children, we make mistakes. We fall short of family expectations. At times with each other we become neglectful, quarrelsome, and selfish rather than thoughtful, cooperative, and generous. Even toward our heavenly Father we are not always as respectful and grateful as we should be. None of these sins is so serious as to exclude us from the family, but that does not mean that we should ignore them. God does not consider them insignificant. He offers us a means of forgiveness. The means he offers is the Holy Eucharist. Within the celebration of the Mass, we acknowledge our sinfulness. With contrition in our heart, we receive the body of the Lord given up for us and his blood poured out for us so that sins may be forgiven. This sacrament forgives our venial sins.

Still more. The sacrament of penance proclaims to us that, no matter what, God reaches out to us prodigal children to embrace us in the warmth of his forgiving arms. Mortal sins must be brought to this sacramental cleansing, but we may always submit our venial sins to the power of this sacrament, especially those which we recognize as serious or particularly troublesome and habitual.

After Jesus' resurrection many signs and wonders occurred among the people through the hands of the apostles, the first ministers of the Church. The signs which we enjoy now are the sacraments. The wonders are the powers granted to the Church to forgive our sins.

On that momentous night when Christ appeared to the apostles, Thomas was absent. Without seeing the risen Christ, he refused to believe. We do not see Christ in the sacraments but we are blessed indeed to believe that through the sacraments of the Church Christ forgives our sins.

Within the act of absolution the priest prays for us: "Through the ministry of the Church may God give you pardon and peace." That ministry of the Church began on the night of Christ's resurrection and has continued through all the centuries and even now graces our lives.

Third Sunday of Easter, C

Feed My Lambs, Feed My Sheep
Ac 5:27-32, 40-41; Rv 5:11-14; Jn 21:1-19

St. Peter is one of the most appealing persons in the New Testament. Most of us can identify with his human foibles. As a disciple of Jesus he was eager but weak, a man of great resolutions who experienced failure. On the night of the passion three times he denied knowing Jesus. After the resurrection three times he was asked by Jesus about his love, and three times Peter protested his devotion.

What is remarkable about this last episode is not that Jesus was so patient and understanding that he was willing to offer Peter a new opportunity to express his love. We fully expect that kind of compassion from Jesus. What is remarkable is the response Jesus made to each of Peter's expressions of love. Jesus did not say, "Peter, if you love me fall down and worship me." He did not demand anything for himself, even though, in the words of the Book of Revelation he was "worthy to receive power and riches, wisdom and strength, honor and glory and praise." In fact Jesus did not think of himself but of us. In a generous and unselfish manner he told Peter: If you love me, "feed my lambs; feed my sheep." Actually that too we should expect of Jesus because he came into the world for us and for our salvation. He offered himself in sacrifice so that by dying he could destroy our death and by rising he could restore our life.

Peter and the other apostles accomplished the mission Jesus had given them toward the lambs and sheep of the Church. They filled Jerusalem with his teaching despite opposition as they chose to obey God rather than men. From Jerusalem the faith spread throughout the world and has come down to us today.

The Church continues to hear the voice of Jesus saying: If you love me, "feed my lambs; feed my sheep." The Church accomplishes this mission through evangelization and teaching, but in an even more profound way the Church accomplishes this mission by means of the Mass, first in the Liturgy of the Word and then in the Liturgy of the Eucharist. We are fed, we are nourished, by both Word and Sacrament, by both the Scriptures and the Eucharist.

Nourishment is necessary to sustain life, to overcome illness, to insure health, to give proper growth, and to give joy to life. What ordinary food and drink do for our human life the Eucharist does for our spiritual life. Jesus said, "Feed my lambs," because we need the nourishment he gives for the spiritual life we received at baptism. Jesus said, "Feed my sheep," because we need nourishment for our faith so that it may not grow weak and die. What the body and the blood of the Lord do for our spiritual life, the Sacred Scriptures do for our faith.

At times the Church may appear as weak as Peter before the day of Pentecost, but the Church, strengthened and guided by the Holy Spirit, has never, and will never, fail to fulfill its purpose of nourishing us through Word and Sacrament. We should never make the mistake of denying Christ or failing to value and accept the nourishment he offers us through the Church in the celebration of Sunday Mass.

Fourth Sunday of Easter, C

The Two Hands of the Priesthood

Ac 13:14, 43-52; Rv 7:9, 14-17; Jn 10:27-30

Every year the Pope designates the Fourth Sunday of Easter as a world day of prayer for vocations to the priesthood. He chooses this Sunday because of its Good Shepherd theme. That theme offers an opportunity to reflect on the priesthood.

In the Catholic Church there is actually only one priest, Jesus Christ. The sacred liturgy, in the Preface of the Mass in which the holy oils are blessed (Preface 20), proclaims our faith. It teaches us that "by the Holy Spirit God the Father anointed his only Son High Priest of the new and eternal covenant. With wisdom and love he has planned that this one priesthood of his beloved Son should continue in the Church."

Although Christ is our only priest, he shares his priesthood in two ways and he does so by means of two sacraments. The Preface goes on to proclaim that "Christ gives the dignity of a royal priesthood to the people he has made this own." This is the sacrament of baptism. It confers upon the baptized the universal priesthood of all the faithful. "From these, with a brother's love, Christ chooses men to share his sacred ministry by the laying on of hands." This is the sacrament of Holy Orders. It confers the ministerial priesthood, a priesthood of service to those who enjoy the royal priesthood.

The Second Vatican Council, in its *Dogmatic Constitution on the Church*, teaches that "Although they differ from one another in essence and not merely in degree, the common priesthood of the faithful and the ministerial priesthood are nonetheless interrelated. Each in its own special way is a participation in the one priesthood of Christ" (10).

The two ways of sharing in the priesthood of Christ are like two hands, but not as if one hand were over the other in a superior position. Such would violate the Gospel value announced by Jesus concerning service. Rather these two ways are like two hands which face each other. They face each other so that they may become joined, one palm against the other, in the gesture of prayer. The priesthood of Christ by which he offers worship to God the Father is exercised when the baptized and the ordained are united in liturgical prayer.

The meaning of the one priesthood is symbolized by arranging the altar so that priest and people may face each other and become joined, as are two hands. The altar is not a barrier between priest and people. The altar does not separate them. Rather what happens there is precisely what brings everyone in the Church together. On the altar is celebrated the sacrifice of reconciliation which has removed the obstacles of sin and established the new covenant of unity and love in the blood of Christ. From the altar we receive the body and the blood of the Lord as the sacrament of unity. The priest prays in the third eucharistic prayer: "Grant that we who are nourished by his body and blood may be filled with the Holy Spirit and become one body, one spirit in Christ."

Priest and people are complementary of one another. Coming together in liturgical prayer they fulfill the priesthood of Jesus Christ.

Fifth Sunday of Easter, C

Jesus Commands One Thing
Ac 14:21-27; Rv 21:1-5; Jn 13:31-33, 34-35

Little children tire of their parents' telling them what to do and what not to do. To them the list seems endless: "Do your homework. Don't bite your nails. Turn off the TV. Get to bed. Wake up. Eat your breakfast. Don't be late for school." Jesus by contrast is satisfied to sum up all he wants to tell us in a single commandment: "Love one another."

The setting for this Sunday's Gospel is the Last Supper. It was the night before Jesus was to die. He had promised to give the Holy Spirit to instruct and guide the Church after his Ascension into heaven, but at this moment of his final meeting with the apostles before his death he was eager to tell them what was closest to his heart. He did so in but a few words: "Love one another." Not only must we never underestimate the importance of this commandment; we must never underestimate its demands. These days some Catholics think that the Church has gone soft. They lament the fact that the practice of fasting and abstinence has been lessened both in its frequency and its severity. They say there is too much talk about mercy and not enough about penance. They miss the "fire and brimstone" approach to preaching. They judge that the Church is lax about allowing frequent communion. They seem to be of the opinion that the "good old days" meant it was a challenge to be a good Catholic.

The truth is that some of the external practices were easy to comply with in comparison with the command of Jesus. When we face what his commandment entails, we see that it is far from easy, especially when we understand what Jesus meant when he declared that his commandment is new. In what way is it new? After all, the Old Testament demanded love for others.

What is new is that Jesus is the model and the measure of our love. That is what he meant when he added, "Such as my love has been for you, so must your love be for each other." That love is truly great. Within the Eucharist we celebrate the love of Christ, his sacrifice. We acknowledge that under the appearances of bread is his body given up for us, and under the appearances of wine is his blood poured out for us. Clearly then we must never underestimate the demands of this new commandment of which Jesus himself is the model and measure.

It was this commandment of love which inspired the preachers of the early Church, like Paul and Barnabas whom we heard about in the first reading, to travel great distances under difficult circumstances to proclaim the good news. It was love which made their hearers accept the faith and persevere in it so that the Church spread throughout the world. It was love which moved the martyrs to give up their lives. It was love which inspired saints to serve others unselfishly without hope of gain. And it is this same love for each other which will make us good Catholics today.

Jesus does not give us a commandment without giving us also the means to fulfill it. That is why in the Mass we not only look upon the sacrament of his body and blood, we also share in it through Holy Communion. Participating in the Eucharist helps us to become more and more like Christ so that we may keep his commandment, "Such as my love has been for you, so must your love be for each other."

Sixth Sunday of Easter, C

The Work of the Holy Spirit
Ac 15:1-2, 22-29; Rv 21:10-14, 22-23; Jn 14:23-29

Sometimes Catholics feel confused in discussing religion when a neighbor challenges them with the question, "Can you find that in the Bible?" The questioner follows the principle which is called *scriptura sola*, the position that Scripture, since it is inspired by the Holy Spirit, is the sole source of faith and practice. The truth is that the Holy Spirit did not stop working when the Bible was finished. The Holy Spirit has been at work through all the centuries of the Church and is still at work.

When St. John completed his Gospel around the year 90 A.D., only the Book of Revelation remained to be composed to complete the contents of the New Testament. Even after almost the entire New Testament had been composed, St. John understood that the work of the Spirit had to continue. In today's Gospel he quotes the promise of Jesus: "The Paraclete, the Holy Spirit, whom the Father will send in my name, will instruct you in everything, and remind you of all that I told you." St. John realized that this promise was kept, not only through the inspiration of Holy Scripture, but through the continued activity of the Holy Spirit in the Church.

St. Luke in this Sunday's selection from the Acts of the Apostles showed how the Holy Spirit was at work during the Council of Jerusalem which had to answer the question whether the disciples of Jesus were obliged to be circumcised and follow the law of Moses or not. They were aware of the Spirit's movement among them, and they answered in the negative. They declared, "It is the decision of the Holy Spirit, and ours too, not to demand any burden beyond that which is strictly necessary."

The Spirit is always at work. In our time the Spirit guided

the deliberations of the Second Vatican Council. The Fathers of this Council, the twenty-first general council of the Church, were keenly aware of the Holy Spirit among them as they sat in the aula of St. Peter's in the Vatican just as the apostles experienced the movement of the Holy Spirit when they met in council in Jerusalem. The first concern of the Second Vatican Council was the liturgy, how we pray as Catholics. They wrote in the *Constitution on the Liturgy*: "Zeal for the promotion and restoration of the liturgy is rightly held to be a sign of the providential dispositions of God in our time, as a movement of the Holy Spirit in his Church" (43).

It must be admitted that not every implementation of the liturgy is what the Council had in mind, nor is every selection of music precisely what is intended by liturgical norms — such is part of our struggle to do what is right and to do it well — but the official prayers of the priest and the people show the hand of the Holy Spirit guiding their composition. Of particular beauty and profundity are the eucharistic prayers, the heart of the celebration of all liturgy.

Understanding that the Holy Spirit is continuously at work in the Church is much more than a way of settling arguments with those who are not of our faith. It is a way of appreciating the wonderful gift which the Holy Spirit has given us in the restoration of the sacred liturgy through his guidance of the Fathers of the Second Vatican Council.

Solemnity of the Ascension, C

The Perfect Adorer of the Father
Ac 1:1-11; Eph 1:17-23; Lk 24:46-53

Our great conviction as Catholics is that Jesus of Nazareth is the Son of God, and that he is divine from all eternity. Our religious instincts move us to worship Jesus, who is Lord and Christ, in all aspects of his earthly life. Today we can broaden our vision to see Christ as the perfect adorer of God the Father.

Today the liturgy presents us with the picture of the almighty Lord and Christ ascending into heaven. He is going home to his Father. From all eternity he has been the loving Son of his devoted Father. During his life on this earth he prayed earnestly to his Father and manifested his love for him. We should in a spiritual way rejoice that Jesus has returned home.

And yet through the power of the Holy Spirit he is still with us, especially during our celebration of the sacred liturgy. In the liturgy he wishes us to join him in his worship of the Father.

Since Jesus is at once both divine and human, he is our link with God the Father. He is our mediator, our intercessor. Jesus is the only priest of our religion. He shares his priesthood with the baptized as the royal priesthood, and with the ordained as the servant priesthood.

Cardinal Pierre de Berulle, the spiritual guide of several saints and many holy people in seventeenth century France, envisioned Jesus as "the perfect adorer of the Father." This truth is vital to our understanding of and participation in the liturgy since Jesus, the Lord and Christ, wishes to lead us in our worship of the Father. The Church teaches us this truth in the *Constitution on the Liturgy*: "Every liturgical celebration is an action of Christ the priest and of his body, the Church. It is, therefore, a sacred action surpassing all others, and no other action of the Church is equal to it" (7).

Christ the Priest is present and active during the celebration of the Mass in four ways. First, in and through all of us who gather in his name Christ prays and sings to the Father, and he urges us to look in the same direction with him, toward the Father. Next he acts in and through the ordained priest who offers the sacrifice in his name and who is the sign of the unity for which Jesus prayed at the Last Supper. Thirdly, he speaks to us through those who read the Sacred Scriptures; through them and the preacher he proclaims that he is the way to the Father, the truth of the Father, and the life of the Father. He is the way we must follow, the truth we must believe, and the life we must live. Finally, through the Eucharist he draws us to himself to offer perfect thanks and praise to the Father; he perpetuates for us his sacrifice of the cross so that we may share in it and join him in his devout sentiment, "Father, into your hands I commend my spirit." The *Constitution on the Liturgy* also teaches that "Christ always associates the Church with himself in the work of giving perfect praise to God the Father and in making his people holy" (7). Pope Pius XII stressed that participation in the sacred liturgy is our chief duty and supreme dignity as Catholics. Although Jesus has gone home to heaven he is still present in the sacred liturgy to lead us in our worship of God the Father.

Seventh Sunday of Easter, C

God's Family at Prayer
Ac 7:55-60; Rv 22:12-14, 16-17, 20; Jn 17:20-26

When a new family moves into a neighborhood, very often the children are the first to become acquainted. Amid their strange surroundings a little boy and girl are delighted to find a child whom they like immediately and with whom it is fun to play.

One Saturday morning the child invites the two into his home. It is lunch time and the child's mother insists that everyone come into the kitchen and join her and her husband for a meal. It is a bright friendly room. There is an atmosphere of welcome about the place and a feeling of love. The boy and girl like the spirit of the family. They find that the parents are very pleasant people who are really nice to talk with. A relationship develops. The kids are at their friend's house as much as they are at their own. They feel part of the family.

When we moved into God's world, we were blessed to have met a child. He is Jesus, the Son of God. The Christian experience begins with an attraction to Jesus which is drawn from the grace of baptism and confirmation. By God's grace we grow in our knowledge and love of Jesus through the Scriptures and the other teachings of the Church. He becomes the center of our lives.

The relationship must then become deeper. Jesus wants to introduce us to his Father. In fact, from his point of view the whole purpose of our relationship with him is to become what he is, a child of God. He invites us into his family home, the Church. There he hopes that we sense the presence of the family Spirit who "gives witness with our spirit that we are children of God" (Romans 8:16). The Spirit makes us feel at home. The Father leads us to the family table where we are nourished by word and sacrament.

This Sunday we hear Jesus praying to his Father. It was the night before he died, the time of his Last Supper. His deep yearning was that we might all be one as he and his Father are one. He wanted us to know that with his Father we should feel at home. During this same supper Jesus instituted the Holy Eucharist, our family meal. As we celebrate this meal, the Holy Eucharist, we should have a deep sense of being part of God's family.

We will feel part of God's family during the celebration of the Eucharist when we look not only at the face of Christ, but also in the same direction with him to the Father. We will feel comfortable when we allow the Spirit to direct our prayer to the Father through our Lord Jesus Christ. We will realize how right it is always and everywhere to give thanks and praise to God our Father. We will find nothing more natural to being a Catholic than to see that through Christ, with him, and in him, in the unity of the Holy Spirit, all glory and honor belong to God, the almighty Father.

God has revealed himself to us as three persons not so that we may have a choice or a preference for our devotion, but so that we may enter into the relationships which God is. God is Fatherhood, he is Sonship, and he is Love. We have been predestined to share the image of God's Son, to be beloved children who feel at home with God our Father.

Solemnity of Pentecost

Pentecost Is Our Epiphany
Ac 2:1-11; 1 Cor 12:3-7, 12-13; Jn 20:19-23

When a child is born, his parents wonder what he will become. They cherish fond hopes in their heart. They want only the best for their child and try to give him their spirit.

Jesus was born as the hope of the whole human race. The Epiphany manifested that he was the Savior, not only of the Jewish people from whom through Mary he had been born, but of the people of all times and all places.

The Church was born on Good Friday, "for it was from the side of Christ as he slept the sleep of death upon the cross that there came forth the wondrous sacrament which is the whole Church." So wrote Pope Pius XII in 1943 in his encyclical, *Mystici Corporis* (the Mystical Body of Christ). But what was to be the future of this infant Church? Pentecost gives the answer.

On the day of Pentecost the Church appeared before the world as the sacrament of universal salvation. Pentecost is the Epiphany of the Church. It proclaims that the Church, though Jewish in origin, is truly catholic; it is universal.

As we celebrate the great Solemnity of Pentecost, we should reflect on the truth that people all over the world have heard the voice of Christ in the Church "speaking in their own tongue about the marvels God has accomplished." In turn these people raise their voices in the rhythms and sounds of a multitude of languages to create a marvelous symphony of thanks and praise to God the Father in the eucharistic sacrifice. By the inspiration of the Holy Spirit people of every race and tongue, of every tribe and nation, have come to know God as their Father and Jesus as their Savior.

The Church not only spans the globe; it also extends back in time through all the centuries to the death and resurrection of Jesus. Slave and free, king and peasant, saint and sinner, have embraced Christ in the Church since the day of Pentecost.

People who lived in the first century of the Christian era had little in common with us. They understood almost nothing of the solar system, and they did not even know that the western hemisphere existed. And yet we share with them our Catholic faith. Even without understanding our language, they would recognize the Mass as the supreme expression of our faith.

People of the second century never rode in a car or flew in a plane, but we are on the same journey as they through this life to the Father in heaven. Our diet would seem strange to them, but they would recognize the Eucharist as the spiritual food and drink of a pilgrim people.

People of the Christian centuries before ours never listened to a recording or consumed artificial vitamins, but with them we have heard the same Gospel and been nourished by the same body and blood of the Lord.

Pentecost is a day of bigness. It should fill us with an expansive sense of jubilation. It is a time for perspective, for seeing ourselves as part of the growing body of Christ by the gift of the Holy Spirit. We are part of those people of all times and places who in Christ Jesus form with him one body and one spirit, the universal Church.

Solemnity of the Trinity, C

Is God Happy?
Pr 8:22-31; Rm 5:1-5; Jn 16:12-15

We use many adjectives in referring to God. We say that God is wise, powerful, merciful, and loving. Before each adjective we may place the word "most." An impressive list can be drawn up to indicate the attributes of God, all of them in the superlative, but a questions remains. Is God happy?

One would think so. God does not have to drive the freeways, he never has to stand in line for anything, and he is not required to pay taxes. With all that, something seems to be missing, even in the revelation of God to his Chosen People. The People of God were surrounded by tribes and nations which believed in many gods. They worshipped the god of agriculture and the god of fertility, the god of peace and the god of war. Some tribes worshipped the sun and the moon and the stars. Each group also had its own national god.

Not so the Israelites. To them God revealed himself as the one, true Lord, the God of all creation. No people were more blessed than they, and yet God still seemed distant and perhaps even lonely in all his majesty. Jesus revealed a fuller picture of God. By coming into our world and manifesting himself as Son of God, he showed that God is actually a Father. God not only possesses all life; he shares that life with another, his divine Son. Uniting Father and Son in an eternal embrace of love is the Holy Spirit. God is not alone. He lives a wonderful life of mutual love. God's happiness is that he is a family.

When I see young parents holding their infant lovingly in their arms to be baptized, and I sense the elation which they feel, then I know that God is happy. When I observe fathers and mothers, their eyes filled with tears of joy, watching their little children receive Holy Communion for the first time, then

I know that God is happy. When I hear parents speak proudly of their sons and daughters who have graduated with honors, then I know that God is happy.

Up to a certain age children believe that their parents can do anything, that they are almost divine. Then they learn that their parents are, as we say, only human, that they have faults and foibles. Parents find their feelings changing when their children are struggling through adolescence and the teens, and many discover that their children can break their heart. All of this should be no surprise. We are not perfect, but God is. The love which is the Person of the Holy Spirit unites the Father and the Son in a never-failing relationship of devotion. From all eternity the sentiment of God the Father is the one he expressed while Jesus lived on this earth: "This my beloved Son in whom I am well pleased."

Our God is not far removed from us. He has drawn us into his happy life. We are privileged to share Jesus' relationship to his Father. Through the sacrament of baptism God has made us his beloved sons and daughters, and through our communion in the body and blood of his Son he nourishes his gift of life.

This Sunday we celebrate the mystery of the Blessed Trinity. It is the reality of a happy God whose life and love we share.

Solemnity of the Lord's Body and Blood, C (*Corpus Christi*)

The Eucharist In Twenty Words
Gn 14:18-20; 1 Cor 11:23-26; Lk 9:11-17

Before television we used to hear of contests on the radio: "In twenty-five words or less write and tell us why you use our toothpaste and you could win a prize." It seemed easy, but it is difficult to say something worthwhile in only twenty-five words.

The great theologian and saint, Thomas Aquinas, was able to summarize the meaning of the Eucharist in only twenty Latin words. His summary, known as the *O Sacrum Convivium* is part of the divine office for the feast of Corpus Christi, the feast we celebrate this Sunday. It has been set to several magnificent melodies, but its real beauty is in its meaning.

This is the original Latin of St. Thomas: *"O Sacrum Convivium in quo Christus sumitur, recolitur memoria passionis ejus, mens impletur gratia et futurae gloriae nobis pignus datur."* Let's take it word by word.

"Convivium" is a banquet. It is not just a meal. It is a happy gathering of people around a sumptuous dinner. This banquet is "sacrum," that is, it is sacred. The "O" is an exclamation which I am tempted to translate as "Wow!" but I guess an English "O" will do.

The next phrase is "in which Christ is consumed." That's plain language. The Eucharist is not bread and wine. The Eucharist is Christ. But it is important that the appearances of bread and wine remain since they symbolize that Christ is our food and drink. That is why St. Thomas says that Christ is "consumed."

Banquets often mark special occasions, such as weddings or anniversaries. The occasion of the Sacred Banquet of the Eucharist is the anniversary of our loving union with the Father through the sacrifice of Christ. It is the living memorial of the Paschal Mystery, the death and resurrection of Christ. St. Thomas expressed this truth by saying that in the Eucharist "the memory of his passion is recalled."

Next St. Thomas indicated the effect of the Eucharist upon us. He wrote that "the mind is filled with grace." Sometimes the Latin word "mens" is translated as "soul." The word to St. Thomas meant the very highest faculty or aspect of the human person, but I feel confident that he would not object to our saying that Christ transforms our entire being. St. Thomas agreed with St. Augustine who said that we do not change the Eucharist into ourselves as we do ordinary food, but Christ changes us into himself. That is God's grace, his gift.

Finally in the Eucharist "a pledge of future glory is given to us." This statement reflects the teaching of Jesus in St. John's Gospel: "He who eats my flesh and drinks my blood has life everlasting and I will raise him up on the last day" (6:54).

It takes me thirty-one words to render a literal translation in English. "O Sacred Banquet in which Christ is consumed, the memory of his passion is recalled, the mind is filled with grace, and a pledge of future glory is given to us." St. Thomas did not win a contest but he should win our gratitude for this summary of the mystery of faith.

The Season of the Year
Cycle C

"The Church celebrates the Paschal Mystery on the first day of the week, known as the Lord's Day or Sunday. This follows a tradition handed down from the apostles and having its origin in Christ's resurrection. Thus Sunday must be ranked as the first holy day of all."
(*General Norms for the Liturgical Year*, 4)

Second Sunday of the Year, C

The New Covenant of Abundance
Is 62:1-5; 1 Cor 12:4-11; Jn 2:1-12

The two young people who were wed at Cana, though nameless, have been immortalized in the Gospel because Jesus was the guest at their wedding. Any couple might be envious of them. And yet the story as told by St. John and as proclaimed to us in the liturgy has a wider meaning than the union of that Jewish man and woman some twenty centuries ago.

The first reading today from Isaiah prepared us for this wider meaning. It is based on a favorite image of God in the Old Testament as the spouse of his people. The prophet says: "As a young man marries a virgin, your Builder shall marry you; and as a bridegroom rejoices in his bride, so shall your God rejoice in you." The story of Cana relies on this imagery and symbolically manifests the new, everlasting covenant between God and his people.

In secular society marriage is considered a contract which is binding by law. In God's view marriage is a covenant which is binding by love. The setting of today's Gospel should make us think of God's covenant with us as one of faithful love like that of dedicated spouses.

The details of the Gospel story reveal that God's love is generous and abundant. At hand were six stone water jars, each holding fifteen to twenty-five gallons. Jesus directed that they be filled to the brim. Cana was a small town. Perhaps there were at most fifty guests, including some disciples of Jesus. When Jesus changed the water into wine the guests had much more than enough, some 150 gallons. God's love is abundant like that. Theologically Cana is related to the Epiphany. The meaning of the Epiphany is that Gentiles as well as Jews are called to be disciples of Jesus. God's love is abundant enough to include everyone in his new covenant.

The new wine at Cana was not only abundant; it was excellent. The waiter in charge observed to the groom: "You have kept the choice wine until now." God too has reserved for us in the Christian era the abundant, choice wine of his new covenant.

The actual union of God and his people awaited a moment beyond that of the wedding feast of Cana. At Mary's behest Jesus embarked upon the events of his public life which inevitably led to "his hour," the time of the Paschal Mystery of his death and resurrection. Jesus opened his arms on the cross to embrace us in a generous, abundant love which is big enough to include everyone. That was the moment of our union.

We renew our relationship of love in the eucharistic celebration. At Cana Jesus transformed water into wine. In the eucharistic celebration he transforms bread and wine into his body and blood as the living memorial of his death and resurrection. In the voice of the priest we hear the words of Christ: "This is the cup of my blood, the blood of the new and everlasting covenant. It will be shed for you and for all…"

Since that beautiful day in Cana every wedding should remind us of God's abundant love for us. Every dedicated couple should make us think of God's fidelity. And above all we should remember that in the Eucharist we celebrate the new covenant, our union with God and one another in the Church.

Third Sunday of the Year, C

Behold the Body of Christ!
Ne 8:2-4, 5-6, 8-10; 1 Cor 12:12-30; Lk 1:1-4; 4:14-21

Some Catholics have been disappointed in recently constructed churches. They find them too stark, unadorned by objects of devotion, and lacking beauty. Others object that older churches are too ornate. Take a lead from the second reading today. Rather than observing the structure and ornamentation of the building, look at the people within the church. With the eyes of your Catholic faith, see them for who they really are: the body of Christ, made up of many diverse members. Within each person is the luster of the person of Christ, the Head of the body which is the Church. That luster shines forth only for those whose eyes are enlightened by the truth that the people of the Church are truly the body of Christ. Within each person is a special and particular beauty. At times I wish we could have a spiritual x-ray vision which would allow us during Mass to perceive that inner beauty. We would then see a couple near us who are struggling to keep a marriage together and who are praying earnestly to recapture the grace of their wedding day, all because they really believe it is God's will that they be two in one flesh. Their faith is beautiful.

We would see a smartly dressed young man. With a special vision we would become aware that he is begging the Lord to free him from an enslaving addiction which is threatening to ruin his life. Just next to him is another young man who is so thankful to God for the blessings of his life that he is asking God to let him know whether he should dedicate his life to the Church as a priest. Within both persons glows a beautiful light of faith. Around us we hear several people who are enthusiastic in saying the prayers and singing the music. They are all different from one another except for the fact that in their late teens they stopped coming to Mass. They all drifted away from the Catholic Church, some joined other religions but most simply started to live pretty much as if God did not exist. Then something happened, something different for each one, that made them realize how much they needed God and his Church. Because they had the seed of faith planted within them, they knew where to turn to find God. They returned to embrace the Church with an enthusiasm which resembled that of those newly initiated into the Church at Easter. We notice the children. Even without x-ray vision we can see their simplicity and their humility. We are reminded that Jesus warns us, "Unless you become like little children, you will not enter the kingdom of God." Children are a living Gospel and they are like lovely flowers adorning the church.

St. Paul reflected on the union of Christ with the people of his Church. He wrote to the Corinthians: "The body of Christ has many members, but all the members, many though they are, are one body; and so it is with Christ." The first reading tells us how happy the people were to have rediscovered the book of the Law (probably Deuteronomy). We should be happy on this day of the Lord to discover the body of Christ among us. At Sunday Mass the reading from St. Paul is fulfilled among us. Look around you. Behold the body of Christ, the real beauty of the church. To this great truth give a fervent "Amen."

Fourth Sunday of the Year, C

To Love as Christ Loves
Jr 1:4-5, 17-19; 1 Cor 12:31-13:13; Lk 4:21-30

A teenage boy was shooting some baskets in the driveway of his home when he lost one of his contact lenses. He looked for it but could not find it. He went into the house and said, "Dad, I lost one of my contacts and I can't find it." His father got up from reading his paper, went outside, and in a few moments returned with the lens. The boy was amazed. "How did you find it?" he asked. His father replied, "You were looking for a piece of plastic. I was looking for $150."

When we do not have the right sense of values, we can fail to find the important realities of life. That is why the people in the Gospel today rejected Jesus. They could not accept a home town boy as their Messiah. They missed out on what was really important. To them Jesus was no more than a piece of plastic.

Something like that was going on in Corinth when Paul wrote his letter to them. They had become enamored of the charismatic gifts. Some could speak in tongues, others could interpret tongues, some had the gift of healing, and others could prophesy. These gifts were good in the themselves, but the Corinthians were failing to value the greatest gift of all, the gift of love.

That is why Paul said to them, "I will show the way that surpasses all others." That way is the way of love. But with St. Paul love was not abstract or merely theoretical. He was not thinking of a honeymoon and romantic love. For him love was practical, down to earth, a day-in and a day-out way of dealing with each other.

"Love is kind." How could he have put it more simply and more directly? We have to be kind to each other: to say "please" and "thank you" and "pardon me." "Love is patient." How hard it is always to be patient with those with whom we live or work, not to let them get on our nerves or annoy us with their concerns when we are not interested. "Love is not jealous. Love is not snobbish. Love is not rude. Love does not put on airs." Every item in his list is practical. Above all love is not self-seeking. Love is generous and unselfish. Finally love never fails. All real love, and not just that between husband and wife, is for better or for worse, for richer or for poorer, in sickness and in health.

It has been observed by spiritual writers that in St. Paul's letter the word "love" can be replaced with the name, "Christ." Christ is patient, Christ is kind, Christ does not put on airs, Christ is not self-seeking, Christ never fails. This truth helps us to realize how high the ideal of love really is and that we cannot attain it on our own. The Eucharist is the means for growing in Christ-like love. When we have received Holy Communion, we must pray, "Lord, transform me and all my affections. Help me to love as you love. Help me with what I find most difficult."

St. Paul observes that the three great virtues are faith, hope, and love. When we get to heaven we will no longer need faith because we will see God face to face. We will no longer need hope because we will have achieved our goal. But we will have the greatest of all the virtues; we will have love. We can begin eternity now by praying for and by putting into practice a Christ-like love for each other.

Fifth Sunday of the Year, C

God's Ways Are Best
Is 6:1-2, 3-8; 1 Cor 15:1-11; Lk 5:1-11

God is consistent. We can depend on God. The Scriptures reveal the actions and the words of God in the past. What God has done in the past is what God does today. What God has said in the past is what God says to us today. What happened to Peter in this Sunday's Gospel has happened to all of us in our own way.

Peter was a fisherman, not for sport, but for his livelihood. He was a professional. He and his mates had worked hard all night, at just the best time for fishing in those waters, but they had caught nothing. Then Jesus the carpenter told Peter the fisherman to lower his nets again. The big problem was that it was now the worst time for fishing. We can hear the protest in Peter's voice: "Master, we have been hard at it all night and have caught nothing." He was at the point of telling Jesus to forget it, when he suddenly realized to whom he was speaking. After a pause, perhaps while looking at Jesus and seeing the insistence in his eyes, Peter said, "But if you say so, I will lower the nets." Peter's faith was like an infant, far from maturity, but it was strong enough to move him to put his emphasis on the "you" when he said "If *you* say so, I will lower the nets." The result of Peter's trust in the Lord was an astonishing catch of fish. Peter thought his way was best but he learned that the Lord's way is best.

Isaiah had learned the same lesson before Peter did. At first Isaiah did not want to accept the mission of being a prophet to God's people. He felt unworthy. He described himself as a man of unclean lips. He would gladly have walked away to follow some other way of life. But God wanted him. One of the seraphim touched Isaiah's lips, a symbol of God's grace. To this grace Isaiah responded. "Here I am," he said. "Send me." He became one of the greatest of all the prophets because he followed God's way.

Upon reflection can we not see that something similar has happened to us? Perhaps you had your heart set on a person whom you wanted to marry. It did not work out. Another person entered your life and now you thank God for your spouse who is the right person for you. Maybe you had a job which you liked. You seemed to have a future with a particular company. But then during a recession there were layoffs. You lost your job. Then a great opportunity suddenly opened for you and you became involved in a wonderful career you never thought possible.

These examples may not fit you. Everyone of us must take time to reflect on how God has acted in our lives in a way far beyond what we had planned or expected. St. Paul thought he was doing right in persecuting Christians. He felt that was his duty as a devout Jew. God had other plans for him as an apostle and author of New Testament letters. He put into writing some of our most important doctrines. God's way was better for Paul.

Sometimes we do not get the great catch of fish. Things seem to go wrong for us. Then we must be patient and give God time to act. From Isaiah's vision of heaven we have taken our acclamation, "Holy, holy, holy Lord, God of power and might. Heaven and earth are full of your glory." That expression of God's magnificence should remind us that God is far above us. His ways are not our ways but his ways are always best.

Sixth Sunday of the Year, C

God Wants Us to Be Happy
Jr 17:5-8; 1 Cor 15:12, 16-20; Lk 6:17, 20-26

There are one hundred and fifty psalms in the Bible, one of which forms our response to the first reading each Sunday. The psalm for today is the very first psalm, which sets the tone for the other one hundred and forty-nine. The first word of the first psalm is "Happy."

God wants us to be happy. Another word for "happy" in the Bible is "blessed." We are happy when we are blessed by God. The psalm declares that to be blessed is to be like a tree planted near running water which yields its fruit in due season, and whose leaves never fade. This imagery suggests a great strength and vitality.

We will be happy with God's strength and vitality if we follow the way God points out to us. The prophet Jeremiah helps us to understand what that way is. He writes: "Blessed (that is, happy) is the one who trusts in the Lord, whose hope is the Lord." He continues in the imagery of the first psalm to say that a person who trusts in the Lord, and whose hope is the Lord, is like a tree planted beside running water.

We know how necessary water is for living things. After a refreshing spring rain, vegetation turns green with life. But in a dry spell during the summer, growing things become brown and barren. It is no wonder that our sacrament of baptism uses the symbol of water since it is in baptism that we first receive the life of God, the gift of his divine grace, and begin to share in his happiness.

But without a continuous flow of God's life-giving water, our lives can turn brown and barren. Without God's grace we become very unhappy. Our chief source of God's refreshing grace is the Mass. During the celebration of Mass, we hear the

Word of God proclaimed in the Scriptures and the homily. God's Word is nourishment for our faith. Second is the Eucharist itself. The Eucharist is nourishment for God's life within us. Nothing can substitute for God's Word and the Eucharist. We are nourished every Sunday by Word and Sacrament. They go together. As the Word enriches our faith, so the Eucharist gives us the strength we need to live in accord with our faith.

We believe we know what happiness is, but its reality is elusive. Sometimes we might think our condition is far from one which brings about happiness, but God has a different way of looking at things. That is why Jesus gives us the beatitudes. They are paradoxical. We tend to think that the opposite of what they say is true. But Jesus insists: "Blest (that is, happy) are you poor. Blest are you who hunger. Blest are you who are weeping."

We can be happy when we are poor if our poverty makes us turn to God and to trust in him. We can be happy when we are hungry if we allow our hunger to make us yearn to have God fill the emptiness of our hearts and not only our stomachs. We can be happy when we are weeping, if our sorrow centers on our failure to do God's will in all things.

God wants us to be happy. Embracing God and following his way of life is the only way to be blessed, to be truly happy.

Seventh Sunday of the Year, C

Forgiveness for All
1 S 26:2, 7-9, 12-13, 22-23; 1 Cor 15:45-49; Lk 6:27-38

Almost everyone knows the story of how in combat David, the youth, overcame Goliath, the giant. By doing so David saved the Israelites from a terrible war with the Philistines. The victory won favor from the people for David, but hatred from King Saul. Saul convinced himself that David was his enemy and would try to usurp the throne. He tried without success to kill David. In today's first reading the tables are turned. David has the opportunity to kill the King, but out of respect for him as the Lord's anointed he refuses to do so. He actually forgives the King for his attacks upon him.

Where today do we find an example like that of David? Surely not among politicians who assassinate each other with words and TV ads during every political campaign. We have an excellent model, however, in the person of Pope John Paul II. After he had recovered from the blatant attack upon his life when he was shot in St. Peter's Square, one of the first things he did was to visit his assailant in prison and offer him forgiveness and reconciliation.

A man falsely accused Cardinal Bernardin, Archbishop of Chicago, of having molested him as a youth. The man soon recanted his preposterous story. It would have been understandable if the Cardinal had railed in indignation against his dishonest accuser. Rather the Cardinal sought him out to forgive him.

These are two extraordinary examples of forgiveness. But we look even beyond these two exemplary men to the person of Jesus. Jesus preached compassion, forgiveness, and reconciliation as we learn in today's Gospel; his teaching is very much the opposite of what we hear and see in our society. Jesus also practiced what he preached. Jesus looked out upon those who crucified him and prayed, "Father, forgive them for they know not what they are doing."

We must be a people who follow the teaching and the example of Jesus. We must be compassionate, forgiving, and respectful. We must be that way publicly and privately. For example, some Catholics do not agree with the Pope and the United States Catholic bishops who are opposed to the death penalty. The Pope and the bishops see clearly that the execution of a human being reduces us to a barbaric state from which the teachings of Jesus would lift us. It is time for Catholics to reject the values of a vindictive society to embrace the principles of Christ. We must leave to God an appropriate punishment for capital crimes.

We are called to follow the teachings and the example of Jesus in what affects us personally. You do not have to live long to have someone hurt you deeply, either by saying terrible things behind your back or by actually doing something which harms you seriously. These hurts we must not foster. We must banish them by offering forgiveness and reconciliation to anyone who has harmed us.

In every Mass we hear the ringing words of Christ: "This is the cup of my blood... It will be shed for you and for all so that sins may be forgiven." Receiving Christ in Holy Communion, partaking of his blood shed for the sake of forgiveness, gives us the strength we need to be a people of forgiveness and reconciliation, and not of hatred and vindictiveness. We can and must be like Christ himself.

Eighth Sunday of the Year, C

Speech Is the Fruit of the Heart
Si 27:4-7; 1 Cor 15:54-58; Lk 6:39-45

We live in an age of marvels such as television, computers, and space travel. Almost every day modern wonders unfold. Who knows what will be next? And yet one of the greatest marvels which we experience every day dates back to the dawn of the human race. It is the wonder of language. In fact, without language it is difficult to see how the marvels of our age could possibly have developed since collaboration among humans would have been extremely difficult, probably even impossible.

Human language did not simply evolve over millennia. Language is the gift of God since it flows from the truth that we are made in the image and likeness of God. It lifts us as human beings far above other creatures, and actually makes us like God. From all eternity God himself utters a Word. That Word we know from revelation is his divine Son who was in the beginning with God and is God. All our human words, no matter what the language, are a sharing in the one Word of God. So precious is God's gift of language that we must not abuse it.

Our words come forth from us as fruit comes forth from a tree. Bad fruit comes from a bad tree. And so Sirach today warns us that a man's faults appear when he speaks. On the other hand, good fruit comes from a good tree. And so Jesus tells us that a good man produces goodness from the good in his heart. Our human words are, or should be, an expression of our goodness.

Of course we humans are free to use God's gifts for right or for wrong. At times we say good things, at times, bad. At times we express respect and love with our words; at times, impatience and hostility. At times we tell the truth; at times, we do not.

We may agree that we should not abuse God's gift, but trying to correct our words without changing our hearts is like trying to produce good fruit from a bad tree. We need change within ourselves. That is what Jesus meant when he said, "Each man speaks from his heart's abundance."

What should be the abundance in our heart? With what goodness should it be filled? With nothing other than the abundant goodness of God. Every Sunday at Mass we hear words, very important words, words which reflect the one Great Word of God. We hear the words of Sacred Scripture. Christ, the Word of God, speaks to us when the words of Scripture are proclaimed during the liturgy. From these sacred words we learn about God and we learn about ourselves. For example in today's second reading St. Paul tells us of our great dignity as children of God. We are so valuable in God's eyes that death is not the end for us. Death has been vanquished by Christ. St. Paul not only proclaims this truth so that our hearts can be filled with the goodness of God but he also shows us how our words must spring from an understanding of that goodness. And so he adds words which should pour forth from our hearts: "Thanks be to God who has given us the victory through our Lord Jesus Christ."

If our heart is filled with the goodness of God, our words will be filled with goodness. We will not use words for evil but for good. We would do well if people who hear us speak could sense that we speak as Jesus did on this earth. To our words, then, they could rightly respond, "Thanks be to God."

Ninth Sunday of the Year, C

Humility, Faith and Communion
1 K 8:41-43; Gal 1:1-2, 6-10; Lk 7:1-10

We Catholics today and a Roman military officer who lived in the time of Jesus seem to have little in common, but the liturgy sees in the dispositions of this unnamed soldier a model for our reception of Holy Communion.

The centurion was humble. Even though he was in the employ of mighty Caesar and part of the Roman occupying force in Judea, he was willing to ask the help of a Jew, the Galilean carpenter turned preacher. This man, who was a Roman, could easily have held Jesus, who was a Jew, in contempt. Instead he actually confessed that he was unworthy to receive a favor from Jesus. But he was desperate. He knew that he was helpless to save his servant and that Jesus worked wonders. By God's grace he had come to believe in the power of Jesus. He had faith, and that faith led him to have hope, to trust that Jesus not only could help his servant, but that he would help him.

Jesus was moved by the man's faith and declared, "I tell you I have not found such faith among the Israelites." He responded favorably to the centurion's plea. Jesus in this instance actually answered the prayer of Solomon in the first reading that all people, and not just the people of Israel, might receive God's favor through their faith.

The Church has adopted the words which the centurion addressed to Jesus and given them to us as a preparation for Holy Communion: "Lord, I am not worthy to receive you but only say the word and I shall be healed." These words which we have repeated many times should make us think of the virtues of the centurion.

First is humility, an acknowledgment that we need Jesus. We need not feel desperate, as did the centurion, but we must recognize that we cannot do without Jesus. Next is faith, a realization that Jesus is the one who can help us, that he does possess divine power. Faith must be coupled with hope, a trust that Jesus not only can but will help us.

We admit that we are unworthy, but we add, "Lord, say only the word and I shall be healed." In our hearts we must hear that word, and that word from Jesus is "Come." "Yes," Jesus says, "come to the altar and there receive my body and my blood."

We must not make the mistake of feeling that we are so unworthy that we should not dare to receive communion. The centurion's humility did not prevent him from asking Jesus for the favor he needed for his servant. To put the truth as simply as possible, Holy Communion is not a reward for having been good; it is a means for becoming good. If we had to wait until we were really worthy of Jesus, we would delay until the day of eternity dawned. No human can at any time or in any way be worthy of the divine.

The Church has interpreted today's Gospel in such a way that it has a practical meaning for us every time we receive Holy Communion. That meaning is that our humility and our faith are pleasing to the Lord and elicit from him an invitation to share in the banquet of his body and blood in the Holy Eucharist. Jesus said that he had not found faith like that of the centurion among the Israelites. Will he find that faith among us Catholics?

Tenth Sunday of the Year, C

The Compassionate Lord of Life
1 K 17:17-24; Gal 1:11-19; Lk 7:11-17

St. Luke the evangelist loved to emphasize the compassion of Jesus. Today's Gospel is one of the best examples of this emphasis.

In restoring the widow's son to life, Jesus manifested that he is the Lord of life, but in St. Luke's mind the story is incomplete without focusing clearly on the widow. Therein lies the emphasis on compassion.

Most widows in the time of Jesus were in dire straits. There was no help from the state: no pension, no welfare, no social security, and generally only meager opportunities, if any, for employment. When Jesus came upon the funeral cortege in today's Gospel, we may assume that someone informed him of the circumstances: a widow was about to bury her only son.

St. Luke very lovingly observes that Jesus was moved with pity upon seeing her. His sympathy went out mainly to the woman, not primarily to her dead son. Jesus understood that this widow's most difficult time was not now, but later when after the burial she would have to return alone to an empty house. He realized that her sorrow would be deepened by fear about her future and how she could possibly survive. Most of all in his mind's eye Jesus could see another widow in a year or so after a crucifixion following the lifeless body of her only son to the tomb. He said to the widow, "Do not weep." From us these words would have sounded hollow but from him they gave both comfort and hope. Jesus spoke those compassionate words to the widow as to his own mother.

Jesus touched the litter which supported the body of the dead man. The bearers sensed that Jesus meant them to stop. The woman waited in anticipation of what Jesus would do.

Then she heard words which were full of compassion as well as power: "Young man, I bid you get up." All eyes turned to the dead man. He sat up and began to speak. But that was not the climax. Jesus' compassion, after all, was for the widow. And so St. Luke carefully adds, "Jesus gave him back to his mother."

St. Paul today remarks on how favored he was that God revealed his Son to him so that he might spread the good news. And how favored we are that through this Gospel according to Luke we have had revealed to us the good news of the love of the Lord. This Lord raised us from the death of sin and presented us to our spiritual mother, the Church, who now nourishes us through the word of Sacred Scripture and the sacrament of the Holy Eucharist.

Notice the difference between what Elijah did and what Jesus did when both confronted death. Elijah called out to God and prayed that he would restore life to the woman's son, but Jesus spoke in his own name and by his own authority. He spoke words of real power. Elijah was indeed a prophet of God, but Jesus is himself the Lord of life. We admire and honor the prophet but to Jesus we cry out in our eucharistic acclamation, "Dying you destroyed our death; rising you restored our life."

We will all one day die. Jesus will not touch our coffin or tell the pallbearers to halt. Instead he will reach out his powerful hand to lift us up from the dead on the day of resurrection. And then we will indeed praise Jesus, the compassionate Lord of life.

Eleventh Sunday of the Year, C

An Enticement to Love
2 S 12:7-10, 13; Gal 2:16, 19-21; Lk 7:36-8:3

What is God really like? Is God distant, remote, inaccessible, far removed from us and our world? Does God care about us or what happens to us? How are we to know what God is like?

The Church strongly teaches us that we are to see the revelation of God in Jesus Christ. Jesus is God's divine Son, his perfect image and likeness. In the fullness of time God sent his Son into our world. He became human like us in all things but sin. In his humanity Jesus is like a blueprint, a plan, which has taken on flesh and blood. We learn what God is like by looking at the person of Jesus.

When we see Jesus in the Gospels and listen to his words, we discover that God is a great lover, that he sent his Son to go in search of the lost sheep, and that he welcomes us as the father welcomed his prodigal son. We learn that as he was dying Jesus prayed, "Father, forgive them." He went so far as to offer excuses: "They do not know what they are doing." That is the kind of God our God is.

In today's Gospel we learn an extraordinary lesson. Jesus shows God as one who not only searches out sinners but uses every means to win our love. Simon the Pharisee believed in God but had a very limited understanding of God. He could not comprehend how Jesus could look with favor upon the sinful woman who washed his feet. He did not realize that Jesus was eager to forgive her sins so that she would respond with love. Jesus wanted to win her heart.[1]

Because much had been forgiven her, she responded with great love. In a sense Jesus, "The Hound of Heaven," pursued the woman as God pursued King David. David had committed the grave sin of adultery and he had compounded his guilt by murder. In one era in some places the practice in the Church was that adultery and murder were not to be forgiven. That was a strictness beyond the practice of God, as we see in the first reading. God sent Nathan the prophet to offer David the grace of repentance. In Hebrew the name "David" means "beloved." God loved David so much that he was determined that he was not going to lose him. God in return for repentance wiped out even the sins of murder and adultery. His forgiveness won the heart of David.

And God wants to win our hearts as well. He did not spare even his own Son so that our sins could be forgiven. In every Mass we hear Jesus proclaim. "This is the cup of my blood. It will be shed for you and for all so that sins may be forgiven." We are to understand that Jesus is speaking to us through the priest. We are the "you" for whom Christ shed his blood.

We must never cease to reflect on the enormity of God's love for us as seen in the cross of Christ. Happy are we because our sins have been taken away. And what does God want from us in return? He wants our love.

---

[1] The translation, "Many sins have been forgiven because she has loved much" contradicts the parable. The meaning is that she loves much because much has been forgiven her.

Twelfth Sunday of the Year, C

The Paschal Mystery Is What Matters
Zc 12:10-11; Gal 3:26-29; Lk 9:18-24

On Good Friday people flock to the churches, and rightly so. They know how important to our religion is the death of Jesus on the cross. On Easter Sunday even larger crowds fill the churches, and rightly so. People recognize that the celebration of the Lord's resurrection has special meaning. But regular church goers notice that after Easter the crowds at Mass grow smaller.

Regular church goers are often tempted to ask, "Where are they the rest of the year?" Judgment we must leave to God, but we should reflect on our instinctive recognition that every Sunday is important to us as Catholics, and that the Mass should be a regular part of Sunday so that we may celebrate our salvation. In fact, the Church teaches that Sunday is the first holy day of all from a tradition which has been handed down from the apostles. Catholics on Sunday without the Mass are like members of an orchestra without their instruments. Neither can fulfill their purpose. Our purpose on Sunday is to celebrate the events of our salvation.

These events, which are the death and resurrection of Jesus, transpired over a period of three days, but now they are one reality which the Church calls the Paschal Mystery. The Paschal Mystery was the whole purpose for the coming of the Son of God into our world. From all eternity the Father had determined that sin and death would not frustrate his plan, that his Son would indeed save us from sin and death through his Paschal Mystery.

Jesus' death and resurrection were so much a part of the Father's thinking that in the Old Testament, long before the birth of Jesus, there were signs of what was to come. Zechariah as the spokesman for God prophesied about a mysterious person for whom the people would mourn as parents mourn over the death of an only son. He said that the people would look upon him whom they had thrust through. We know who this person is. It is Jesus, the only Son of God, who died on the cross and whose side was pierced by a lance.

St. Luke presents Jesus in the Gospel as on a journey up to Jerusalem. His face is ever turned toward the Holy City since it was there that the prophecy Jesus himself uttered three times was to be fulfilled: "The Son of Man must endure many sufferings... be put to death and then be raised up on the third day."

We acknowledge the meaning of the death of Jesus in our eucharistic acclamation: "Dying you destroyed our death; rising you restored our life." When Jesus' side was pierced, water and blood poured forth. The ancient tradition of the Church sees in the water a symbol of baptism and in the blood a symbol of the Eucharist. St. Paul today reminds us that we who have been baptized have clothed ourselves with Christ. At baptism we received a white robe, the symbol that we had been clothed in Christ, that we had taken on a new life, a life which was won for us by the Paschal Mystery and now is nourished by the Eucharist.

In another of our acclamations we say of our reception of the Eucharist, "When we eat this bread and drink this cup we proclaim your death, Lord Jesus, until you come in glory." Every Sunday we celebrate the Paschal Mystery which is a reality that has been uppermost in the mind of God from all eternity. We come to the Mass every Sunday to celebrate the Paschal Mystery.

Thirteenth Sunday of the Year, C

Clearing the Road to Heaven
1 K 19:16-21; Gal 5:1, 13-18; Lk 9:51-62

Before highways can be constructed, work crews must clear the roadway. Sometimes trees have to be cut down, boulders have to be moved, and hills have to be leveled. Whatever interferes with the laying of the highway must go.

Jesus had something like that in mind when he invited people to be his disciples. He expected them to remove from their lives whatever stood in the way of following him. His enigmatic statement, "Let the dead bury their dead," did not mean that he opposed the burial of loved ones. In one sense his declaration means that those who reject him are like dead people since they have rejected the Lord of life, but it was also Jesus' way of saying that we must decide that nothing may be more important than loyalty to him.

The first reading today describes an episode from the Old Testament in which a man had to make a decision. Elijah's cloak was a symbol of his prophetic office. When he threw it over Elisha, he was inviting Elisha to succeed him as prophet in Israel. Elisha seemed to hesitate for a moment. He thought of his parents. What should he do? His freedom allowed him to make his own decision. A strong resolution burned within his heart. He slaughtered his oxen and burned his plowing equipment. That meant that he gave up his means of livelihood. He then fed his people in farewell to them, and left to follow Elijah. We might say that he burned his bridges behind him.

Jesus invites us to do much the same, to follow him unreservedly. At baptism he placed a white garment over us. It was a symbol that we were a new people with a new life, a life of true freedom. Jesus wants all of us to be free of all obstacles to full discipleship, but freedom is a somewhat complex reality.

We live in a free society but these days we witness and must endure the abuse of freedom. Our society has canonized the phrase, "Freedom of choice." It is used to justify choosing abortion over the right to life. In fact a former U.S. Senator declared in his dogmatic manner that "Freedom of choice is the most fundamental of human rights." He was wrong — dead wrong. His idea of freedom is not what Jesus intends for us.

The kind of freedom Jesus gives us is for the sake of love. Jesus does not force us to become his disciples, to be devoted to him, to love him above everyone and everything. He grants us freedom to choose because love which is forced is not love at all.

Faithful to the intentions of Jesus is St. Paul who teaches us that "we have been called to live in freedom, but not a freedom that gives free rein to the flesh." This "free rein" is actually a slavery. If we are addicted to drugs, to illicit sex, to avarice or violence, we are not free. Matters need not be that grave. When we allow a habit of gossip, the vice of arrogance, or a spirit of selfishness to rule us, we have in effect abused our freedom. Sin is a slavery and the opposite of freedom.

In our eucharistic acclamation we acknowledge that Jesus paid a great price for our freedom: "Lord, by your cross and resurrection, you have set us free." Jesus freed us from sin so that of our own free will we may love him unreservedly.

Fourteenth Sunday of the Year, C

Who Are the Laborers for the Lord's Harvest?

Is 66:10-14; Gal 6:14-18; Lk 10:1-12, 17-20

A man observed that just once he would like to hear the word "vocation" from the pulpit as referring to a calling from God other than to the priesthood or the religious life. Here is that one time: Every Catholic has a vocation from God.

Today's Gospel has often been interpreted in a narrow sense. When Jesus directs us to ask the harvest master to send workers to his harvest, many think that he wants us to pray for more priests. Indeed he does, but his intention is not limited to that calling.

The Second Vatican Council has called all Catholics to full, active participation in the liturgy and in the mission of the Church. That is a vocation. In the Mass which was celebrated before the Council the priest did almost everything by himself. He was assisted by a small boy, the altar server, but the people were present in a passive role. The priest said all the prayers, read all the Scriptures, offered the canon in silence, and gave Holy Communion by himself or with the help of another priest. Only the altar boy responded to the prayers of the priest; the congregation kept silence. Lay people were not allowed to read the Scriptures or to say any of the prayers or to assist with Holy Communion. And what surprises many people who are not familiar with the previous missal, or who have forgotten its prescriptions, is the fact that the priest alone said even the "Our Father." That's right; the people were not allowed to say the "Our Father." This passive role of the people to a large extent reflected their lack of involvement in the mission of the Church. For a work to be considered Catholic, a priest had to do it.

The Second Vatican Council decreed that in the restoration and promotion of the sacred liturgy the aim to be considered above all else is the full, active, and conscious participation by all the people (see the *Constitution on the Liturgy*, 14). But participation in the liturgy is incomplete until it leads to participation in the mission of the Church.

The ordained priesthood is essential to the Church. That cannot be changed. But the Holy Spirit through the Council is now calling all Catholics to be responsible members of the Church. No more leaving everything to the priest. No more avoiding those who challenge our faith by telling them they really should talk to a priest. No more fearing to manifest the Catholic faith at work or anywhere else. No more excuses that our faith is personal and private and should not influence us in politics. The truth is that all of us are called, especially through the sacrament of confirmation, to be active, involved, and responsible Catholics.

The Church fulfills the image of Jerusalem as a mother (see the first reading). The Church through her union with Christ produces children and nourishes them through word and sacrament. Like a good parent, the Church is also a teacher and a guide. From this image and reality of the Church everyone of us must draw guidance and strength to be active Catholics.

Jesus tells us that our names are inscribed in heaven. In that we should rejoice. But until the Lord comes again in glory to bring us to heaven, we must remember that God's work on earth through his Church must truly be our own.

Fifteenth Sunday of the Year, C

Who Is the Best Samaritan?
Dt 30:10-14; Col 1:15-20; Lk 10:25-37

Jesus loved to tell parables when he preached, and so it is not surprising that to the question, "Who is my neighbor?" Jesus did not give a direct answer. Instead he told a parable.

This parable is so familiar and so powerful that it has given an expression to a language. To say that someone is a Good Samaritan is to say that he helps people in need. In the story the Samaritan who stopped and helped the man who had fallen in with robbers proved himself to be the kind of neighbor Jesus had in mind, even though the Samaritan did not know the afflicted man and the afflicted man did not know him.

To his parables Jesus often gave an unexpected twist. The twist to this parable is the meaning which Jesus gave to the word "neighbor." It is the fact that the hero is a Samaritan. Remember that the story was being told to the Jews who despised Samaritans. They saw them as traitors and heretics. Those who heard Jesus must have been shocked. They were dismayed that he proposed to them the least likely person as a hero.

Some of the early Fathers of the Church put still another twist on the story. They saw in the person we call the Good Samaritan an image of Jesus himself. In other words, they thought that the least likely person represents for us the most likely person to help. And help us Jesus did.

The human race was waylaid by sin. Sin had stripped us of our dignity as human beings. It had robbed us, taking from us the grace of God. It had attacked us so severely that we all were like a person who is half dead. Jesus lifted us up, not on a beast, but on his own shoulders and brought us to the Church so that we could be cared for until he returns in glory on the day of our resurrection.

But after Jesus brought us to the Church, he did not leave us to go on his way. He is with his Church all days even until the end of the world. Through the ministry of the Church in baptism Jesus heals the wounds of our sins, restores the life of grace, and gives us the dignity of the children of God. In confirmation Jesus strengthens the life of grace within us; he confirms our identity as children of God and heirs of heaven. Jesus comes to us in the Church through word and sacrament: the word of Sacred Scripture and the sacrament of his body and blood are our spiritual nourishment.

The word "neighbor" literally means someone who is near. Jesus proved himself to be more than a neighbor, more than someone who is near to us. He has made us part of his body, his mystical body, the Church. In him we continue in being; as the second reading teaches us, he is Head of the body, the Church.

As we go through life, sin will continue to stalk us, waiting for an unguarded moment when it can attack us in our weakness. But we need never be alone in our struggle. It is vital that we learn the lesson of today's responsorial psalm: "Turn to the Lord in your need, and you will live." When we turn to the Lord we will realize that he is not too mysterious and remote for us. Jesus is not merely the *Good* Samaritan. He is the best.

Sixteenth Sunday of the Year, C

Sitting at the Feet of Jesus

Gn 18:1-10; Col 1:24-28; Lk 10:38-42

I think that when we hear the story of Martha and Mary many of us are inclined to feel sorry for Martha. Mary had left all the work for Martha to do while she enjoyed her conversation with Jesus. When Martha complained, Jesus seemed almost to scold her, even though mildly, perhaps shaking his head from side to side as he said: "Martha, Martha, you are anxious and upset about many things. Mary has chosen the better portion." But what exactly was it that Mary had chosen? Was it simply to play the part of a gracious, lovely hostess while Martha sweated over a hot stove?

When St. Luke wrote that Mary sat at the feet of Jesus, he was not describing her posture but her relationship with him. "To sit at the feet" of someone meant to be that person's disciple. In the Jewish culture of Jesus' day it was unheard of that a woman would be the disciple of a rabbi. Religion, or at least its external observances, was left to men. Jesus broke a tradition of long standing because that tradition was not right. He had come to call all people, women equally with men, children as well as adults, and even those who were thought of as sinners, to be his disciples. He insisted that Mary had made the right choice. She understood his invitation and accepted it. Martha felt obliged to maintain her stereotype, to agree that her place was in the kitchen. Jesus was practical enough to realize that food had to be prepared, and so he told Martha that one dish, something simple, would be enough. Then he added, not only for Martha, but for everyone of all times: "Mary has chosen the better portion and she shall not be deprived of it." Jesus wanted Martha to make the same choice.

Mary represents all women in the Church, but in a larger

sense she is a model for everyone. We are called to be disciples of Jesus, to offer him the warm hospitality he experienced in that home in Bethany, to listen to him as intently as did Mary, to make him the priority of our lives, and to allow nothing and no one to deprive us of our relationship with him. Abraham offered hospitality to the angels who were messengers from God. We are urged to offer hospitality to Jesus, who is the Son of God.

We should understand that in a profound sense we sit at the feet of Jesus at Mass during the Liturgy of the Word. The Second Vatican Council solemnly teaches us that "Christ is present in his word, since it is he himself who speaks when the Holy Scriptures are read in the church" (*Constitution on the Liturgy*, 7). Jesus wishes us to focus our attention on him, to hear his word in faith, to absorb it and to apply it to our lives. Then we are nourished with a sacred food, the Eucharist, which is prepared not by Martha, but by Jesus himself.

Perhaps we find the example of Mary difficult to follow. It is easy to allow the preoccupations of daily living to distract us from hearing and following the teachings of Jesus. It is tempting to allow the false values which are presented to us in our materialistic society to turn us aside from the truths of our faith. We must be faithful about coming to Mass because here we can put aside distractions to concentrate on what is really important to us. During our liturgical celebration our place of worship should become our Bethany where we learn to be true disciples.

Seventeenth Sunday of the Year, C

With Jesus We Pray "Abba"

Gn 18:20-32; Col 2:12-14; Lk 11:1-13

The Lord's Prayer, the "Our Father," has taken on an appropriate prominence during the celebration of Mass. One reason is that, thanks to the changes brought about by the Second Vatican Council, we all may say or sing this prayer in our own language. (It is hard to realize that previously in the so-called "Tridentine" Mass the priest alone said this prayer and he did so in Latin; no one was allowed to join him.) People offer this prayer while standing alert, sometimes extending their arms, sometimes raising their eyes toward heaven, sometimes joining hands with a neighbor, but always it seems with a special attention.

The version of the Lord's Prayer we hear in St. Luke's Gospel is slightly different from the one we use at Mass, which follows St. Matthew's version (6:9-12). We should not be surprised at the difference. For one thing, the prayer is so important that we may rightly presume that Jesus taught it on several occasions, and most likely not always in exactly the same words. For another, the prayer had been part of the liturgy for over a generation before any of the Gospels was written. The prayer was offered by memory, and consequently with slight variations, until St. Luke and St. Matthew wrote down the version in common use in their respective communities.

All of this leads to an important conclusion. What is new or special about the prayer is not the nature or number of the petitions within the prayer. After all, the Jews often prayed that God's name might be hallowed and that his will might be done. Psalm 51 from the Old Testament is an eloquent and fervent prayer for forgiveness which preceded the prayer for forgiveness in the "Our Father."

What is special about the prayer is the unique way in which Jesus addressed God. He called upon the Lord, the almighty, the creator of heaven and earth, the judge of the living and the dead as "Father." And not exactly as "Father," but as "Abba," which means "Papa" or "Daddy." It was the way in which a little child, with intimate love and pure familiarity, addressed his parent. Of all the many words of Jesus which are recorded in the Gospels, surely "Abba" is among the most sacred.

Think how different the prayer of Abraham is from that of Jesus. Abraham, the father of the chosen people and our father in faith, dared to approach God to beg him to spare the people of Sodom and Gomorrah. He was so bold that he even bargained with God. But he did not dare to address God as Jesus did. He would have thought it brazen to have said, "Come on, Dad. Have a heart. Take it easy on Sodom and Gomorrah." No one had addressed God as "Abba," as "Dad," until Jesus did.

And yet we are invited, actually we are told, to address God as "Abba," our loving Father. The reason we can do so is that God has given us new life in company with Christ. It is the family life of the Blessed Trinity, the life we received at baptism when we were made members of the Church, God's family here on earth.

Whatever our posture or gestures may be during the Lord's prayer at Mass we must realize how blessed we are to address God as Jesus did, to call him our "Abba."

Eighteenth Sunday of the Year, C

Praying as Catholics with the Pope
Ec 1:2; 2:21-23; Col 3:1-5, 9-11; Lk 12:13-21

In his book, *Crossing the Threshold of Hope*, Pope John Paul II answered the question, "How — and for whom, for what — does the Pope pray?" He responded by referring to the opening sentence of the great *Constitution on the Church in the Modern World* of Vatican II. This is not surprising since as a bishop at the council he was on the committee which framed this document which is known in Latin as *Gaudium et Spes*. This is the sentence the Pope had in mind: "The joys and the hopes, the sorrows and the anxieties of the people of this age, especially those who are poor or in any way afflicted, are the joys and hopes, the sorrows and the anxieties of the followers of Christ." This sentiment is in perfect accord with the warning of Jesus, "Avoid greed in all its forms." Greed prompts us to pray for selfish reasons rather than for those who are in need as does the Pope.

The Pope, of course, as the pastor of the universal Church, must not omit anyone or any need from his concern, especially in his prayer. And yet what is true of the Pope in this regard is true of each one of us in our own way since we all bear the name "Catholic," a name which indicates that we are a universal Church, and not one which is limited to any nation or culture or ethnicity.

Our Catholicism and our effort to overcome greed are manifested by how we pray during the liturgical celebration of the Eucharist. Of special significance is the Prayer of the Faithful. This name indicates that the prayer is an exercise of the priesthood of the faithful which flows from the sacrament of baptism. It is also known as the "General Intercessions." This name indicates that we are to pray for all of humanity and not merely for our own private intentions. We offer petitions for the

Church both locally and throughout the world, for civil authorities, for those oppressed by various needs, for all people, and for the salvation of the world. (See the *General Instruction of the Roman Missal*, 45.)

The Eucharistic Prayer also relates to that opening sentence of the *Constitution on the Church in the Modern World*. The third eucharistic prayer in particular seems almost to strain not to omit anyone: "Lord, may this sacrifice advance the peace and salvation of all the world. — Strengthen in faith and love... the entire people your Son has gained for you. — In mercy and love unite all your children wherever they may be. — Welcome into your kingdom... all who have left this world in your friendship."

Of course we may and should pray for our own needs and those of our loved ones, and yet we need the reminder from St. Paul that we must set our hearts on what pertains to higher realms. We rise to those higher realms when we are generous and unselfish in our prayer. It must be added that prayer by itself for those in need is not enough. We also need action which is inspired and motivated by prayer. Others may snub the poor, look down upon those on welfare, despise the immigrants, and choose to live in isolation from human misery, but not Catholics. We believe that "the joys and hopes, the sorrows and the anxieties of the people of this age, especially those who are poor or in any way afflicted, are the joys and hopes, the sorrows and the anxieties of the followers of Christ."

Nineteenth Sunday of the Year, C

Fear Not, Little Flock
Ws 18:6-9; Heb 11:1-2, 8-19; Lk 12:32-48

Throughout his life Jesus followed the Jewish form of greeting which was customary at that time, "Peace be with you." It was a way of saying, "Hello, how are you?" After his death and resurrection, Jesus transformed this greeting into a gift of serenity in the midst of this life's uncertainties. When Jesus greeted his disciples after his death and resurrection and said "Peace be with you," his words became an assurance that all was well. Jesus offered peace because he had won the victory over our twin enemies, sin and death.

Jesus offers us the same assurance which he gave to his disciples. He says to us in today's Gospel, "Do not live in fear, little flock." And yet fear is part of life. President Franklin Delano Roosevelt in his inaugural address on March 4, 1933 said to the American people: "… the only thing we have to fear is fear itself." The United States at the time was sunk in a deep economic depression, the likes of which we have not seen since. Wealthy business men were reduced to selling pencils on street corners. Women who had cherished their elaborate homes found themselves without a place to live. A past of foolish economic maneuvers had brought about a terrible present and suggested nothing but a desolate future. Despite the President's reassuring words, many Americans thought they had much to fear.

What about us? Does our faith in the words of Jesus calm our fears, not about the economy, but about the great issues of life and death? The Letter to the Hebrews in the Mass of this Sunday tells us that "faith is confident assurance concerning what we hope for, and conviction about things we do not see." What is our faith about the future based on? What is the source of our conviction? It is the past.

In 1933 the past begot fear in the hearts of Americans. For us the past should strengthen our faith. Think about the great ancestors of our faith: Abraham and Sarah, Isaac and Jacob and all the devout people of the Old Testament. They were seeking a homeland. They found it, not primarily on this earth, but in heaven. They finally discovered they had nothing to fear. Their destiny should fill us with confidence.

When we look to the era when Jesus was on this earth, what do we see? We see that by dying he destroyed our death and by rising he restored our life. We see that by his cross and resurrection, he has set us free; he is the Savior of the world.

After the "Our Father," we pray for the gift of peace: "Deliver us, Lord, from every evil and grant us peace in our day." Just before Holy Communion, the priest prays, "Lord Jesus Christ, you said to your apostles: I leave you peace, my peace I give you. Look not on our sins but on the faith of your Church and grant us the peace and unity of your kingdom." When we offer a sign of peace to each other, we share in the offering of peace which Christ gave to his disciples.

Our faith is based on the reality of all that God has done, first in the events of the Old Testament and then in a special way in the death and resurrection of his Son. The only thing we have to fear, is not fear itself, but a lack of faith.

Twentieth Sunday of the Year, C

The Movement of the Spirit in Our Time
Jr 38:4-6, 8-10; Heb 12:1-4; Lk 12:49-53

These days "tension" is a word which is in the active vocabulary of most people. We recognize tension at work, tension within a marriage, tension about making ends meet. Tension occurs when forces move in opposite directions. A simple example is a rubber band: pull the ends away from each other and you produce tension. If the tension continues to increase, the rubber band will snap. Jesus warned that his doctrine would bring about tensions which would end in divisions, even within families.

In the family of the Church there is tension, especially in many places regarding the liturgy. We ought to be living like a happy family, in unity and peace, but forces are pulling in opposite directions, one wishing to move forward with the restoration of Vatican II and the other wanting to go back to earlier theology and practices.

Here is straight talk. Moving backwards is not the right direction. Wanting to believe that the Pope is ultra-conservative and regrets where Vatican II has been leading the Church is not only a vain wish; it is an affront to the Holy Spirit. In fact, the Pope seems to dismiss the strident voices of complaint against the Council without so much as a nod in their direction.

At an important meeting of the world's Cardinals in the summer of 1994 Pope John Paul II declared: "The liturgy is doubtless at the center of the Church's life. The process of liturgical renewal in the spirit of the Second Vatican Council is continuing under the direction and supervision of the Congregation of Divine Worship and the Discipline of the Sacraments."

The Pope acts in accord with the solemn pronouncement of the Council's *Constitution on the Liturgy*, a pronouncement which should inspire every person of the Church and must guide every bishop and priest: "Zeal for the promotion and restoration of the liturgy is rightly held to be a sign of the providential disposition of God in our time, as a movement of the Holy Spirit in his Church. It is today a distinguishing mark of the Church's life, indeed of the whole tenor of contemporary religious thought and action" (43).

Perhaps you have been spared the grief of reading attacks by Catholics upon the Second Vatican Council, such as "the Second Vatican Council was the door through which the devil entered the Church to bring about the worldwide revolt against the order of God." If you have been so spared, thank God for that favor. If you have in any way been swayed by these charges, dismiss them as evil. Follow the advice of the Letter to the Hebrews: "Let us keep our eyes fixed on Jesus who inspires and perfects our faith."

Of course there have been abuses against the liturgy but that is no excuse for attacking the restored liturgy itself. We do not abandon the judicial system of our country just because some judges and juries fail to act in accord with justice. The abuse is not the system, but a contradiction of it. Do not end up on the wrong side against God as did the princes who wanted to put Jeremiah, God's prophet, to death. The promotion and restoration of the sacred liturgy is God's work through the Holy Spirit. Do not be the cause of tension in the Church. Make sure you are pulling in the same direction as the Holy Spirit.

Twenty-first Sunday of the Year, C

Getting Through the Narrow Door
Is 66:18-21; Heb 12:5-7, 11-13; Lk 13:22-30

Is it hard to get into heaven? Jesus seems to say it is when he warns, "Try to come in through the narrow door." His warning is somewhat confusing since he also says that "People will come from the east and the west, from the north and the south, and will take their place at the feast in the kingdom of God." The prophecy from Isaiah today says much the same thing. In other words, there will be a lot of people for the kingdom. How are all of them going to make it through the narrow door?

I think about what happens on a freeway (or expressway) when there is a bad accident. The police close off three lanes; only a single lane is open which is like the narrow door. All the traffic slows down and at times comes to a complete stop because of the bottleneck. As I think of the narrow door Jesus referred to, I see people all bunched up like cars on the freeway, moving very slowly, trying to squeeze through the one open lane. Drivers are upset. They are fussing and fuming and making obscene gestures at each other. Cars and tempers are overheating. The bottleneck is a pain in the neck. Sin is like the accident on the freeway which causes all the trouble.

This is not an inviting scene, this image of what it means to get to heaven. But when I think more clearly about the image of the narrow door, I realize that actually only one person has to get through the door. That person is Jesus. And through the door to heaven he has passed in the Paschal Mystery of his death and resurrection. We do not have to force our way through the narrow door. All we need do is make sure we are united with Jesus. Many bodies do not have to get through the door, only one, and that is the body of Christ, the mystical body of Christ, the Church.

Jesus, however, gave a second warning. People, Jesus said, will protest to the master of the house, "We ate and drank in your presence. You taught in our streets." But the master will reply, "I do not know where you come from. Away from me, you evildoers."

This is disturbing because we eat and drink in Jesus' presence: at Mass we partake of his body and blood. Obviously a merely passive participation in Mass is not enough. Receiving Holy Communion without a devotion which moves us to allow Jesus to transform our lives is of little spiritual value. What we do at Mass, especially in receiving communion, must influence the way we live. Jesus does not teach in our streets, but he does teach in our church during the Liturgy of the Word. That is why we must take to heart the lessons of the Scriptures, such as that from today's Letter to the Hebrews: "My children, do not disdain the discipline of the Lord nor lose heart when he reproves you; for, whom the Lord loves, he disciplines."

And yet with it all, the indispensable requirement is that we be faithful people, that we remain united with Christ in his mystical body, the Church. That is the way to make sure that we will make it past all the fuss and bother of this world into the eternal kingdom of heaven.

Twenty-second Sunday of the Year, C

Humility Leads to a High Place
Si 3:17-18, 20, 28-29; Heb 12:18-19, 22-24; Lk 14:1, 7-14

A simple but impressive ceremony occurs during the Good Friday liturgy. After the people have gathered, the priest and ministers prostrate themselves in silence before the altar. It is an awesome expression of humility before the Lord. The priest and ministers lying before the altar look like dead men. But then they stand to show that they have been raised from the death of sin to newness of life in Christ.

This ancient ritual is now expressed in a less dramatic way during the penitential rite of the Mass. Before God and each other we acknowledge our sinfulness and our need for God's mercy. In a sense we prostrate ourselves before the Lord. It is our way of fulfilling the instruction of Jesus, "When you are invited to a wedding party, go and sit in the lowest place." Jesus' instruction is in accord with the wisdom we hear from the Book of Sirach: "Conduct your affairs with humility. Humble yourself the more, the greater you are, and you will find favor with God."

And find favor with God we have. Through his Son's offering of himself on the cross, the Father has raised us up to new life. When we have humbled ourselves during the penitential rite — after we have spiritually prostrated ourselves or taken the lowest place — Christ says to us, "Come up higher." Then we can take our place with the dignity Christ has conferred upon us. We can participate fully in the sacrifice which is the great wedding banquet of the Lamb of God.

Perhaps some of us are one-sided in this matter of humility. We may emphasize our sinfulness and our unworthiness to such an extreme that we seem to have forgotten what Christ has done for us in raising us up from sin. Christ calls us to true, not false, humility. On the other hand, some of us may be a little smug, a little self-satisfied, like those who immediately took the highest places at the wedding feast. Christ calls us not to pride, but to humility.

Balance is needed when we think about whether we are worthy or unworthy. The liturgy gives us that balance by encouraging us on the one hand to admit our sinfulness and assuring us on the other hand that Christ has raised us up from the death of sin.

During the second eucharistic prayer the priest says to God in the name of us all: "We thank you for counting us worthy to stand in your presence and to serve you." The Latin is actually very strong. A literal translation would be: "We thank you for making us worthy to stand up straight before you, face to face."

Humble people must be careful not to suggest that Christ did not do a very good job in redeeming them. We must never think that we are still miserable creatures who are not, and can never be, pleasing to God.

Just before communion the priest declares, "Behold the Lamb of God who takes away the sins of the world. Happy are those who are called to his supper." This supper is not the Last Supper. It is the great wedding supper of the Lord in heaven (see Revelation 19:9). Happy indeed are we, lowly though we are in ourselves, that through the Eucharist we will be led to a high place in heaven where we will enjoy the great wedding banquet of the Lamb of God.

Twenty-third Sunday of the Year, C

Being Prepared to Be Faithful Disciples
Ws 9:13-18; Phm 9-10, 12-17; Lk 14:25-33

Behind today's second reading is an interesting episode. A slave by the name of Onesimus escaped from his master, Philemon, and fled to St. Paul for safety. Paul was eager to protect the runaway slave, but he realized that something of higher value than the freedom of Onesimus was at stake. He was concerned that the master, Philemon, act as a true disciple of Jesus Christ.

Paul could easily have hidden Onesimus or even demanded in the name of Christ that Philemon grant him freedom. Instead Paul sent Onesimus back to Philemon, somewhat, I imagine, to the slave's chagrin and the owner's surprise. With the slave Paul sent a letter, part of which we have heard today. The point of the letter is that Paul did not want to force virtue upon Philemon, that he wanted instead to invite him to be generous. Giving up a slave meant surrendering valuable property. It was a challenge for Philemon. Paul concluded his letter by saying, "Confident of your compliance, I write you, knowing that you will do more than I say."

Actually we are not sure how Philemon responded. Did he release his slave or not? Did Philemon perhaps remind Paul that slavery was legal and that he had a right to keep his slave? Did he complain that Paul really did not understand the economics of his situation and that his slave was necessary for his financial success? We do not know whether Philemon responded with the generosity which Paul expected of him as a disciple of Jesus.

What we do know is that as disciples of Jesus we are called to be generous in our response, not to live according to the minimum or to look for excuses for not being the kind of Catholics we should. In the Gospel Jesus warns us through the examples about building a tower and going to battle that we have to be prepared for the Christian experience. Heaven is our promised inheritance but that lies in the future. Meanwhile here on earth we are expected to be faithful disciples who must hear and heed the words of Jesus, "Anyone who does not take up his cross and follow me cannot be my disciple."

Perhaps our cross is to endure the pain involved in giving up our own slavery to alcohol, tobacco, or drugs. Our cross may be to embrace the discipline we need to overcome gossip, to forgive someone who has injured us gravely, or to be kind and thoughtful toward someone who drives us crazy.

God does not force us to be virtuous any more than Paul forced Philemon to give up his slave. Even when bad things happen to us, God does not compel us to accept them as a cross. We have to make the effort to see that we can turn something awful into something valuable by joining our sufferings to those of Christ.

In every Mass we remember the death and the resurrection of Christ in such a way that through the Holy Eucharist his sacrifice is a reality before us on the altar. When we hear the words, "This is my body given up for you," we should in our hearts say to God our Father, "Yes, this is my body too and with your Son I offer myself to you." When we hear the words, "This is the cup of my blood," we should say, "And this is my blood too which I wish to shed out of love for you, if such is your will." We must be prepared to be faithful disciples of Jesus Christ.

Twenty-fourth Sunday of the Year, C

The Father Will Do Anything for Us
Ex 32:7-11, 13-14; 1 Tm 1:12-17; Lk 15:1-32

When parents love their children, they are willing to do anything for them. It seems to happen, however, that children seldom realize how deep their parents' love is for them. Both sons in Jesus' parable today failed to understand their father's love. Neither comprehended that his devotion to them precisely as his sons could never change, no matter what. The father could not even imagine altering his relationship with his sons.

We usually think first of the younger son, the one who is known as the prodigal son, the son who wasted his inheritance. When he realized his folly, he prepared a little speech to give to his father. In it he would recognize that he was no longer worthy to be called a son, that he would become a hired hand. When he arrived back home and attempted to give his speech, the father would have none of it. He threw his arms around the young man, kissed him, and called for a celebration. He insisted that his son be given shoes to wear, a sign that he was back as part of the family and not a servant since only family members wore shoes in the house. (An old spiritual sang, "All God's chillun got shoes.")

The older son we somewhat sympathize with. After all, he had not left home but had continued to work dutifully for his father. He refused to join the party for his younger brother, and the reason he gave for his refusal revealed that he too had failed to understand his relationship with his father. He protested, "For years now I have slaved for you, yet you never gave me so much as a kid goat to celebrate with my friends." His father was flabbergasted because his son thought of himself as "slaving" for him with an expectation of a reward. He was not serving his father out of love. The father responded, "You are with me always and everything I have is yours." What really reveals the father's feelings is the fact he addressed the angry son tenderly. He did not admonish him. He looked at him and said two words, "My son."

The father in the parable was a remarkable man. When the younger son decided to return home, he ran out eagerly to welcome him. When the older son refused to come into the house for the celebration, the father went out to him and pleaded with him.

Even more remarkable is God our Father. To begin to understand and appreciate our God, we must remember who we are. We are children of God, his beloved sons and daughters. God will never change his loving relationship with us, even if we abandon him. No matter how foolish we may be in life, no matter how far we may wander from God, our Father reaches out to us by his grace.

Every Sunday God welcomes us to his house, the church. Since God is our Father, his house is our family home. Here he invites us to the family celebration, the sacred meal at which his divine Son speaks to us in the words of Scripture and nourishes us in the Eucharist. We call this sacred meal a celebration, a joyful and happy event because we acknowledge that we were once dead in sin but that Jesus by dying has restored us to life. We have become part of God's family, his beloved children, and God will never change that relationship. God loves us and he has shown that he will do anything for us. Can we ever be so foolish as to forget that God is our Father and we are his children?

Twenty-fifth Sunday of the Year, C

Taking More Initiative than the Worldly
Am 8:4-7; 1 Tm 2:1-8; Lk 16:1-13

At this time of year major league baseball teams are intent on the pennant and the World Series. In particular the teams which are leading their divisions are at a point where they are eager to trade for that one player who, they think, is just what they need to field a team which can finish first. They are willing to undergo considerable expense, either in trades or salary, to get that player. They take the kind of initiative which Jesus commends today in the rich man's manager.

The Gospel seems to suggest that Jesus approves dishonesty on the part of the manager. Some commentators observe that in all likelihood the manager was actually surrendering his commission and not cheating his boss, even though he had done a poor job of managing the boss's affairs. The boss gave no sign that he felt cheated. In fact, he commended his employee for being enterprising and for taking initiative.

Jesus' point was this: here is a man who wants to guarantee his future after he loses his job. He does not just sit around and moan about his fate; he does something to win favor with his boss's debtors. Jesus in this Gospel is not concerned about initiative in business any more than he is concerned about winning in major league baseball, but he does hope that we are concerned about our eternal salvation. More than that, he expects us to work as hard for spiritual values as some people do for financial gain.

Today's Scriptures suggest two areas in which we should grow spiritually. They are prayer for those who are in need and justice for the poor. The two are closely linked. The second reading today is one of the sources of our Prayer of the Faithful at Mass. Our prayer should reflect the broad, expansive nature of the prayer recommended in the Letter to Timothy. We need to include everyone in our prayer, and yet we should have a special emphasis on the poor, the downtrodden, and the despised of this world.

Prayer must lead to action, in particular the kind of action advocated by Amos, the prophet of social justice. He condemned those who through their unjust practices "trample upon the needy and destroy the poor of the land," and he admonished those whose only thought was financial gain. Amos would not have favored the outlook of Calvin Coolidge who said that "the business of America is business." And neither should we. Our business should be sharing with others who are in need, being the advocates rather than the critics of those who live in destitution, and recognizing that God calls us to share our talents and blessings with others.

Catholics ought always to be known as the people who take the side of the poor and who are generous in helping them. We are called to be the ones who "make friends for ourselves with the poor through our use of this world's goods." We are rightly expected to be the ones whom God can trust with "elusive wealth" because we know how to share it with others.

Above all, Catholics should show initiative and enterprise not only in praying for those in need but in reaching out to help them as best we can. That will ensure that we have only one master, the great, good and generous Father of our Lord Jesus Christ.

Twenty-sixth Sunday of the Year, C

Lazarus Would Never Be Complacent
Am 6:1, 4-7; 1 Tm 6:11-16; Lk 16:19-31

During Mass we often hear Jesus teach by means of parables. It can be helpful to ask ourselves, "Who am I in the parable?" This Sunday Jesus tells a powerful story about the rich man who ignored the poor man at his doorstep. The rich man in the story has no name (he has been given the nickname "Dives," which is simply the Latin word for "rich"). Perhaps the lack of a name is a sign to us that we should ponder whether we are that man who was so complacent, so self-satisfied, that he did not even notice Lazarus at his gate, even though it was obvious that Lazarus was very ill, that he was covered with sores, and he was so hungry that he longed to eat the scraps which fell from the rich man's table.

But there is another way to see ourselves in today's parable. Before we too readily agree that we should be alert to see and care for all those who are in grave need, we may do well to recognize that all of us are Lazarus. To be more precise, we have been in his predicament in a spiritual if not a physical way.

Without our redemption by Christ we were even worse off than Lazarus. We had no external sores but within we suffered the effects of sin. We lacked proper nourishment, not of mere scraps, but of the holy body and blood of the Lord. We were outside the gate of the Church, and without Christ we would never have been able to cross the threshold of his house here on earth in order one day to enter his eternal home in heaven.

God took pity on us. He sent us his Son as our great High Priest, our Mediator, who spanned the great abyss which Abraham told the rich man separated him from heaven. God has given us the faith to believe in the redemptive power of the death of Christ and to embrace the truth of his resurrection which is the source of our sure and firm hope. God has given us the wisdom to embrace the Eucharist as the sacred body of the Lord given up for us and his precious blood poured out for us. Spiritually we were like Lazarus in his physical misery but we have become like him as he was lifted up by angels. We are blessed indeed that Jesus was as not as indifferent to us as Dives was to Lazarus. To make the application which Jesus intended in the parable, let us imagine Lazarus has come back to earth. Do you think he would ever be as neglectful as was Dives, the rich man? Do you think he could ever ignore someone now who is in as wretched condition as he was? Do you believe Lazarus would be anything other than a person of compassion who would do much more than give a beggar the scraps from his table?

But we do not have to imagine Lazarus coming back from the dead. We are Lazarus, everyone of us. All that God has done for us should be the motive for our being generous to those in need, kind to those who are without comfort, and loving toward everyone as God is toward us. In the Preface of the Mass the priest proclaims in our name: "Father, we do well always and everywhere to give you thanks." Our liturgical prayer of thanksgiving should move us always and everywhere to treat everyone with the kind of generous love which God has shown to us in the person of his Son, our Priest and our Redeemer.

Twenty-seventh Sunday of the Year, C

Who's in Charge Anyway?
Hab 1:2-3; 2:2-4; 2 Tm 1:6-8, 13-14; Lk 17:5-10

We live in a violent, hate-filled world. It is a world of drive-by murders and drug crazed people. It is a world in which babies are aborted and little children are abused and killed by their parents. It is a world of political and economical corruption. Is there more evil in the world now than in former generations, or is it that the media make us more aware of what is going on?

Habakkuk, a Jewish prophet, lived six centuries before Christ. It was a time which in its own way was really as bad as our own. In Judah there was widespread political intrigue, corruption of morals, social injustice, contempt for the poor, and, worst of all, a creeping idolatry which ignored the God of Abraham, Isaac, and Jacob, the God who had saved the Israelites from slavery in Egypt and who had formed them into a people with whom he had made a solemn covenant.

Habakkuk the prophet was disgusted. Almost no one among his people showed any wish for repentance and renewal. Habakkuk, to put it plainly, was fed up. So he turned to God in prayer, but not the polite and compliant kind of prayer which seems appropriate before the majesty of God. Habakkuk complained bitterly to God. His patience was just about at an end. He prayed, "How long, O Lord? I cry for help but you do not listen! I cry out to you, 'Violence!' but you do not intervene."

Other people may have prayed to God this way before Habakkuk, but the Bible makes no mention of them. Habakkuk seems to have embarked on a new, bold way of speaking to God. His insistence with God is remarkable but God's response is even more remarkable. He did not thunder down words of rebuke upon this puny creature of his. God did not demand, "How dare you speak to me this way?" Rather God asked Habakkuk to be patient. Then he added, "The just man, because of his faith, will live."

Habakkuk was a man of faith. He believed that God the Creator was responsible for his creation. He called upon God who had made a covenant with his people to remember his faithfulness and his love for them. Habakkuk did complain, that is true, but he complained to the right Person, to the one true God who alone could clean up the mess in the world. He believed that God is in charge. Habakkuk was a man of great faith.

Faith is a gift. The apostles feared that their faith was not strong enough. Perhaps they were thinking of someone like Habakkuk when they asked Jesus, "Lord, increase our faith." That plea for greater faith must surely be our own when we pray at Mass, especially when, in the Prayer of the Faithful after the homily, we ask God to right the wrongs of our society.

Our prayer should be filled with a boldness which comes from faith. St. Paul assured Timothy, "The spirit God has given us is no cowardly spirit, but rather one that makes us strong, loving, and wise." That spirit we received at our baptism. It should move us to pray to God with respect but also with tenacity, not only at Mass but whenever we pray. A prayer that is strong, loving, and wise acknowledges that God the Creator is the right person to complain to because God is the one who is in charge.

Twenty-eighth Sunday of the Year, C

Give Thanks and Praise to God
2 K 5:14-17; 2 Tm 2:8-13; Lk 17:11-19

The Mass is the great, central act of our religion as Catholics. Because the Mass is an action of Christ the Priest and of his body, the Church, it is a sacred action surpassing all others. Nothing can equal the power of the Mass or substitute for its importance. (See the *Constitution on the Liturgy*, 7.)

The Mass is so rich that we do not seem to be able to settle on a single designation. The Mass is the unbloody sacrifice of the cross, it is the Lord's Supper, it is the living memorial of the Paschal Mystery, it is the sacrament of the death and resurrection of Christ, it is truly his body given up for us and truly his blood poured out for us, it is the sacred banquet in which Christ is consumed, and it is the pledge of resurrection to eternal life. Amid all these splendid indications of the Mass, many priests and people since the Second Vatican Council have settled on one word, and that word is "Eucharist."

"Eucharist" is from a Greek verb used in the New Testament which can be translated as "to give thanks." It involves more than the gratitude which we owe at times to our fellow human beings since it concerns our relationship with God; for this reason when the priest says, "Let us give thanks to the Lord our God," the response is "It is right to give him thanks and praise." Adding the word "praise" alerts us to the truth that we are offering thanks to God. We are recognizing our relationship to our Father in heaven who is also our Lord and God.

To remember to give thanks is beautiful; to forget to do so is ugly. When only one of the ten lepers who had all been cured came back praising God in a loud voice, Jesus asked, "Where are the other nine?" We can almost hear the note of disappointment in his voice. But we need not disappoint Jesus and his Father. Remember that the Mass is our Eucharist, our thanksgiving to God.

We all have our own reasons to offer thanks to God in the Mass. Today we may wish to thank God for the gift of life in a new baby, or the blessing of health restored to an elderly person. We may want to thank God for employment after a long layoff, for the resolution of an old family argument, or for the graciousness of a devoted friend. Every Sunday we need to reflect on our personal motives for thanksgiving but then we should remember that it is right always and everywhere to give thanks to God simply because God is God. Thanksgiving expresses our relationship with God.

Thanksgiving is what Naaman the Syrian wanted to offer to God. He was cleansed of leprosy by bathing seven times in the waters of the Jordan river. He asked for two loads of the earth of Israel so that he could build an altar upon it in Syria, his home, in order to offer a sacrifice of thanksgiving to God. His experience is a symbol of our baptism. We have been washed clean in the waters of baptism and been given a share in the priesthood of Christ. Baptism calls us to be a people who worship God, who offer him thanks and praise. But we need no special soil, no particular location, for the offering of thanks to God. Wherever Mass is celebrated, there is the greatest offering of thanks and praise to God. For us it is right always and everywhere to give thanks to God, and we have the means to do so in the celebration of the Eucharist.

Twenty-ninth Sunday of the Year, C

People and Priest Praying Together

Ex 17:8-13; 2 Tm 3:14-4:2; Lk 18:1-8

It is pretty easy to break a single thread, but putting thousands of threads together forms a strong cord which withstands attempts to cut it in two. Prayer is like that. When we pray together, especially during the celebration of the liturgy, our prayer possesses strength. God is pleased with that kind of prayer. When we pray together, God the Father readily sees within us the person of his Son, the Head of the body which is his Church. Liturgical prayer together as the body of Christ is the best possible prayer.

Today's first reading symbolizes liturgical prayer. Moses needed strength to continue praying during a battle with the Amalekites. As long as Moses kept his hands raised in prayer, the Israelites had the better of the struggle, but when he let his hands rest, the Amalekites seized the ascendancy. Then Moses' brother Aaron and his friend Hur helped him to keep his hands raised in prayer and the Israelites won the battle.

Moses with his hands raised in prayer looked like a priest today with his hands raised in prayer during the liturgy of the Mass. A priest will not grow tired as did Moses, but everyone at Mass should spiritually hold up the arms and the hands of the priest. People and priest must pray together. The priest does not pray for himself alone. He is a leader, the presider, who prays for the sake of the people. At times people and priest say or sing prayers together, as with the Gloria and the acclamations. At times the people respond to the prayers which the priest says in the name of everyone. At times people are to listen attentively and pray in their hearts, particularly during the eucharistic prayer.

The priest is the liturgical sign of unity who signifies that our prayers ascend to God as from a single people. We are like the thousands of threads which form a strong cord. Not only the priest at Mass but every person needs and deserves the support of fellow Catholics, especially in order to persevere in prayer when we feel that God is not answering us. We believe that our help comes from the Lord, but at times it is hard to act in accord with that belief.

Jesus understands our weakness. That is why he tells us a parable on the necessity of praying always and not losing heart. The widow in the parable was persistent; she refused to give up. Jesus does not want us to give up either, no matter how hard or how long we have been praying for something. In order to persevere in prayer Jesus wants us to pray together, especially during the Mass.

We come to Mass for many reasons, and probably everyone of us has motives which are distinctly our own, each one of them valid and important, but above all we must be alert to put into practice the lesson of this day's liturgy.

As Catholics, as people of the Church, we have responsibilities toward one another. Aaron and Hur did not abandon Moses when he grew tired. They did not think that Moses ought to pray alone or that they had to be attentive to their own individual prayers. God is pleased with prayer which is strong because we are all praying, not as isolated individuals, but together as Catholics, as people of the Church, united by the Spirit as the one body of Christ.

Thirtieth Sunday of the Year, C

Humble Prayer Pierces the Clouds
Si 35:12-14, 16-18; 2 Tm 4:6-8, 16-18; Lk 18:9-14

In the Gospel according to St. Luke Jesus teaches us about prayer. First we learn to pray with Jesus to the Father in what we call the "Lord's Prayer" or simply the "Our Father." We learn that we must remember to give thanks and praise to God, and that we must persevere in our petitions to God.

Today Jesus teaches us the truth which was proposed in the Book of Sirach, that "the prayer of the lowly pierces the clouds; it does not rest until it reaches its goal." God favors prayer which is humble. Such is the lesson within the parable of the two men who went up to the temple to pray. God was not pleased with the prayer of the proud Pharisee. Actually it was no prayer at all but only a list of self-congratulations. But God was pleased with the humble tax collector. His was a sincere prayer for mercy.

Jesus took delight in making the least likely candidate for imitation the hero of his stories (remember it was a hated foreigner, the Good Samaritan, who was the hero of an earlier parable). Everybody despised the tax collectors, the ancient version of the IRS, but this man acknowledged his sins and begged God for mercy.

Jesus chose this hated tax collector to be the hero because he addressed the parable "to whose who believed in their own self-righteousness while holding everyone else in contempt." The Pharisee in the parable represented such people. He had the worst form of "I" trouble. He could see only himself in a favorable way.

Although he thanked God for not making him like the rest of men, he was hypocritical. He did not mean what he said. He really saw himself as a self-made man who did not need anyone, not even God. It was the fundamental mistake, the originating sin of our first parents who thought they could put themselves in place of God. Self-made people are like cars which we call "lemons." They have serious defects because they had incompetent manufacturers and are doomed to repeated failures.

The tax collector was not a "lemon," but he was like a car which has endured careless driving and a lack of maintenance. The only solution is to bring the car back to the dealer for a complete overhaul. The tax collector made the right choice. He went to the right person for the repairs he needed. He made no excuses. He diagnosed his own problem and asked God for the grace he needed in his simple prayer, "O God, be merciful to me, a sinner."

The tax collector's prayer was one of petition, a plea for help, the type of prayer we often offer to God. Authentic petitions express the kind of humility of which Jesus approved. We ask God favors because we know he is the right person to turn to, that he has the power to help us. That is one half of humility: to acknowledge God's power which is greater than any power in the universe. The second half of humility is to admit that we need God, that we cannot go it alone, that we depend on God's love as well as on his power. Humble prayer expresses God's power and our need.

Our humble prayer goes right to heaven because the prayer of the lowly pierces the clouds and does not rest until it reaches its goal.

Thirty-first Sunday of the Year, C

We Are Like Zacchaeus
Ws 11:22-12:1; 2 Th 1:11-2:2; Lk 19:1-10

Some people were often dismayed by Jesus' behavior. In today's Gospel the bystanders disapproved of the favorable attention which Jesus paid to Zacchaeus, who was branded as a sinner. In fact, they were shocked and they murmured against Jesus.

Despite the disapproval of the crowd, Zacchaeus made the right decision. He realized that it was Jesus to whom he had to turn in order to straighten out his life. He understood that Jesus was full of love and mercy. Zacchaeus also had determination. He was not going to let anyone or anything interfere with his meeting Jesus, not the objections of those who judged him unworthy, nor his small stature which prevented him from seeing Jesus over the heads of the crowd.

I imagine Zacchaeus to have been like a child when a parade is passing by. He is surrounded by adults who block his view. He jumps up and down but still cannot see what is happening. Zacchaeus knew that no one would help him but he had an idea to help himself. He ran on ahead and climbed a sycamore tree so that he could see Jesus. There he was above the crowd, trying to catch his breath, perched perhaps precariously, when to his amazement he not only saw Jesus; he actually heard Jesus speaking to him. Jesus called him by name. Zacchaeus wondered how Jesus knew who he was. Had Jesus heard of his terrible reputation? Had someone pointed him out to Jesus? Then he realized what Jesus was saying, "Hurry down. I mean to stay in your house today." He was so thrilled that he scampered down, ignoring the scrapes from the bark of the tree, and he escorted Jesus to his home. He pledged to repent, to change his conduct in accord with the teachings of Jesus. It was the happiest day of his life.

What Jesus did for Zacchaeus, he has done for us. He has entered our world, which in truth is the home of sinners. We are blessed indeed by this shocking behavior by the Son of God. Whether others are scandalized or not, we have made the right decision in seeking Jesus out, lifting ourselves above the heads of those who ignore Jesus or who hold the Church in contempt. With the eyes of faith we see Jesus as our Savior, and with the ears of faith we hear him speak to us. On the day of our baptism he called us by name. He knew who we were because his Father, our Creator, had pointed us out to him. We became God's sons and daughters.

Then in a reversal of roles, Jesus does not become our guest, as he was of Zacchaeus, but we become his guests. Baptism opens for us the door to his home, the Church, where Jesus our host invites us to a sacred meal, his body and his blood in the Holy Eucharist. We have this enormous privilege every Sunday, or even every day if we wish.

Jesus expects that we will change whatever we must in order to follow his teachings, just as Zacchaeus did. At the conclusion of Mass we are told, "Go in peace to love and serve the Lord." That is our commission to be faithful to the will of God.

We are not dismayed by Jesus' behavior. We are delighted that he has come to search out and to save what has been lost. Like Zacchaeus we are the beneficiaries of God's love and mercy.

Thirty-second Sunday of the Year, C

A Mystery Greater than We Know

2 M 7:1-2, 9-14; 2 Th 2:16-3:5; Lk 20:27-38

Mysteries are part of life. How does it happen that our planet rotates at just the right distance from the sun so that we are neither consumed in fire nor frozen in cold? Why is it that rain falls and the earth yields its fruit? What makes gravity work? These are marvels which the human mind can describe but can neither understand nor explain. Not least of all wonders is the human race. We are among the greatest marvels and the deepest mysteries of the universe.

We began our existence in our mother's body as a single cell, tiny, seemingly insignificant, clinging to the precarious but precious gift of life, searching for a safe place to nest within our mother's womb. We grew, we developed, and we were born. Then we grew more, we developed more, and we became clearly that creation which Psalm 8 describes as little less than the angels. Do not these marvels point to the possibility of even greater marvels?

Not so for the Sadducees of this Sunday's Gospel who did not believe in the resurrection of the dead. They thought they could trap Jesus by posing a question which seemed to make the resurrection absurd. A woman had been married to seven husbands in succession. The question was whose wife would she be after the resurrection. Their mistake was to think the doctrine of the resurrection means that people will rise to live a life identical to the one they possessed before they died. Jesus in but a few words corrected their notion by teaching that, although before the resurrection we are a little less than the angels, after the resurrection we will be like the angels. We will have changed. We will have gone through a development not unlike that which in our mother's womb prepared us for birth.

Our development is taking place even now, especially through our reception of the Holy Eucharist. We receive the body and the blood of the Lord who died but who has been raised up. It is the risen, glorified Lord who is our spiritual nourishment to sustain and enrich our life of grace. When we receive Holy Communion we should remember the firm promise of Jesus, "Those who eat my flesh and drink my blood will have everlasting life and I will raise them up on the last day." We wait in joyful hope for the coming of our Savior, and we say to him in the words of the responsorial psalm, "Lord, when your glory appears, our joy will be full."

Belief in the resurrection has given hope and courage to those who have gone before us. Devout people, like the seven brothers in today's first reading, readily went to death rather than deny their faith. What is amazing is that their own mother urged them to accept death. All this happened because of a God-given hope of being restored to the fullness of life in the resurrection on the last day.

We are challenged, not to die for the faith, but to live according to our faith. Exactly how our resurrection will take place is a mystery hidden in God, but we can be sure that it will be a great marvel because we will share in the resurrection of Jesus Christ.

Thirty-third Sunday of the Year, C

God's Power and Love Control the Universe
Ml 3:19-20; 2 Th 3:7-12; Lk 21:5-19

A certain religious sect, the members of which seem to like to knock on our doors, has predicted the end of the world five times — all within the twentieth century. Scientists assure us that one day, billions of years from now, the world will end because the sun, a source of energy, will exhaust its fuel. The Church teaches that the world, and indeed the universe will end, but not in the way or at the time that either this religious sect or some scientists believe.

Jesus taught that the time for the end of the world is hidden within the plan of God the Father. In fact, Jesus dismissed questions about when all of this will happen as insignificant. And so the Church teaches us that "we do not know the time for the consummation of the earth and of humanity" (Vatican II's *Constitution on the Church in the Modern World*, 39).

The Scriptures and other teachings of the Church call us to understand that God purifies what he has created, but he does not destroy it. God directs what he has made toward perfection, not annihilation. And so the Church also teaches us through the Vatican Council that "We do not know how all things will be transformed. As deformed by sin, the shape of this world will pass away, but God is preparing a new dwelling place and a new earth where justice will abide and whose blessedness will answer and surpass all the longings for peace in the human heart."

An example of how God works underlies today's Gospel. Jesus predicted that the Jerusalem temple would be destroyed. This prophecy was fulfilled about forty years later, on August 9 in the year 70 A.D. to be exact, when Roman soldiers set fire to the structure. It was a sorrowful day for God's people, and yet we believe that the physical temple was replaced by Jesus himself who said, speaking of his own body, "Destroy this temple and in three days I will raise it up."

The temple was a magnificent building wherein the worship of sacrifice was offered to God. Now throughout the world we worship the Father in spirit and in truth because of our union with Jesus Christ in the liturgy. Jesus more than fulfilled both the beauty and the purpose of the temple. In somewhat the same way the world, and the universe, will be brought to perfection when Christ comes again in glory.

The truth about the end of the world is based on both the power and the love of God. God's power gives him complete control over the universe, and his love for his creation moves him to bring it to perfection. That perfection will be achieved when Christ comes again. "The Lord will come to rule the world with justice."

During the liturgy of the Eucharist we acknowledge that Christ has died, Christ is risen, and Christ will come again. As people of faith we should look forward to the second coming of Christ without anxiety; we should not dread it as some think we should. That is why we also pray to God the Father, "Lord, protect us from all anxiety as we wait in joyful hope for the coming of our Savior, Jesus Christ."

Solemnity of Christ the King, C

Brothers and Sisters of the King
2 S 5:1-3; Col 1:12-20; Lk 23:35-43

Sometimes we Americans wonder why the English bother with their monarchy. The fact is that the Queen, it seems to us, is little more than a figure-head with almost no authority. And yet within us there is some kind of wish for a person whom we can look up to, someone who personifies dignity and wins our respect, a person who makes us feel better about ourselves.

Many Americans found that kind of person in the election of John F. Kennedy as President of the United States. He was young, handsome, intelligent, and articulate. He was married to a beautiful woman who, it seemed to us, had become his Queen and who had presented him with beautiful children, a prince and a princess. The White House became known as Camelot. The United States had a family to whom many Americans attributed royalty.

But on Friday, November 22, 1963 the dream was shattered. During four days Americans sat stunned before their television sets, watching again and again the pictures of the unbelievable assassination and the woeful funeral ceremonies which helped to convince us that the President's death was real. Since then stories have gradually been unfolded which reveal that all was not perfect as we had imagined. The dream of Camelot was shattered and the illusion of royalty was dimmed.

All along we had been looking in the wrong direction toward the White House in Washington, D.C. as if it were a palace. We should have been looking back to Calvary because the cross is truly the throne of Christ the King. His death was not a tragedy, as was that of JFK. It was a triumph over our twin enemies, sin and death. Above the head of Jesus on the cross, Pilate the Governor had placed an ironic inscription: "This is the King of the Jews." We replace that inscription with our profession of faith: "Christ Is Our King." To him we pray: "Remember us when you enter upon your reign."

That prayer has already been answered because through Christ we have redemption. We have been rescued from the kingdom of sin. Our eucharistic celebration this Sunday "gives thanks to the Father for having made us worthy to share the lot of the saints in light. He rescued us from the power of darkness and brought us into the kingdom of his beloved Son."

God has done much more than make us subjects of Christ the King. He has transformed us through his gift of grace into his brothers and sisters. The brothers and sisters of a king are princes and princesses. We are royal people, possessed of a dignity and worth which only God can grant.

We do not need an earthly sovereign to give us self-respect. Our King is truly royal. His kingdom is not an imaginary Camelot. It is an eternal and universal kingdom, a kingdom of truth and life, a kingdom of holiness and grace, a kingdom of justice, love, and peace. Our King is Christ the Lord.

A PLEDGE OF ALLEGIANCE TO CHRIST THE KING

This Sunday is an appropriate time to pledge our allegiance to Christ the King. The following suggested form, which is based on the Preface of the Eucharistic Prayer for this Solemnity, may be used at Mass by having the people repeat the lines of the pledge after the priest or other minister.

> We pledge allegiance to Christ the King.
> We embrace his eternal and universal kingdom.
> We acknowledge his kingdom to be one of truth and life,
> of holiness and grace.
> We wish to do what we can through prayer and action
> to bring to the world his kingdom
> of justice, love, and peace.

Solemnities, Feasts, and Special Observances

[Note: the homilies for the Solemnities of the Trinity and the Body and the Blood of the Lord (*Corpus Christi*) can be found following the homilies for the Solemnity of Pentecost in each of the three cycles.]

The Feast of the Lord's Presentation, February 2

Death Leads to Eternal Life
Ml 3:1-4; Heb 2:14-18; Lk 2:22-40

For some reason the young seem to have an affinity for the old. Maybe that is one reason, among others, why little children and their grandparents usually are very compatible. All this seems somewhat strange in view of the fact that little children are at the beginning of life while old people are at the end of life.

When Mary and Joseph brought Jesus to Jerusalem forty days after his birth for his presentation to the Lord, an old man called Simeon was moved by the Holy Spirit to go to the temple at that moment. As soon as he saw the infant Jesus, he took him into his arms. Mary and Joseph did not object. They could see that the two somehow belonged together, the infant at the beginning of life and the old man at the end of life.

It seemed as if Simeon had waited all his many years for this one, precious moment. Looking up to heaven, he blessed God in these words: "Now, Master, you may dismiss your servant in peace." He knew he was holding the Savior in his arms; he was ready to die.

The Gospel does not tell us precisely what the faith of Simeon included. Did he have a clear hope of everlasting life? Did he believe that he would be raised, body as well as soul, to the fullness of life in heaven? In a way, it is good that we have been given no precise information about his faith because he is a model for us of total trust in God, an abandonment to God's will, whatever it may be, an embracing of death as a sure but mysterious path to God. The Church has adopted his prayer, "Now, Master, you may dismiss your servant in peace," as part of her night prayer in preparation for death.

Also in the temple was an elderly woman, Anna, who was granted the grace to acknowledge the Christ Child. She became an early Christian preacher since "she gave thanks to God and talked about the child to all who looked forward to the deliverance of Jerusalem."

Simeon is a model of faith for us, but Anna, the elderly prophetess, represents the Church. From the very beginning the Church has talked about Christ; she has proclaimed him as Savior in every age. Even now the Church, almost two thousand years old, continues with youthful enthusiasm to point out Christ to us, heralding him during the celebration of the Eucharist as the victim who was slain to overcome death, "the Lamb of God who takes away the sins of the world."

The Church reminds us how blessed we are, even more blessed than Simeon, for we do not merely embrace Jesus; we actually receive his body and blood, our spiritual nourishment, the divine vitality which is the pledge of everlasting life. We hear the declaration, "Happy are those who are called to his supper." This is not the Last Supper, but the eternal supper, the great wedding banquet of the Lamb of God in heaven (see Revelation 19:9).

There is an affinity between Jesus and us even though like the Church he is, so to speak, approaching the age of two thousand. Actually Jesus is now without age, having entered into eternity. In the Church and through the Eucharist he is leading us to everlasting life in our heavenly home.

Holy Thursday

The Heart of Our Faith
Ex 12:1-8, 11-14; 1 Cor 11:23-26; Jn 13:1-15

Tonight we celebrate the institution of the Holy Eucharist. How different our religion would be without the Holy Eucharist. Perhaps one of your first thoughts is the realization that there would be a certain emptiness about our churches without the presence of the Blessed Sacrament. More profoundly there would be no Mass, the heart of our worship. There would be no First Communion days for little children, brilliant in their white clothing and beautiful in their innocence, no joy of reconciliation for the sinner through the sacrament of penance completed by returning to communion after a long absence, no yearning for the spiritual nourishment and strength which the Eucharist alone can give. No martyr would ever have died for the Eucharist, and no one with intense conviction would ever have declared: "It is the Mass that matters." We would never have heard those beautiful words of Jesus, "Take and eat. This is my body given up for you. Take and drink. This is the cup of my blood, shed for you and for all so that sins may be forgiven." The Christian Paschal Mystery, the death and resurrection of Jesus, would have been lost in a cold and lifeless past, for it is of the Eucharist that Paul wrote, "When you eat this bread and drink this cup, you proclaim the death of the Lord until he comes."

But Jesus was determined not to conclude his life on earth without first giving us the Holy Eucharist, the sacrament of his death and resurrection. In fact, during his life the Eucharist gradually became his preoccupation. When did the idea of the Eucharist first occur to Jesus in his human mind? Perhaps when he was a child eating with his parents, the warmth of that human experience fanned a flame in his mind. The time of Passover when Jesus was twelve was a turning point for him when he spent three days in the temple. Something happened to him during that experience as he was moved closer to the realization that he would become the new temple, and that he would be both priest and victim of his sacrifice.

Many circumstances made him think of the Eucharist, such as his dinner in the home of Zacchaeus and all the meals he took with his disciples. Jesus realized that human hunger is for something greater than food. By the time of Passover in the year before he died, the concept of the Eucharist was clear in the mind of Jesus. He was preaching along the Sea of Galilee. St. John in his account was careful to note that Passover was near. After the multiplication of the loaves and fishes Jesus for the first time promised the gift of the Eucharist. Jesus said: "The bread that I will give is my flesh for the life of the world. He who eats my flesh and drinks my blood has life everlasting and I will raise him up on the last day." Feeding the five thousand led Jesus to think of the Eucharist and to make a solemn promise which he fulfilled on this night.

Every act of love, every gesture of affection, every sign of unselfishness and generosity, made him think of the Eucharist. The reason is that the Eucharist is the sacrament of his death, the greatest act of love the world would ever see. Every act of love in the life of Jesus was caught up in that one moment of his death, a moment which is a reality for us in the eucharistic sacrifice.

Holy Thursday (alternate)

A Eucharistic Life
Ex 12:1-8, 11-14; 1 Cor 11:23-26; Jn 13:1-15

We may tend to romanticize the early Christian communities, but they were not perfect any more than we are perfect. As a matter of fact the Corinthians were not entirely an exemplary community. Such is not surprising. Corinth was a seaport city and was about as corrupt as any city of New Testament times. One could find any vice there, even religious prostitution. And yet we are indebted to the Corinthians because they evoked from St. Paul some of his most beautiful and profound expressions of Christian doctrine. St. Paul protested to the Corinthians that when he preached to them they were not ready for solid food, only for milk, and that they were not ready for solid food at that time when he was writing his letter. And yet in his first letter he went on to present the doctrine of the Church as the body of Christ, the beautiful hymn on love, and the most complete treatment of the resurrection found in the New Testament.

Most important to us at this moment, we are indebted to the Corinthians for the first account in the New Testament of the institution of the Eucharist, an account which precedes by about eight years the narrative found in the Gospel of Mark. St. Paul's presentation was occasioned by the disgraceful way in which some of the Corinthians conducted themselves during the fraternal meal which served as a context for the celebration of the Eucharist.

First the Corinthians were guilty of factions. They formed themselves into little, exclusive groups. The basis for these divisions is not clear. It may have been ideological, but probably was social and financial. The rich and the poor, the noble and the peasant, did not associate with each other. Secondly they lacked a sacrificial spirit. Some overindulged in food and especially in drink in the fashion to which they had become accustomed during their pagan days. Christianity had not changed their hedonistic tendencies. Thirdly, some violated charity by not sharing with others so that some people were actually left in their hunger.

These were the failings which St. Paul singled out, not heresies or sexual excesses or any other vices of which the Corinthians were guilty. He singled out these three failings — factions, the lack of a sacrificial spirit, and the violation of charity — because they were directly contrary to the meaning of the Eucharist. Paul wrote: "Shall I praise you? Certainly not." Then he gave the reason why he could not praise their actions: it was because of the Eucharist.

The meaning of the Eucharist is to make present that act by which Jesus opened his arms on the cross to embrace all in his love, to bring to fruition his prayer that all may be one. We may enjoy a beautiful eucharistic celebration with excellent music and full participation. And such is very important to our lives. But Jesus also expects a sacrificial spirit from us in imitation of his own, not that we have to suffer physically, or even emotionally, but we must be willing to be unselfish people. After all, the Eucharist is the cross; when we eat this bread and drink this cup we proclaim the death of the Lord. Eucharistic people do not base their existence on their own convenience or on their own preferences. They are generous, unselfish, and giving, like Jesus himself.

Good Friday

The Explosion of Love
Is 52:13-53:12; Heb 4:14-16; 5:7-9; Jn 18:1-19:42

A long time ago in a galaxy far away a star exploded. Over uncountable centuries because of its intense gravity the star had been building mass from neighboring celestial bodies. Then at a time before the creation of the human race, before there was anyone on this earth who could look up to the heavens with intelligence and understanding, this immense star exploded.

On the night of February 23, 1987 an astronomer by the name of Ian Shelton was working in an observatory in northern Chile. He looked up to the sky and saw a new star. It was a supernova. For the first time a human being was seeing the light of that star which had exploded in the distant galaxy. Ian Shelton was witnessing an event which had occurred 170,000 years ago. It had taken that much time for the light of the explosion to reach us.

Less than two thousand years ago in a tiny country on the other side of the world, an event took place which to all appearances seemed utterly insignificant, just another Roman execution of a Jewish upstart. It was all over in a matter of a few hours, and most of the bystanders were inclined to think no more of the affair. Without faith they could not even begin to understand the meaning of what they had witnessed.

We look back upon this event with the eyes of faith. We believe that on Calvary there was an explosion of God's love. A new brilliant light had come into the world to show the meaning and purpose of life. A tremendous power had been unleashed — the power of God's love.

On the night before he died, Jesus looked up to the heavens. He saw, not a supernova, but the Passover moon, the full moon. He knew that it was time for the fullness of God's love.

The hour had come for him to pass from this world to the Father. He had loved his own in this world, and would show his love for them to the end, to the very end of his life on the cross. But he wanted this powerful love to touch all of God's people.

And so it was that on Holy Thursday night he gave us the gift of the Eucharist, the sacrament of his Paschal Mystery, the sacrament of his death and his resurrection.

When we celebrate the Eucharist, we do not merely look back on something which happened in the past. Although the light of the star which exploded 170,000 years ago is still reaching the earth, the star itself was long ago consumed in a huge thermonuclear fire. Not so the death of Jesus. The Eucharist brings Jesus' death itself to us, not merely its light. Through the Eucharist we are in contact with the saving death of Jesus. The Eucharist is his body given up for us, his blood poured out for us. When we eat this bread and drink this cup, we proclaim the death of the Lord until he comes.

I cannot imagine what even an all-wise and all-powerful God could do more to express and communicate his love. If the events of this Holy Week do not move us to deeper faith and greater love, I do not know what will. So that we may never forget but may always grow in our appreciation, Jesus has given us the Eucharist, the sacrament of his Paschal Mystery. The death of Jesus which we commemorate on Good Friday is a reality for us in the celebration of the Holy Eucharist.

Good Friday (alternate)

Witnesses to the Death of Jesus
Is 52:13-53:12; Heb 4:14-16; 5:7-9; Jn 18:1-19:42

Today in the liturgy we hear proclaimed an extraordinary narrative, the story of the passion and death of Jesus Christ. There is a difference between being a witness *of* this event, and a witness *to* this event.

A small number of people were witnesses of the death of Jesus: the Roman soldiers, the chief priests, and some of the residents of Jerusalem. They were like people today who see an accident on the highway. Most drive by after only a pause to satisfy their curiosity. Some may stop to help the victims. A bold person may even tell the police that he is willing to testify in court because he was, he says, a witness of what happened. But the wisest person does not see any transcendent meaning in the event; if anything, he is frustrated by what appears to be a senseless accident.

At the foot of the cross stood a few people of faith: Mary, the mother of Jesus, some other women, and John. They became witnesses to the death of Jesus because through God's grace they began to penetrate its meaning, to see that here was more than an execution, that this death would wipe out sin and death and transform lives. They came to realize this event was a mystery of faith.

The cross stands at the turning point of human history. God's love was poured out upon his creation from the very beginning and was never recalled; his grace was constantly offered to every human person and was never lacking to anyone of good will. And yet because of the death of his Son, God entered into a new covenant with us. This covenant was a pledge of undying love which was sealed in the blood of Jesus Christ.

"For our sake Jesus opened his arms on the cross; he put

an end to death and revealed the resurrection. In this he fulfilled the Father's will and won for him a holy people," the people of the new and everlasting covenant (cf. Second Eucharistic Prayer).

English is the only language which designates this Friday as "Good," and a wise and perceptive practice it is. God the Father through the gift of faith moves us to go beyond appearances and to see the death of Jesus as more than a tragic execution, as a powerful sign of the love of our great, good God.

The sacrifice of the cross is so important to us that Jesus has left us the living memorial of his death in the Holy Eucharist. When we offer the Mass we stand with Mary and the women and John at the foot of the cross.

In our celebration of the Eucharist we are called to be witnesses to the death of Jesus. We are witnesses to this death when we proclaim the mystery of faith: "Christ has died, Christ is risen, Christ will come again." We are witnesses to his death when we proclaim: "Dying you destroyed our death; rising you restored our life." "Lord, by your cross and resurrection you have set us free; you are the Savior of the world."

This memorial of Good Friday is intended to deepen our appreciation of the cross so that we may enter more fully into the mystery of faith which we celebrate in the Holy Eucharist.

Mother's Day

Mother Mary Is the Great Model
Readings from the Mass of the Sunday

Mother's day is an American original. In 1903 the mother of Anna Jarvis died in Philadelphia. One year later on the anniversary of her mother's death, Anna spoke to a friend about an idea she had about establishing a yearly day in honor of mothers so that they would never be forgotten. Anna began writing letters to influential people to get them interested in her plan. Because of her efforts the city of Philadelphia in 1909 observed a city-wide Mother's Day for the first time. The idea was so popular that in 1913 Congress decreed that Mother's Day should be celebrated nationally every year on the second Sunday of May. Since then we have never failed as a nation to honor mothers on the second Sunday of May, and the idea has spread to other countries as well.

As Americans we can be proud of our creation of Mother's Day. As Catholics we see a deep meaning in this yearly celebration. If ever there were a contest to determine the best mother of all times, every Catholic would vote for Mary, the Mother of Jesus. Mary is the model for mothers. Of course some will point out that Mary is not a very practical model since she was the perfect mother. She was conceived without sin, she had Jesus for a Son, and Joseph for a husband. Hard to beat that combination. And yet a model should be a high ideal, not some insignificant and easily attainable example. Every Catholic mother rightly looks to Mary for inspiration.

Mary is not only the model for mothers; she is also the model for the Church. At times we refer to the Church as "Holy Mother the Church." That is an appropriate title. What Mary did for Jesus, the Church does for us. Mary conceived Jesus in her womb, gave him birth from her body, nourished him with the milk of her breast, and taught him at her knee. When Jesus grew up and began his public ministry, Mary became his best disciple. She stood at the foot of the cross and accompanied the lifeless body of her Son to the grave with the sure hope of resurrection.

The early Fathers spoke of the baptismal font as the womb of the Church. In that font the Church conceived us and gave us birth as the children of God and brothers and sisters of one another in God's family on this earth. The Church nourishes us with the body and blood of her Lord, and teaches us by means of his Word. The Church invites us to stand with her at the foot of the cross in every Mass we celebrate since the Eucharist makes present for us the sacrifice of the cross. The Church, on the day of our funeral, will accompany our lifeless body to the grave in the sure hope of resurrection.

Mother's Day goes back to the resolve of Anna Jarvis when her mother died in 1903. Our Catholic Mother's Day goes back to the very beginning of our faith when Mary conceived Jesus by the power of the Holy Spirit. Mary is the model for every Catholic mother and for the entire Catholic Church.

Solemnity of the Sacred Heart

The Mass and the Sacred Heart

Dt 7:6-11; 1 Jn 4:7-16; Mt 11:25-30

You may have grown tired of seeing hearts on bumper stickers, but you never have a doubt about their meaning. Long before the bumper sticker craze, the Church adopted the symbol of the heart to emphasize the divine love which Jesus expresses in a human way.

The Friday which follows the Sunday known as Corpus Christi is the Solemnity of the Sacred Heart of Jesus. Jesus is divine as he is begotten in eternity by God the Father, and he is human as he was conceived by the Holy Spirit in the womb of Mary. As divine Jesus is without limitation. He and his qualities are infinite. Catholic piety has hit squarely upon the area in which Jesus wanted us to perceive, as far as our limited faculties allow us, one divine quality which he expressed in a human way. Our genius as a Church is manifested in our liturgical Solemnity in honor of the Sacred Heart. We could have had a feast of the Sacred Intelligence or the Sacred Omnipotence (why not?), and yet as a Church which is guided by the Holy Spirit we have selected the symbol of love.

Love is the meaning of life. It is not a means to anything; it is an end in itself. This is no wonder, since God is love. Jesus wanted to express divine love in a human way and that is why he died for us. In the beautiful words of the second eucharistic prayer, "He opened his arms on the cross" as a gesture of his all-embracing love.

The love within the heart of Jesus moves him to draw us all to himself. He has given us the gift of his body and blood so that we may grow more and more like him, to become more fully what he is in perfection, the Son of God. The love in his heart is a filial love, the love of a Son for his Father. His love for us is such that he wants us to have within our hearts the same kind of love that he has. He wants us to join him, our eldest brother in God's family, in his love for our heavenly Father.

In the prayers for this Solemnity we refer to the Sacred Heart as "the pledge of all that we are called to be," and we ask that we may "open our hearts to share his life." We are called to be children of the Father with Christ. The life we share is the divine life which flows from the Father to the Son as a parent's gift to a child.

In every celebration of the Mass Jesus invites us to join him in his sacrifice, the offering of himself in perfect love to the Father. During the Mass we should make the effort to be one with Christ in his love for his heavenly Father. As his body and blood are offered in sacrifice to the Father, so we should offer ourselves in union with him so that we may become "an everlasting gift" to God.

In one sense it is a shame that this Solemnity is always on a Friday when only a few are at Mass, and never on a Sunday. And yet every Mass can be considered a celebration of the Sacred Heart of Jesus. As we prepare for Mass, we do well to offer the prayer, "Sacred Heart of Jesus, make our hearts like unto yours."

Birth of John the Baptist

What's in a Name?
Is 49:1-6; Ac 13:22-26; Lk 1:57-66, 80

This Sunday at Mass we have an unusual celebration, the Solemnity of the Birth of John the Baptist. It is observed on June 24th. In the year 2001 it falls on a Sunday and replaces the usual Sunday Mass. The only other birthdays which the liturgy observes are that of Jesus on December 25 and that of his mother Mary on September 8. The liturgy obviously believes that the birthday of John the Baptist deserves our special attention.

The Gospel tells the story of how John received his name.

William Shakespeare in his play *Romeo and Juliet* wrote, "What's in a name? That which we call a rose by any other name would smell as sweet." Actually in biblical names there is often a rich meaning.

When the time came to circumcise this child, neighbors and relatives expected him to be named after his father, Zechariah. But his mother insisted, "No, he is to be called John." This was the name indicated by the angel who had appeared to Zechariah to promise that he and his wife would have a child despite their advanced age.

The name, "John," in Hebrew is "Yehohanan." It means "The Lord is gracious" or maybe better, "The Lord shows favor." After the child was given this name, Zechariah offered a beautiful prayer of thanks and praise to God, which is always included in the Church's Morning Prayer (see Luke 1:68-79). Within the prayer, Zechariah turned to his little son and said, "You, my child, shall be called the prophet of the Most High, for you will go before the Lord to prepare his way, to give his people knowledge of salvation by the forgiveness of their sins."

John the Baptist had the privilege as the herald of Jesus to point him out as God's gift to us, the Lamb of God who takes away the sins of the world. Jesus in his person reveals to us the gracious favor of God the Father and fulfills the meaning of the name "John."

The birthday of John the Baptist relates to the birthday of Jesus. The Church selected the time of the winter solstice to celebrate the birth of Jesus because from that time the days gradually grow longer; the amount of daylight increases. The Church selected the time of the summer solstice to celebrate the birth of the Baptist because from this time the days gradually grow shorter; the amount of daylight diminishes. This symbolizes the words of the Baptist in speaking of Jesus, "He must increase while I must decrease" (John 3:30).

The names of John's parents are not without significance. "Elizabeth" means "God has sworn" or "God has promised by oath," and recalls the solemn promise God made to send the Messiah. "Zechariah" means "God remembers," and indicates the faithfulness of God in keeping his promise.

During the celebration of the Mass this Sunday in which we recall the birth of the Baptist our hearts should be filled with thanks and praise to God for the gracious favor he shows to us in the person of his beloved Son.

Because of all of the events which led up to and followed the birth of John the Baptist, we too have a name of great significance, and that name is "Christian."

Solemnity of Saints Peter and Paul

United in Christ
Ac 12:1-11; 2 Tm 4:6-8, 17-18; Mt 16:13-19

There is an old saying: "That's robbing Peter to pay Paul." In a family money may be taken from the food budget to pay for clothes for the kids at the beginning of a new school year. That is robbing Peter to pay Paul.

On this solemnity we should not rob Peter of his primacy in the infant Church in order to pay our regard to Paul for his theological depths, nor should we rob Paul of his place in the New Testament in order to pay our respect to Peter as the rock of the Church. And yet these two disciples of Jesus are significantly different from one another.

Peter was with Jesus from the beginning of his public ministry. Paul did not encounter Jesus until five or more years after his death and resurrection when he was thrown to the ground by the blinding light on the road to Damascus. Peter would be the first to admit that he had been weak when he denied that he even knew Jesus. In fact, one legend has it that Peter wept such abundant tears of repentance that he wore furrows in his cheeks. Paul was strong, even tempestuous, sure of himself even to the extent of bragging about his credentials as a true apostle.

The greatest difference between them is that, at least in the beginning, they were on opposite sides of the most profound and bitter disagreement in the first generation of the Church. Most of the Jewish converts believed that in order to be a disciple of Jesus people had to be circumcised and follow the law of Moses. They seemed to think that Christianity, which at the time had not yet even been given a name (see Acts 11:26), was little more than a new sect or form of Judaism. In effect, they believed that new disciples had to become Jewish in order to become Christian. They came to be know as the Judaizers. Paul vehemently opposed their position. He insisted that Jesus had done something new. He understood the meaning of Jesus' saying that one cannot put new wine into old wine skins. He taught that Jesus by his cross and resurrection had set us free of the constraints of the Old Law. There was now a new covenant in the blood of Jesus. He believed that the Church was open equally to Jews and Gentiles without distinction.

Peter did not exactly believe what the Judaizers taught, nor did he contradict what Paul insisted on, but he was a little weak about insisting on the truth. Paul especially became upset with Peter when he seemed to lean toward compromising with the Judaizers. Before long the Church had to call a council in Jerusalem to settle the matter (Acts 15). Before the council met Peter enjoyed a vision which convinced him of the correctness of Paul's view (Acts 11).

What was it then which really united these two men, despite their differences? It was nothing more complex or less profound then their complete love for Jesus Christ and his Church. That truth is vital for us. Whatever may be our differences in the Church today, we must keep our eyes fixed on Jesus and his great gift to us of the Church, the new and everlasting covenant. In any dispute we must ask: "Does my position add to dedication to Jesus and his Church or not?" We cannot rob Peter to pay Paul, and we cannot abandon the truth in order to adhere to our own opinion.

Independence Day, The Fourth of July

Catholics Make Good Americans

On the Fourth of July we commemorate those events whereby thirteen English colonies became the United States of America. From that time the thirteen have increased to fifty to become, we at least would like to believe, the greatest nation on earth.

Since 1886 the Statue of Liberty has stood on Liberty Island in New York Harbor as a symbol of the ideals of our country. The "lady" holds aloft a lamp, as if to beacon people to her shores. Graven on a tablet within the pedestal upon which the statue stands is the famous poem by Emma Lazarus which reads in part: "Give me your tired, your poor, your huddled masses yearning to breathe free, the wretched refuse of your teeming shore. Send these, the homeless, tempest-tost to me."

And to the lady's shore came the Irish and the Italians, the Germans and the French, the Polish and the Scandinavians, some Jewish, some Catholic, some Protestant. These people struggled in a strange land, wanting to preserve their language and customs but knowing that they had to adapt to their new homeland. They made their contribution to the riches of our country, sometimes materially but more importantly humanly and spiritually.

These pioneers would not recognize the attitude of some of their offspring who have entered into the mainstream of American life. Many contemporary Americans, despite their origin from immigrants, have erected, so to speak, their own statue to represent America, not one holding a beacon of welcome, but one with hands and arms raised to say to immigrants, "Halt! Go back! We do not want you in our country!"

This attitude of exclusion extends even to those Americans who are not white or who speak English with an accent or perhaps not at all. Our foreign ancestors are crying out to us: "If we had been excluded from the United States, you may have been born but not as an American." The fact is that the vast majority of our citizens would not be part of this country if it had been determined that to be an American one's ancestors had to be British and to have come here on the *Mayflower*.

Chauvinism and xenophobia have made our national boundaries to be like a collar which is too small with a neck tie which someone is pulling tighter until the oxygen is cut off and you die.

Catholics should be the best Americans according to the origins and the traditions of our country. The reason is that to be Catholic means to be universal, not exclusive, to be like Jesus who opened his arms on the cross to embrace all men and women. The Church is not limited to any nation or group of people. You don't even have to be Italian to be Pope.

The United States, more than any other country in the world, has the opportunity to be in a secular way what the Church is in a spiritual way — not a melting pot but a home in which all people have a place, not just those who are of a certain color or speak a certain language. Catholics accept the principle of the separation of church and state but that does not mean that we should leave to others the shaping of our country. The best way for us to be good Americans is to be good Catholics, not to heed the strident voices of bigotry and hate, but to have the mind and heart of Christ.

Feast of the Transfiguration

The Paschal Mystery
Is One of God's Great Mysteries

Dn 7:9-10, 13-14; 2 P 1:16-19; Mt 17:1-9

William Bennett in his *Book of Virtues* repeats an old Jewish folk tale about two naive city boys who had never seen a farm. One day they decided to wander into the country. There they saw a farmer plowing. They said to each other that this man must be insane to be tearing up a beautiful green field. Then they saw him sowing seed, an act which also mystified them, especially when the farmer next covered over the seed as if burying it. Laughing at the farmer's foolish actions, they returned to the city.

Later they went once again to the country. Now they admired the standing crop of wheat in the farmer's field, but to their amazement they saw him cutting down the stalks. This was too much for them. They went home where they opened a loaf of bread to make sandwiches, with no understanding of how bread came to be.

These boys were amazingly simplistic, but with all of our technical knowledge today, we understand very little of the workings of God's world. Scientists can describe what we experience but they do not explain it. Why does the earth rotate? What makes gravity work? Why does fire burn and water cool? In particular, what makes a seed buried in the earth grow into a tree with the help of soil, sunshine, and rain? The fact that all of these things work is more amazing than the ignorance of the two city boys.

There are great mysteries in the universe. Today we celebrate one of God's great mysteries, which we call the Paschal Mystery. The Father's plan was that his Son would go from suffering to joy, from humiliation to glory, and from death to life. Jesus died. Then he was buried, planted like a seed in the earth. His Father's glory, like the sun, and the Spirit's life-giving power, like the rain, came upon him and he rose from the dead in glorious splendor.

The transfiguration of Jesus was a gift to the apostles to prepare them for the ordeal of Jesus' death. It was meant to strengthen their faith on that day of trial, so that remembering Jesus' glory on the mountain they could endure his death with hope for his resurrection. And yet the scandal of the cross was too much for them until Jesus had actually risen from the dead.

We are blessed to look back in faith upon the Paschal Mystery, to believe that Jesus died and yet was raised up, to realize that the transfiguration was a prelude to the resurrection. All of this has taken place for our benefit, for our salvation.

When loved ones go before us in death, we may be inclined to think that this awesome fact of life makes about as much sense to us as the planting of seed made to the two city boys. When faced with our own impending death, we may be tempted to fear that we will be buried like a seed but left to rot in the soil.

Can it all be true, this wonderful promise of resurrection to the fullness of life? Jesus has given us a sacrament of resurrection, a guarantee for our faith and a strength for our hope. Jesus promised, "If you eat my flesh and drink my blood I will raise you up on the last day." We stand in dignity to receive Holy Communion since standing is the sign of our faith in the resurrection. God who guides all the mysteries of the universe will not fail to lead us to the fullness of life.

Solemnity of the Assumption of Mary

The Assumption Is a Truth for Our Times
Rv 11:19; 12:1-6, 10; 1 Cor 15:20-27; Lk 1:39-56

The Solemnity of the Assumption of Mary, body and soul, into heaven celebrates an important dogma of our faith. This dogma emphasizes for us a truth for our time and for our society.

A not very bright picture of our era has developed. Its beauty and brilliance have been obscured by the dark hues of a "twisted and depraved generation" which treats human life with disdain, even contempt.

There is no need to elaborate upon the atrocities of our times: terrorism, drug traffic, gang warfare, abortion, molestation of children, abuse of women, xenophobia... The litany is a long one and after each acknowledgment we must raise our eyes to heaven and plead, "Lord, have mercy."

Upon this bleak and depressing world picture shines a brilliant star which reflects the revealing light of God's attitude toward his marvelous creation of human life. This star is Mary who was taken body as well as soul into heaven after her death. As the highly favored daughter of God, she did not have to wait until the final day of resurrection in order to enjoy the blessings of her Father's heavenly home in the fullness of her humanity.

The assumption of Mary illustrates how precious in the eyes of God is the entire human person, body as well as soul. And yet Mary is so extraordinary that we may wonder whether we ordinary people can really share in a privilege like her own. Is it too much to hope that we will actually enjoy a privilege like hers? The prayers of this day's liturgy answer that we have good reason to be quite confident that we, like Mary, will be raised to the fullness of life.

In the opening prayer of the Mass, after expressing faith

in the Assumption, the priest says in our name: "May we see heaven as our final goal and come to share Mary's glory." In the Preface we proclaim: "Today the virgin Mother of God was taken up into heaven to be... a sign of hope and comfort for your people on their pilgrim way."

Mary is a sign of hope that we will share in the resurrection of Christ. To put it simply: of course Christ was raised from the dead; he is divine. But what about us? Mary, though sinless, is a human person; she is not divine. And yet God the Father was pleased to raise her from the dead. That truth, the Church assures us, contains the comforting promise that God will raise us too.

Our pilgrim journey is symbolized at Mass by our processing toward the altar to receive the body and the blood of the risen Lord. Standing to receive communion is a liturgical expression of our faith in the promise of Jesus, "I will raise you up on the last day." The Assumption assures us that in God's eyes our entire humanity is precious and that we are that "you" of Jesus' promise: "I will raise *you* up on the last day."

Solemnity of the Assumption (alternate)

This Mother Is the Image of Her Son
Rv 11:19; 12:1-6, 10; 1 Cor 15:20-27; Lk 1:39-56

One of the most beautiful aspects of our Catholic religion is our devotion to Mary. That devotion is an integral part of the true Christian spirit. We are privileged to fulfill the prophecy which Mary uttered when she visited her relative, Elizabeth: "From this day all generations will call me blessed" (Luke 1:48). Mary has indeed been blessed by God. That is why the angel said to her, "Rejoice, O highly favored daughter." And that is why we honor her.

On August 15th we celebrate Mary's Assumption into heaven, the truth that she was taken body as well as soul to heaven to be with her Son, and to see even with bodily eyes the awesome countenance of her heavenly Father.

To put this Solemnity of Mary's Assumption into perspective, it is helpful for us to see that the major liturgical feasts of Mary parallel those of her Son. No human person planned this relationship of feast days; it developed over time and was guided by the Holy Spirit in the Church.

Notice the parallels: We celebrate the human conception of Jesus on March 25th. We celebrate the immaculate conception of Mary on December 8th. December 25th is Jesus' birthday as September 8th is Mary's. There are feasts of both presentations in the temple, that of Jesus on February 2nd and that of Mary on November 21st.

During Holy Week we remember the passion and death of Jesus, and on September 15th we remember the sorrows of Mary. Jesus' resurrection from the dead, celebrated on Easter, is fulfilled in Mary by means of her Assumption, the solemnity which we celebrate today.

We honor Jesus as King on the last Sunday of the liturgical year and we honor Mary as Queen one week after the Solemnity of her Assumption. We recognize the love of Jesus in the image of his Sacred Heart and we recognize the love of Mary in the image of her Immaculate Heart.

Ordinarily children take after their parents. They look like them. They perhaps have a manner of speaking or walking similar to that of their parents. Above all they learn from their parents. Jesus undoubtedly had some of Mary's physical characteristics. As a child Jesus learned from Mary, as he also learned from St. Joseph. But when Jesus grew up and entered upon his public ministry, the roles were reversed. Mary became Jesus' chief and best disciple. She fulfilled the preordained plan of God that she should become conformed to the image of her Son. The mother had become the disciple. Though Mary preceded her Son in time on this earth, as all parents precede their children, in eternity and the plan of God her Son comes first.

Mary's discipleship and her conformity to her Son are illustrated by the parallel of their feast days. This parallel puts our honoring of Mary in perspective and reminds us that Mary's holiness consists in becoming like her Son in all things. That, of course, is God's plan for us as well.

As Catholics we should relish our devotion to Mary. Celebrating the liturgical feasts of Mary and seeing them in relationship to the liturgical feasts of her Son direct us in developing the true Christian spirit.

Labor Day

Sunday Is Our Labor Day

In the United States and Canada, the first Monday of September is celebrated as Labor Day. It has been observed that the name is somewhat ironic since it is a holiday, a day on which no labor is done.

Of course we are all happy to accept a holiday, a day free from work, but for us as Catholics we may conclude that we have a kind of Labor Day every Sunday. On the first day of the week, by a tradition which goes back to the very beginning of our faith, we gather to celebrate the sacred liturgy of the Holy Eucharist.

"Liturgy" is a Greek word which has been restored to our Catholic vocabulary since the time of the Second Vatican Council. It means "the work of the people." Students of physics may recognize in this Greek word the origin of the technical word, "erg," which is a measure of energy.

When we come to Mass on Sunday, we must make sure that we exert energy, that we do not reduce the meaning of the word, "liturgy," to irony. The Church urges us to observe Sunday as a day of rest, not so that we may do nothing, but so that we may enter whole-heartedly into the celebration of the sacred liturgy. Our vigor during Mass should be at high measure.

The Second Vatican Council declared that "the Church desires that all the faithful be led to that full, conscious, and active participation in liturgical celebration called for by the nature of the liturgy." The nature of the liturgy is that it is the spiritual work of God's people. All are expected to do their share of the work. The Council, therefore, insisted that "in the reform and promotion of the liturgy, the full, active participation by all the people is the aim to be considered above all else, for it is the primary and indispensable source from which the faithful are to derive the true Christian spirit" (*Constitution on the Liturgy*, 14).

The Council also made clear the meaning of "active participation" by stating that the people take their part in the Mass "by means of acclamations, responses, psalmody, antiphons, and songs, as well as by actions, gestures, and bearing" (30).

Actually the call for full participation is not new. Pope Pius XII as long ago as 1947 declared that people were not to be present at the Mass as silent spectators but that they were to recognize that participation in the sacred liturgy is their chief duty and their supreme dignity (*Mediator Dei*, 80).

Sunday Mass should be a joyful, energetic experience for us. The Mass is like an oasis in the midst of a busy, hectic, and sometimes hostile world. But it should still be work. This work requires us to direct our attention to what we are doing and to work hard so that we may do it properly. Coming to Mass is not like going to a movie or watching TV. Such entertainment is largely passive; we sit back and relax and expect to be entertained. At Mass we are not to let the priest and ministers do all the work. Everyone is called to that full, active participation which the nature of the liturgy demands.

Sunday is our day for liturgy. Sunday is our day for spiritual work. Sunday is our spiritual Labor Day.

Solemnity of All Saints

What Makes a Saint?
Rv 7:2-4, 9-14; 1 Jn 3:1-3; Mt 5:1-12

The people whom we honor on All Saints day are not self-made people. They have been made holy by God through their co-operation with his grace. They became like Christ who is the model of all holiness. God the Father's plan for all of us is that we should become conformed to the image of his Son. St. John wrote, "See what love the Father has bestowed on us in letting us be called children of God! Yet that is what we are."

But not all saints are the same. Since no single saint can possibly reflect all the wonder which is Jesus Christ, each saint tends to specialize in one of his characteristics. Examples are rather easy to think of. St. Francis of Assisi, the poor man, reflects Jesus who was so poor that in his missionary journeys he had no place to lay his head. St. Teresa of Avila was a mystic who is recognized by the Church as a doctor of prayer. She was like Jesus who went off and spent whole nights in prayer.

St. John Chrysostom, the patron of preachers, continued the mission of Jesus who declared that he was sent by the Father to preach the good news to the poor. St. Vincent de Paul was like Christ in his great concern and affection for the needy and the outcasts of society.

St. John of the Cross was true to his name and like Jesus endured great suffering for God. St. Damien the Leper as his name suggests was like Jesus who reached out to touch and cure those who were afflicted with the most feared disease of his time.

The saints tell us, "It can be done. Mere human beings can by the grace of God become holy." The saints in heaven are not few in number. They are "a huge crowd which no one can count from every nation, race, people, and tongue." They like us "have washed their robes and made them white in the blood of the Lamb" through the sacrament of baptism. This great sacrament is our initial conformity to Christ. It makes us children of God and heirs of heaven. It is the beginning of our journey on the way to holiness.

We — like the many women, men, and children who have gone before us in faith — can become saints. We should never minimize the reality of God's call nor underestimate the power of his grace.

A young woman died at the age of twenty-four. She had never traveled from her home in a small French village except once when her father took her at the age of sixteen to Rome. She was not a great missionary. She was not a martyr. In fact, she did nothing at all which seemed extraordinary. And yet she is St. Therese of Lisieux, the Little Flower. How did it happen? She determined to do everything, even the most insignificant thing, out of pure love for God. It was her way, her little way of spiritual childhood. She was a child of God who became like the Son of God in her simplicity.

What is our way? How are to live like Christ? Each of us must determine that for ourselves. But we must remember that saints are not self-made. Our power comes from the Holy Eucharist. When we receive the body and the blood of the Lord, we receive the grace to become like Christ, each one of us in our own distinctive way. Remember: the saints tell us that it can be done. Through Christ we can all become truly holy.

Solemnity of All Saints (alternate)

The Church Means "Here Comes Everybody"
Rv 7:2-4, 9-14; 1 Jn 3:1-3; Mt 5:1-12

James Joyce, in his novel *Finnegan's Wake*, expressed the mark of the Church's universality by writing that the Catholic Church means "Here comes everybody." The Church is not Italian or Irish any more than it is Iranian or Polish. The Church is universal.

St. Luke in the Acts of the Apostles (11:26) attests that we were called "Christians" for the first time at Antioch in Syria. St. Ignatius, the bishop of Antioch who died around the year 109, records the first reference to our being called "Catholics." In other words, within less than a century from the day of Pentecost, Christians considered universality to be important enough to be recognized in the very name of the Church which Jesus Christ founded on the Rock which is Peter.

The simple, clear concept that the Church means "Here comes everybody" applies to the Church in its three stages: in heaven, in purgatory, and here on this earth.

The first stage is celebrated on the first of November, All Saints day. The saints in heaven are that "huge crowd which no one can count from every nation, race, people, and tongue." They stand before the throne of God "dressed in long white robes," the symbol of their baptism, and they hold "palm branches in their hands," the sign that they have conquered sin and death by sharing with Christ the Paschal Mystery of his death and resurrection.

On the second of November we remember those who have gone before us in death. They are the second level of the Church. We pray for "our brothers and sisters, who have gone to their rest in the hope of rising again," and we ask that God "will bring them and all the departed into the light of his presence" to join the saints in heaven.

Meanwhile, we see ourselves as the pilgrim Church throughout the world. We are the third stage or level. We pray that God will make us grow in love together with the Pope, the pastor of the whole Church, and with our bishop, the pastor of the local Church. We ask our heavenly Father to make us worthy in his mercy to share eternal life with Mary, the Virgin Mother of God who is the model of the Church, and with the apostles upon whom the Church was founded, and with all the saints who by doing God's will throughout the ages have shown us how to live as members of the Church on earth.

These two days, All Saints and All Souls, are very significant to our spirituality as Catholics. They emphasize in a special, annual celebration the mark of the Church's universality. They should help us realize that every eucharistic prayer reflects this mark, and proclaims that Christ is the binding force of the Church in heaven, in purgatory, and on earth, and that the Eucharist, because it celebrates the death and resurrection of Christ, forms us into one body, one spirit in Christ.

At Mass look around you at the men and women, the girls and boys of the congregation. They are members of the one, holy, apostolic, and catholic Church. Others like them have gone before you in death. All of us are on our pilgrim way to enter our eternal home, the Church in heaven.

All Souls Day

God Wants Us to Pray for the Dead

A politician died, so the story goes, and his wife put a notice in the obituary column which read: "Los Angeles, today my husband, Willoughby Dubius, departed for heaven at 3:30 A.M." The next day a notice appeared in the paper: "Heaven, 8:30 P.M. Mr. Dubius has not yet arrived. Whereabouts unknown."

Perhaps whoever put the second notice in the paper needed to be patient. Nowhere in Scripture or the other teachings of the Church do we find any doctrine which declares that we are static after death, that death immediately means either heaven or hell. Even after death God gives us the opportunity to grow in his grace, to become better suited to enjoy the blessedness of heaven.

I think we can all acknowledge that when we have concluded life in this world we are probably not quite good enough to go directly to heaven but surely not bad enough to go to hell. Does that mean we must remain in some nebulous condition, suspended as it were between the state of paradise and that of perdition? Those who believe in God's mercy can give a resounding "No" to that question. God applies to us the reconciling grace of his Son's sacrificial death as we pass through a state of purification when "we are washed clean in the blood of the Lamb." We call that state purgatory.

We pray for the dead in purgatory just as we pray for each other on this earth. Our faith tells us that it is right to ask others for prayers, and we follow that teaching especially when we face a special need, as when we must undergo serious surgery or when we are faced with a difficult decision. We help each other by means of prayer, and we help those who have gone before us in death in the same way.

By a constant tradition, the Church has always prayed for the dead. In every Mass during the eucharistic prayer we offer intercessions for those who have gone before us. We pray: "Bring all the departed into the light of your presence" (second eucharistic prayer). We pray: "Welcome into your kingdom our departed brothers and sisters and all who have left this world in your friendship" (third prayer). We pray: "Remember those who have died in the peace of Christ and all the dead whose faith is known to you alone" (fourth prayer).

Each year on the second of November we are invited — no, we are urged — to pray even more fervently for the dead. We are privileged to participate in the highest form of prayer, the Mass. Although death seems to be a separation, it does not make us lose contact with those who have gone before us. We are united with them through the communion of saints. Our voices raised in prayer are their voices before God, our hands lifted in prayer are their hands lifted up to God, for in Christ we form one body.

In the Mass of All Souls day after communion we pray: "Lord God, may the death and resurrection of Christ which we celebrate in the Eucharist bring the departed faithful to the peace of your eternal home." Prayer for the dead is one of the most beautiful aspects of our Catholic faith. The older we get, and the more we see loved ones preceding us in death, the more we can appreciate the opportunity God gives us to pray for the dead.

Thanksgiving Day

An American Original, A Catholic Experience

Our custom of celebrating a day of Thanksgiving traces its origin back to the year 1621 when Governor Bradley of the Plymouth Colony appointed a day of public praise and prayer after the first harvest. The practice soon spread throughout the other colonies. President George Washington at the request of Congress proclaimed the first national observance on Thursday, November 26, 1789. Now it is traditional for the president to publish a Thanksgiving Day proclamation every year.

Thanksgiving Day, like Mother's Day, is an American original, and it is the only American holiday which has an inescapable religious character. As such it poses a problem for some of our fellow citizens, so much so that it is a little surprising that they have not mounted a drive to abolish it altogether. After all, as one wag questioned, whom does an atheist thank on Thanksgiving Day?

We as Catholics know whom to thank, and we know how to go about it. We acknowledge that all life and every good gift comes from God. He is the one whom we thank. We come together today to celebrate the Mass as our thanksgiving to God. That is the right way to express our thanks. In fact, every Mass is our great act of thanksgiving. The word, "Eucharist," is Greek and means "thanksgiving."

We realize that it is right always and everywhere to give thanks and praise to God, and yet it is appropriate and helpful for us as American Catholics to observe this special day once a year as Thanksgiving Day. Today we appropriately give thanks to God for the principles upon which our country was founded. They are expressed in the Declaration of Independence: "We hold these truths to be self-evident, that all men have been created equal, that they are endowed by their Creator with certain unalienable Rights, that among these are Life, Liberty, and the pursuit of Happiness."

While giving thanks as Americans, we must be careful that we do not slip into a mentality of nationalism or complacency. Motives for thanksgiving imply responsibility, and those who thank God for temporal favors must also recognize duties toward those who are in need.

George Washington himself created the proper spirit of this day in his first Thanksgiving proclamation. He set aside a day which, in his own words, was to be "a day of public thanksgiving and prayer to be observed by acknowledging with grateful hearts the many and signal favors of Almighty God." He went on to urge his fellow citizens "to beseech God to pardon our national and other transgressions, to promote knowledge and the practice of true religion and virtue, and to grant unto all mankind a degree of temporal prosperity as he alone knows to be best."

On this day we can follow the advice that we should count our blessings. When we have added them all up and reached our sum, we should look up to heaven and with Christ as our priest we embrace the words of the third eucharistic prayer: "Father, calling to mind the death your Son endured for our salvation, his glorious resurrection and ascension into heaven, and ready to greet him when he comes again, we offer you in thanksgiving this holy and living sacrifice."

Solemnity of the Immaculate Conception

God's Artistry at Work

Gn 3:9-15, 20; Eph 1:3-6, 11-12; Lk 1:26-38

The Solemnity of the Immaculate Conception is an Advent celebration. Mary was conceived immaculate for that moment of which we heard in today's Gospel when she conceived Jesus by the power of the Holy Spirit at the announcement of the angel.

Some of the Fathers of the Church and early theologians, including St. Bernard and St. Thomas, had a problem with the idea of the immaculate conception of Mary. They saw Jesus as the Savior of all human beings without exception. If Mary had been conceived immaculate, it would seem that Mary did not need Jesus. Such a possibility is unacceptable even for the mother of Jesus.

It was left to a Franciscan theologian, John Duns Scotus (1265-1308) to arrive at a solution by analogy with human experience. He observed that a physician is valued who can cure an illness, but he is even more highly regarded if he can prevent an illness. Jesus as the Savior of Mary used a form of preventive medicine. Even though Mary preceded Jesus in time and was born before he shed his saving blood on the cross, she came under his redemptive power. Mary was preserved free from sin by the foreseen merits of her Son. She was in God's eternal plan. Even before she could do anything to merit God's love, in the very moment of her conception, Mary was preserved free from sin as a beautiful work of God's artistry.

Mary's immaculate conception is more than a work of God's art to be admired by us. It shows us the gratuity of our own calling by God. That gratuity is expressed in the second reading selected from the Letter to the Ephesians. God chose us in Christ before the world began to be his adopted children.

We cannot merit that choice. Becoming children of God the Father is his gift to us as the immaculate conception was his gift to Mary.

In 1854 Pope Pius IX defined the dogma of Mary's Immaculate Conception. The doctrine had been celebrated liturgically for centuries. In fact, the beauty of the doctrine evoked from William Wordsworth in 1821 these memorable verses:

> Mother! whose virgin bosom was uncrost
> With the least shade of thought to sin allied;
> Woman above all women glorified,
> Our tainted nature's solitary boast....

Boasting, in a sense, could be done by God since Mary is his great artistic creation. In order to praise God for his work the movement to declare the dogma was given impetus by the revelation of the "miraculous medal" to the Daughter of Charity, St. Catherine Laboure, in 1830 at Paris. After the declaration, devotion to the Immaculate Conception was intensified by the apparitions to St. Bernadette Soubirous at Lourdes in 1858. Now Mary under the title of the Immaculate Conception is the patroness of the United States.

This Solemnity of the Immaculate Conception invites us to give thanks and praise to God for the wonder of this privilege granted to Mary as his most favored daughter. At the same time we are urged to praise and thank God for the wonder which has made us his children.

ST PAULS

This book was produced by St. Pauls/Alba House, the Society of St. Paul, an international religious congregation of priests and brothers dedicated to serving the Church through the communications media.

For information regarding this and associated ministries of the Pauline Family of Congregations, write to the Vocation Director, Society of St. Paul, P.O. Box 189, 9531 Akron-Canfield Road, Canfield, Ohio 44406-0189. Phone (330) 702-0359; or E-mail: spvocationoffice@aol.com or check our internet site, www.albahouse.org